LIVE·Syst.

Doncaster
Metropolitan Borough Council

DONCASTER LIBRARY AND INFORMATION SERVICES

Please return/renew this item by
Thank you for using yo

D1420854

EAST END
Memories

JENNIE HAWTHORNE

Foreword by WILLIAM WOODRUFF
Author of *The Road to Nab End*

SUTTON PUBLISHING

First published in 2005 by
Sutton Publishing Limited · Phoenix Mill
Thrupp · Stroud · Gloucestershire · GL5 2BU

British Library Cataloguing in Publication Data
A catalogue record for this book is available from the British Library.

ISBN 0-7509-3996-6

Typeset in 11/14pt Garamond.
Typesetting and origination by
Sutton Publishing Limited.
Printed and bound in England by
J.H. Haynes & Co. Ltd, Sparkford.

CONTENTS

LIST OF ILLUSTRATIONS

FOREWORD

by William Woodruff

Here is a wonderful book about a girl born in poverty in London's East End, who never gave up the struggle to survive and do something with her life. Jennie Crawley (Hawthorne) was born in 1916 in Bethnal Green, one of the East End's tougher boroughs. Her resolute English Protestant mother was a 'Mrs Mop', who spent her life cleaning up after others. Her irresolute, gullible (yet most lovable) Irish Catholic father – who forever sought the job that in a world depression did not exist – happily drank his way through life's difficulties. We are told that he wore a smile that only a saint could have possessed.

The hand-to-mouth existence under which the Crawleys lived would have tested any saint. The author describes her father's 'fight for jobs at the docks; the bodies covered in rags that came alive as we passed them under the arches on our way to our Whitechapel school; the lice crawling over the head of the girl at the desk in front . . .'. Hunger often was the worst burden to bear. Sometimes the child was overcome by the sight and scent of other people's food. She recalls the Dutch herrings taken from great smelly barrels, the saveloys and hot salt beef, and cucumbers pickled but not too sour, the jellied eels, 'such a lovely glassy green . . .'. Food in those far-off days was a benediction, 'like berries from a bush or apples blown from a tree'. The desperate conditions of the late 1920s and early 1930s would eventually give rise to the extreme fascist and communist groups of the East End, which Jennie Crawley's Catholic Church denounced.

Regardless of the setbacks, Bethnal Green, to a child, was a magical place, vibrant and alive. Every day her street became awash with a tide of humanity: a fairground, where every kind of people played their part. Sharp wits were everything.

This book brings out the extraordinary ethnic mix of the East End. From 1900 until 1910, large numbers of Jews fleeing poverty and persecution in Eastern Europe had swarmed into the East End. Long columns of refugees from Poland, Lithuania, Russia and Italy followed. Irish refugees fleeing mid-nineteenth-century famine had preceded them. At school in the 1920s Jennie swam happily in a sea of immigrants. 'There was hardly an "English" name among us.' Fighting for a living, these groups did not have the time or the incentive to fight each other. Waving a Union Jack on Empire Day, and celebrating St Patrick's Day with bunches of shamrock, she says, they somehow found homogeneity.

In 1926 Jennie Crawley made her First Communion, which 'stood out like a peak in the valley of our lives' – not least because of the feast that followed. Mrs Silverman, an elderly Jewish friend whom Jennie helped, celebrated the occasion by giving her a gold-plated necklace with tiny Jewish charms. Neither of them could have possibly imagined that the necklace would later land Jennie into trouble on a trip to pre-war Nazi Germany.

It is to the credit of this girl that she allowed nothing to stifle her love of life, or lessen her determination to improve her lot. Discarding self-pity, and with enormous strength of will, she began to excel at school. After passing test after test, in 1937 she eventually took up residence at Oxford University. 'I was as smitten by Oxford's beauty', she writes, 'as a besotted lover'.

Alas for Jennie, her dream was not to be. Fate intervened and the world went to war. Because of family affairs and the need to hang onto a job, she found herself back in Bethnal Green.

Several times during the war her life hung on a thread. She was in a street, she tells us, 'that got blown to bits . . . the survivors were screaming for help. We could not help them for we had to be dug out ourselves.'

Despite incessant bombing and the unbearable miseries of war, life went on and the war went on and the Cockneys of East London, of whatever ethnic background, remained unbowed. In all the chaos, Jennie hung onto a job, found a husband and started a family. In 1946, a year after the war in Europe had ended, Jennie Crawley, now Mrs Hawthorne, joined her Air Force husband in Germany.

East End Memories is a tale well and vividly told. It provides an absorbing and lasting picture of a girl's struggles to find a place in society, a society now gone. Its added value is that, in viewing society from the bottom of the social pile, Mrs Hawthorne is able to draw upon the life she lived. There is no make-believe here. The writer's aim has been to capture the life of a poor East End community at a particular moment in time. In this, she has succeeded.

William Woodruff
Author of the best-selling *Nab End* books

INTRODUCTION

The tale unfolded in the following pages covers the period from the First to the Second World War, a period of the greatest social and scientific changes the world has ever known. Cheap air flights, TV, mobile phones and personal computers have transformed the lives of ordinary people everywhere. In my childhood, there were no refrigerators, frozen foods or take-aways, no dishwashers, tumble dryers, no ball-point pens with which to sign a name, and no credit cards either. Most working-class homes lacked electricity: lighting came from gas mantles or candles. Alexander Fleming discovered penicillin only in 1928 and we had not heard of antibiotics.

Social changes took a little longer to make their impact but were even more revolutionary. Marriage came first and sex afterwards. Babies arrived yearly, so Marie Stopes and her teaching were more in demand than Viagra or IVF are today. The word 'gay' had a different connotation and closets were not for coming out of but for putting clothes in. There were no meaningful relationships except chaste ones within the family circle, and divorce was only for film stars.

This is the world in which I grew up. It is probably alien to today's teenagers, their parents and even grandparents, but my story has a wider relevance. Our expectations and aspirations, along with those who had them, were killed off by two terrible wars. Today, people aim, hope and often work hard for material comfort and personal happiness. The two do not always go together. If happiness proves elusive, I offer two sayings heard in my youth, one from my husband's Irish aunt, which goes,

'Money doesn't make you happy, but with it you can be d——d miserable in comfort.' The other sounds like a biblical phrase, but isn't. It comes from my Cockney mother, who replied, when we asked for something beyond her power or inclination to give: 'He that expecteth a lot, receiveth nothing.' Neither entirely true, but useful to remember if dreams ever become nightmares.

1

AS IT WAS AND NEVER SHALL BE

When I was born, in October 1916, Bethnal Green had everything: museum, stalls, shops, neighbours and friends, even a bit of greenery too in Victoria Park, and the gardens surrounding the museum. Along a few lucky streets there were some humble plane trees, their leaves mangy and worn as sick old cats, but still able to provide a haven for the homely sparrow. Everything was there.

Now, with old landmarks gone, I am as disorientated as an explorer with an unserviceable compass. The 'Red Church', so called not because of any Communist leanings but because of the colour of its brick, is a block of flats. Brick Lane is packed with lively young couples going to curry joints, every one the recommended Restaurant of the Year. Further towards Whitechapel are purveyors of beautiful saris and eastern silks. Sandwiched in between is probably the smallest police station in the British Isles, its main advantage being the cornucopia of cheap food that surrounds it.

In my childhood, the area was a magical place, vibrant and alive. Club Row, on the opposite side of the road, teemed with dogs and birds and bicycles and slick sellers of sick china. Wrestlers squirmed and squiggled and squeezed their way out of vice-like grips. Houdini-type men let themselves be tied up in ropes and chains and sacks so tightly held together by leather belts that I watched, terrified. The men would suffocate. They would die in their sacks in front of my very eyes. They would never get free again. Watching the second-by-second death-defying squirms within the sacks, I held my breath and prayed. The Houdini look-alikes came safely out and after resurrecting themselves went round with a hat.

Other men looked at your hands and felt your arm muscles and guessed your weight in a loud voice. It mingled with the bell-ringing and high-pitched chant of the Lascar trader singing 'Indian Toff-ee-ee', and the Jewish woman's invitation in Yiddish to buy her wares, 'drei a penny bagels'. A bearded old man pushed his pram round and round the streets with a gramophone that kept repeating 'mazal tov', the Jewish words for good luck.

The weight guessers always gave you your money back if they were wrong. When women looked at your hands, they pretended for a 'tanner' or less to tell your fortune. All your wishes came true, though you might have to wait a lifetime for that to happen and climb over many hurdles on the way.

I listened, even more fascinated, to the men at the stalls, their voices coaxing you to buy something you didn't want at all. Clever voices they all had, wheedling, bullying, coaxing, persuading, loud and raucous, soft and sad. When you listened to them you suddenly realised how badly you needed the things they were selling: horrible vases made into the shapes of nasty-looking cats and dogs and even nastier-looking children . . . yet people liked them.

On other stalls, clocks that worked ticked away happily without any regard for the time-keeping of the face next door; clocks that didn't stood mute, silently grumbling in a world of noise. Next to them were bits of miscellaneous junk, parcels of gramophone records, and cutlery, splendid and proud in green-lined cases or tied up in tarnished batches of six. Before the men began to speak, you were ready to pass by those stalls, not wanting anything at all.

How was it that voices so different could all alike be so persuasive? I was forever tempted to buy something: clothes or shoes perhaps, but, like my father – never my far more sensible mother – was such a sucker for so many bad 'bargains', I feared to try my luck again even if I had a 'bob' or two on me.

Bakers were a paradise on earth. Outside their front windows, the delicious aroma of Sunday dinners cooked for people with money but no ovens filled the air. Inside, different scents arose from the piles and piles of assorted bread in different shapes and sizes: crunchy fresh loaves, shiny and crisp with poppy seeds on top and some with seeds inside too; milk loaves with white, soft centres covered by a dark brown crust; long, thin loaves, tins and cobs and twists. Famous bakers in the area, like Goides, produced these and other epicurean wonders such as their unforgettable cheese cake. Where can you find their like today? In New York perhaps . . . a long way to go for a slice of bread.

Blooms, a Kosher restaurant, was also noted for its Jewish delights. Morris Bloom, a pre-First World War immigrant to England from Lithuania, learnt the art of meat pickling in his home town and brought this expertise to the snack bar he opened with his wife Rebecca in Brick Lane. Their son, Sidney, left Raine's Foundation School at the age of 16 to help them. The salt beef, chicken and sausages they sold proved so popular that the family moved to a larger site in Brick Lane. After the death of his father, Sidney took over new premises in Whitechapel High Street and named it M. Bloom (Kosher) & Son. The premises were never without a queue for the take-away provisions. Also on offer was the usual Jewish fare like lokshen, chicken livers and cholent. Strangely I don't remember ever having gefilte fish or latkes in the restaurant, which was always full with famous personalities, manic waiters and exuberant diners.

Bakers – Jews and non-Jews – sold bagels too: lovely crispy rolls shaped like a doughnut ring with a hole in the middle, but tasting far more delicious. Though dearer and succulent enough they were never quite as saliva-inducing as those from the old woman advertising her wares in Yiddish in the street. And of course, there were matzos, big packets of them, looking like sheets of white paper which had been lightly browned in the oven and then pricked up and down in straight lines. How good they tasted with a squidge of white Dutch butter. You never even connected those unleavened crunchy crackers with the feast of the Passover, when Jews remember their flight from Egypt, with no time to bake bread.

Pretzels were on sale, as well as mouth-watering piecrust with the steam still rising from its currant-filled centre. Having earned my halfpenny from a Jewish momma for turning off her gas tap on the eve of her Sabbath, I would be unable to resist that piecrust, would buy a slice, hold it for a second, warm in my hand, then dig my teeth in for a taste of heaven.

My imagination on fire, I wandered round, following the sight and scent of food: Dutch herrings from great smelly barrels, and saveloys and hot salt beef, and cucumbers, pickled but not too sour; jellied eels, such a lovely glassy green, from Tubby Isaacs' stall, or Kelly's in Bethnal Green Road. The eels slid off your tongue, juicy and cold in summer, and in winter warmed you up if you ate them with hot mashed potatoes, flecked with parsley, vinegar and pepper, or warmer still, pie and mash instead.

Butchers' shops boasted sheeps' heads, faggots and pigs' trotters; Kosher ones dangled delicious chickens invitingly in their front windows. Into barrels of salt or pickled herrings, a fat Jewish sales lady fished for a catch, slapped it with onions into a page of newspaper and thrust it into your waiting palm. How you longed but did not dare to have a taste on the way to the hungry stomachs at home.

In spite of the shops filled with food, the threat of hunger, real hunger, hovered over so many people in those far-off days that food itself was a benediction, like berries from a bush or apples blown from a tree, a favour showered upon you, worthy or not, by some heavenly supervisor. My mother felt she had to give thanks − it didn't matter to whom − usually some form of grace after meals to an unknown invisible Creator. Somebody, somewhere, had to be thanked. She did not use the Catholic grace, 'Bless us O lord and these thy gifts which we are about to receive through thy grace, Amen,' and she did not know the Selkirk one which she would have loved: 'Some have meat and cannot eat, Some cannot eat that want it, But we have meat and we can eat, Sae let the Lord be thankit.' No, Mum's grace came straight from her heart, usually in the form of 'Thank God for my good dinner, Amen.' She said it after any food, well cooked or not, that gave enjoyment, no matter at what time of the day.

If you were really, really hungry, a kindly trader at Spitalfields Market nearby might give you some not-too-rotten fruit or vegetables. But everything was nearby. We needed no buses or trains. The street was our playground. Our feet, unaided, took us to whole new kingdoms. Ships from all parts of the globe packed London's great river. Its long grey waters, stretching up towards the Cotswolds and down beyond the Essex marshes, boasted so many cranes on the docksides that a Hudson Institute statistician must have wept for joy. Steamers chugged off to far-away Margate or Ramsgate. France was a dream, and package flights to Spain, like a trip to the moon, belonged to science fiction.

At night, the naphtha flares from the stalls lit our way for occasional Saturday night outings to Smarts' or Excelsior cinemas to see more heavenly romances than this world dreams of. Our young eyes occasionally glanced away from Raymond Navarro's attractions or the exploits of Charlie Chaplin or Rin Tin Tin, to the courting couples sitting in such odd positions in the back rows.

When darkness fell, the great heart of the City stopped beating and died. As if by magic it became a deserted park where no man loiters and no birds sing. But how gracious and spacious it seemed in the sleazy summer. I walked past the Old Lady in Threadneedle Street and imagined I owned the world.

Against these joys was the all-pervading hardship and squalor which, childlike, we took for granted: our fathers' fight for jobs at the docks; the bodies covered in rags that came alive as we passed them under the arches on our way to our Whitechapel school; the lice crawling over the head of the girl at the desk in front; the mice that jumped out of our shoes when we got up in the morning; the cockroaches hidden in the cracks between the walls and ceilings of the homes where we lived, and which were fought, not by a spray of ICI insecticide, but a lighted candle, taken round by an ever-tough mother in nightly forays which she occasionally won.

2

MY MOTHER

In 1901 my mother, Susan Cole, was 10 years old. Her father, Philip, was severely disabled, and would never have a full-time job again; her mother, Ellen, was dead. Shattered by the death of his wife, the loss of his strength and of his job, Philip barely coped with the mundane chores of everyday life. He had tried for numerous jobs in vain. The employers where he had had the accident that maimed him sent occasional food parcels. While these kept coming, the family didn't starve. His children helped him with any work that they could find, any errands they could run. Their schooling suffered and they often went hungry, but the rent was paid.

My mother was hardest hit: the loss of her mother when she herself was so young; cruelly knocked about and starved by gin-soaked Aunt Aggie who, instead of using the money given her to feed the child in her care, used it to drown her own sorrows in drink. Mum developed rickets, and bow legs which were still obvious in her later life.

School, which might have given her a respite, merely proved another hellhole. Like her brothers and sister, and many other children of her generation, she worked long before the school-leaving age of 12, earning a few pence by sweated labour of one kind or another.

One of her jobs was to clean part of a warehouse owned by one of the Jewish families who had settled in the East End after emigrating from Russia. The warehouse was a big square room on a corner site, with two large windows facing two sides of the street. Stuffed to the brim with old rags, this room was linked by a wooden corridor to the kitchen where the

7

family ate. Bales of cloth, on top of each other, were piled up in shelves each side of the corridor and reaching to the ceiling. The house, off Hackney Road, was some distance away from both Susan's home and her school in the Jago district of Shoreditch.

Susan did the cleaning for the family early in the morning, before school opened. Alongside her Jewish faith, Mrs Abrahams followed the creed of housework expanding to fill the time available . . . and a bit more. 'Do this little job,' she would say to her young *shikseh*. 'It won't take a minute. Just a *lek un a shmek*. And when you've finished, could you do that little job?' By the time one little job and another little job were done, Susan was often late for school. One day she was sent for by the headmistress.

'Punctuality is the politeness of kings,' intoned the head, not only irrelevantly but incorrectly. 'You just can't turn up at school when it suits you, you've been late twice already this week. You must get up earlier. And from now on, every time you're late, you will stand up in the hall as a lesson to others not to be lazy, like you.'

Susan stood silent, head down, hands rubbing the tears that kept coming to her eyes.

'Do you hear me, girl?'

Susan nodded. The headmistress got out a big white clown's cap on which was a large letter 'D' for 'Dunce'. She put the cap on the head of the 10-year-old motherless girl and made her stand on a bench in the school hall all day long wearing it.

Later on, Mum recalled little of her schooldays, not even the name of the headmistress who meted out this punishment. She learnt to read, write and count, and forgot everything else save the day when, at 10 years old, she wore a dunce's cap in front of the whole school.

As an adult she was a tough and wiry fighter, ready to speak her mind against anything she thought wrong. As a child she wanted only to keep out of the way of 'trouble', but the punishment of wearing a dunce's cap in the hall made her an easy target for bullying, especially as she was very small for her age. She lost all the many fights that followed. School became a nightmare, to be avoided as much as possible.

When not yet 15 years of age, my mother became a servant in the Waterman family. The fate was not a harsh one. On the contrary, it turned out to be a lucky break for Susan to have been employed by the Watermans. Though she felt like an emigrant who has to leave a once beloved country, it was a decision she was never to regret. She learnt much during her employment there which had a big impact on her later life and on those of her children and grandchildren.

The Watermans, poorer but more religious, cultured and musical than most of their middle-class neighbours, lived in a large Edwardian house in Seven Kings near Ilford. Suburban Essex was then almost a remote country area for an East Ender like Susan, who had never travelled much more than a mile from home.

Mr Frederick Waterman was 'something' in the City. He had large hazel eyes, a handsome profile and a head of thick dark hair, just turning grey, which gave him an air of wisdom and distinction. His rugged face looked as if it had been carved out of granite, as firm and clean-cut as that of an ascetic Jesuit priest. But it was his voice, deep, soft and seductive, that fascinated Susan. By contrast, Fred's wife, Gertrude, several years older than her husband, had, in spite of a sweet expression, an almost frightening aristocratic voice and manner.

Over the next seven years the Watermans, then with a son and daughter, had two more daughters. Susan did all the heavy housework and looked after the children when the parents went out. Once a week the family enjoyed musical evenings at home in their front room. They could all sing or play an instrument: the piano, cello or violin.

Fred Waterman's singing fascinated Susan. In between serving drinks and sandwiches for the evening parties they gave for their friends, she stared at him, goggle-eyed. When he got to the lines, 'on thy bosom, the fair lilac blossom,' or even better, 'on away, awake beloved' from Coleridge Taylor's 'Hiawatha', she became aware of a whole new world – and not only of music. She adored Frederick Waterman like a god.

He was not unaware of the devotion he inspired in the young servant and in which he sometimes almost erotically basked, but the High Church background of philanthropy and duty instilled into him from youth did not allow him, like many men in less scrupulous families, to take advantage of an innocent girl. And Susan, so worldly wise, so knowledgeable in the ways and language of the street, was quite naive in others.

Gertrude Waterman had a different appeal from her husband. A wonderful housekeeper and manager, she patiently taught her young maid-of-all-work her own skills. Susan loved cooking. Once a month she went home to her father. Another batch of 'relations', realising that there was a spare room for part of the month, moved back in with him during the vacant days, and hoped the landlord wouldn't notice.

In the Watermans' house, Mum saw for the first time in her life, linen cupboards. She loved opening those cupboards to see the neat piles of clean sheets and pillowcases and to be assailed by the warm, sweet scent of lavender. Another wonder was the mahogany wardrobes and chests of drawers where members of the family each kept their own clothes and some of their possessions.

She polished all of these and learnt how to sweep the carpets – throwing down tea-leaves to prevent the dust from rising – to iron 'goffered' pillowcases with their tiny little pleats, to polish the brass door handles, the silver and glass, and to lay a table with the right knives, forks, spoons and glasses and put them all in the correct places.

During her time at the Watermans' she took me down to their house several times, so at an early age I glimpsed a world quite unlike that of Bethnal Green. The first of many visits occurred when I was quite young. I was absolutely fascinated by the sense of space everywhere, the gleaming kitchen with its array of pots and pans, the soft carpets in other rooms, and most of all by the toy cupboard. It seemed wonderful to have a cupboard just for toys and games. As I grew older, other things impressed me, especially the paintings on the walls. They were not copies by famous artists of the period, but the work of various members of the family, principally Fred Waterman or his middle daughter, Dorothy.

The skills which my mother learnt at the Watermans' house were unfortunately of little use in trying to keep clean a slum infested by cockroaches, fleas, bugs or other pests. Cats that were good 'mousers' kept scuttling creatures at bay, though sometimes when Susan put her shoes on in the mornings, her toes felt inside them a sleepy, lazy mouse that had somehow escaped the cat. Trying to keep a tenement building clean was an altogether different skill from any of those learnt in Seven Kings.

Susan and other tenants in cramped rooms sometimes used the services of Albrecht, the baker. He had premises near Gosset Street and charged only a few pence for cooking dinners (expertly too) in his big ovens. On Sundays, the aroma from his ovens sent you into paroxysms of pleasure – and if you had no pence, pangs of frustration or despair. During the week he added piecrust to his other goods. That cost a halfpenny, or a penny for a larger slice. 'Ha'p'orth of piecrust,' you asked of him, proffering the coin that was the 'wages' you, as a *Shabbas goy*, picked up from the stoves of the *fromm* Jewish mommas, for turning out their taps on the Sabbath.

In return for your halfpenny, or penny, Albrecht passed you a slice of hot fluffy pastry, fresh from the oven and full of currants. He was still selling piecrust when I was in my teens: absolutely salivatingly delicious. Even thinking of it today, along with real bagels, makes my taste buds tingle.

At home in Bethnal Green, Mum's culinary style was unusual and unhygienic. She brushed aside any complaints with the words, 'They say you've got to eat a peck of dirt before you die.' Who said it and when, nobody dared ask, but then the only suffering ever connected with food was not poisoning but hunger.

When money was around – an important proviso – there was compensation enough for her in the food that she saw on the tables in the

Watermans' and Jewish houses where she had worked, and which sometimes appeared on our own: rice served as a vegetable, which few other Gentile families ever had (and which I hated), challah (plaited bread) and bagels, schmalzes herring, gefilte fish and latkes, which she always made herself, and matzos bought in any street-corner grocer's.

3

A NEW LIFE

While she was working for the Watermans, Susan met my father, James Crawley. How and where, I do not know. But who could resist him? Susan certainly couldn't. He was the handsomest member of a most handsome and beautiful Irish family. Like that of his sisters – not of his only brother, whose hair was a mousy brown shade – Jim's hair was thick, curly and black. Black has many shades, and Jim's hair had a blue sheen in it that rivalled the feathers of a raven. He went grey very early, in his thirties, but the new colour enhanced rather than detracted from his good looks.

Mum sometimes used to brush it back and say, 'The grey looks nice. It's a pity you're not grey all over. You've got a bit of black hair at the back.'

To this he replied, 'Don't worry, my love. Grey it will be soon enough. And then I'll go bald. Will that suit you better?'

His heavy-lashed eyes were of an unusual hazel colour, almost green, with little dark flecks in them. No wonder my mother thought him the best-looking man around, and when I was older, so did I. But he was as gullible as he was lovable, the ideal victim for a con man or a fraudster, constantly being taken for a ride by any smooth talker. It was a wonder he ever had any money left for drink after he got his wages as a carman. As for any practical tasks in the home, he was quite hopeless, though improving a little as he got older. He illustrated that line in Hilaire Belloc to perfection: 'A lost thing could I never find, Nor a broken thing mend.'

Jim was some four years younger than Susan and earned a pittance. Employed as a delivery man for the railway, he drove a horse, sometimes two, with a cart. He had little money and, unlike an engine driver or station master, for instance, no status either. But the job was safe. No carman ever got the 'sack' from the railway, any more than did a dustman from the local council. Poorly paid though such jobs were, they were greatly sought after for the security they gave the wage earner and his family. Like coal mining (the Bevin Boys) in the Second World War, Jim's job was a 'reserved occupation', which meant no call-up for military service if ever a war should come. That was unlikely: something nobody in the East End even thought about. A safe wage packet was far more important.

At the end of one long evening, Susan arrived home late and exhausted. Her father was out. The room was unbearably hot. She opened the window, and noticed yet another crack in the ceiling. That meant her lighted candle must wage another battle with any invaders. The wallpaper and ceiling would be still more scorched and browned by her light, but for a time at least, the room would be partly pest free. The trouble was that as you managed to get rid of one lot of pests, others took their place. Still, she must have another go. That nasty crack in the ceiling over the mantelpiece meant a comfortable nesting place for all manner of horrors.

She made herself a cup of tea, and drained it rapidly. Taking the cup outside to the wash-house, she rinsed it, then came back to the kitchen table and pushed it against the mantelpiece. She lifted a chair onto the table and scrambled up onto it. From this vantage point she could comfortably reach the crack in the ceiling.

In her hand, she held a small candle. Jutting uncomfortably into her stomach, as usual, was the wooden mantelpiece, draped with some pretty material. The Watermans had given it to her for curtains. It looked much nicer where it was. She took out a match from the box on the mantelshelf, struck it, lit her candle and put the box back on the shelf.

Holding the lighted candle, she stretched forward to the crack in the ceiling.

As her hand moved along the gap, the chair began slipping away from under her feet. In a panic, she grabbed the mantelpiece to save herself from falling, and let go of the lighted candle. The candle fell onto the drapery, the box of matches on the mantelshelf.

In seconds, the drapery became a fireball. It fell down, in no time setting alight the old coconut mat by the side of the fireplace and engulfing the chair by the table. Tongues of flame began licking everything in their way, feeding on themselves and stretching perilously across the floor. Susan scrambled down from the table and opened the kitchen door.

'Fire! Fire! Get down quick!' she yelled to the tenants upstairs, before diving back into the blazing room.

She tore down what was left of the burning drapery and threw it out of the window. The coconut mat followed. She shut the window and turned the table upside down. Her face, her hands, her hair, seemed on fire.

The upstairs tenants and neighbours rushed to help, filling with water any utensils they could find, and throwing it with almost happy abandon over everything in sight. Soon anything that remained unburnt was soaked. Little was left of the room. It looked an empty shell.

Her father arrived with a friend. He pressed inside the gawping crowd and stood at the door of the ruined kitchen. 'Good God Almighty! What's 'appened 'ere?' Neighbours hastened to enlighten him.

'And what about Susan? She's all right, is she?'

He looked round and saw her pushing to get out from the smoking room, her face blackened by soot and debris, her hair and eyebrows singed.

'You all right, Susie?'

She nodded, almost in tears. 'I'm all right, Dad. But everything's gone, everything.'

'Not everything,' he said. 'We're still alive and kicking, though for how long, God only knows. Germany's invaded Belgium and England's declared war.'

4

BATTLE LINES

The First World War precipitated a great change in Susan's life. Her older brother, recalled from service in India, managed, with Fred Waterman's help, to spend his last day's leave with Susan. It was a poignant farewell. Her mother had died in her thirties, her sister as a teenager and her younger brother in his twenties. Now her last remaining sibling was going out to stem the seepage in France. Arriving in March, he was reported 'missing, believed killed', in May 1915, about par for the course. Shattered, Susan found comfort with Jim. She would leave the Watermans and start a new life.

At this time a strong sense of family unity existed in the East End. It was almost like a mafia, with its own rigid ideas of right and wrong.

Mixed marriages between Gentiles and Jews were initially unacceptable to both sides – save, perhaps, between the prospective bride and groom. Gentiles tended to grow more tolerant over the years, a Jewish father, never. Marriage between Protestants and Catholics was frowned upon rather than forbidden. Only worse than either was the disaster of no marriage at all . . . a man disappearing and leaving behind a pregnant unmarried woman. Fathers were particularly hard on 'erring' daughters. Black and white unions were so rare that they aroused more wonder than disfavour. The only black man that I ever saw in my childhood, for example, was a Doctor Jelly (probably not his real name), whose presence in a nearby street was greatly appreciated by the many who used his services for their families.

Living together before marriage was acceptable as a custom of the gentry and occasionally for working-class couples who did not flaunt the fact too obviously. Running off with somebody else's husband or wife was frowned upon at least in theory, though often envied by those unable to manage a similar action.

When a local shopkeeper's wife left husband, son and thriving business, one of the most prosperous in the district, for a fellow who proved a rogue, it kept people gossiping for years afterwards. Why did she do it? Such 'elopements' when there were no TV soaps to see or discuss proved as much a source of interest and never-ending topic of conversation among the local community as the latest murder case.

My grandfather considered an Irish Catholic the most undesirable suitor possible for his daughter's hand. Even if she married a Jew – slightly better, but not much – at least she'd never go short of a penny or two. All that Jim Crawley could offer was a job that paid peanuts. As for his religion . . . though my grandfather Philip Cole rarely entered a church, he considered himself staunchly Church of England.

Like many of his co-religionists, he would have nothing to do with any popery and was determined never to have a Catholic son-in-law, any more than a Jewish one. He prophesied all manner of disasters if the wedding took place, threatening to return from the grave after his death and haunt Susan if she went ahead and married that good-for-nothing fellow.

Why Dad should have been so ill received when, unlike many young East Enders, he was lucky enough to have a fairly safe – if low-paid – job, is difficult to say, but the thought of her father's ghost haunting her after his death was a terrible threat indeed to my mother.

She was the most superstitious person imaginable, and remained so right into her adult life, always seeing signs and wonders in the tea-leaves and everywhere else. Even when I was long past my teens she still remained frightened of thunderstorms and would go anywhere to avoid hearing them, sometimes even under the bed. Yet she stayed at her hospital cleaning job in Bethnal Green throughout the Second World War, sticking out all the air-raids and bombings, and only running off to the underground tube shelters in Liverpool Street or Bethnal Green when she finished work in the evenings. In those shelters, hearing neither air-raid warnings nor German bombers, and surrounded by lots of lively Cockneys, she was content. How could she foresee that the Bethnal Green tube shelter would become the scene of the worst civilian casualty of the war?

Fred Waterman was as helpful as ever in this difficult time which Susan faced in wanting to marry an Irish Catholic. Fred and his wife advised their one-time maid that she was now a capable young woman with a little money of her own. They told her that whom she married was for her to decide and she should make her own choice. Fred, himself Church of England, equally stringent in his ideas of right and wrong as Susan's father, and with a strong sense of duty, made it his business to visit Philip Cole and have a few words with him. He did his job so well in 'upgrading' Susan's prospective groom that the way was made clear for a wedding and, surprise, surprise, a wedding in a Catholic church.

His fine bone structure enabled my father, Jim Crawley, in spite of the many hardships he suffered, to retain his good looks far longer than most men of that generation. The patrician quality of his face was such that, had he possessed the accent and the bearing, he could easily have passed for a haughty member of the aristocracy. However, his gait was strangely unsteady, even when he was sober, rather like a sailor trying out his legs on land after a long journey at sea.

He married my mother in November 1915. The war was still going on but it would surely be over soon. The Watermans, generous as ever, helped Susan with her wedding dress and the wedding breakfast (as the repast after the ceremony is so quaintly called, no matter what the time of day that bride, groom and guests sit down to eat it). Who came, or how many, I do not know. A friend of Susan's soldier brother may have come with the guests.

With many misgivings, in spite of Fred Waterman's little homily, Philip gave his daughter away. When all was said and done, he loved her dearly, this last surviving member of his family. The wedding took place in St John the Baptist Catholic church in the Registrar's district of Hackney. Susan thought that sounded more 'refined' than Bethnal Green.

Many East End families, particularly Jewish ones, splashed out extravagantly on weddings. Gentiles spent a lot on funerals – they took place only once in a person's lifetime and showed respect for the departed. Sometimes spouses or relations were still paying for these ceremonies in one way or another for years afterwards, and the amounts often became a subject for family jokes, particularly Jewish ones. ('Marriage is like a violin. When the music is over, the strings are still there.')

The only photo I have of my parents' wedding shows it to have been quite a lavish affair. Susan carries a beautiful bouquet, probably created by the very deft and artistic florists who lived in Bethnal Green. It consists of large chrysanthemums and tiger lilies, set off by gypsophilia and some fern trailing artistically down the front of her bridal gown.

The dress was probably also made locally, perhaps by one of her sister Bessie's seamstress friends with whom Susan still kept in touch. It reached up to her neck and down to her ankles. She wears white shoes and stockings. Framed by the uplifted veil and headdress, her face looks even smaller than it actually was, and there is a quality of pathos about her smile that is like the woman in the painting, *Nameless and Friendless*, by the nineteenth-century painter Emily Mary Osborn. That work hangs today in a Liverpool museum and depicts so well a scene rarely portrayed, of the so-called genteel poverty of that period. The Trades Union Congress building in Holborn should get a copy to hang alongside its more masculine-oriented pictures.

However, Susan was neither nameless nor friendless on this occasion. The only shabby thing about her wedding photo seems to be where it was taken: against a portion of a wall that appears to be in imminent danger of collapse. My father stands against a part of the wall with a brick missing. The black cavity above his head gives him the appearance of an Egyptian wearing a fez. He sports a dark suit with white collar and tie, and a large chrysanthemum in his buttonhole. He is much taller than my mother and, in spite of his gentle half smile, still manages to convey a seriousness appropriate to the occasion.

In another photo, now lost, there are bridesmaids, possibly the older Waterman girls. Round-faced and chubby, with large smiles and beautifully dressed, they are sitting down cross-legged, each with her own bouquet.

The young couple began their married life in shared rooms, as was the usual practice, and eventually graduated to two rooms and a kitchen in Nelson Street, where I was born. This small terrace of about sixty houses was situated between Hackney Road and Bethnal Green Road, and built in the form of an incomplete square with three sides instead of four. Two entrances came off St Peter's Street. They led nowhere except into and out of Nelson Street, both ends of which ended in a cul-de-sac, so that traffic rarely entered. An ideal playing area for children, the street has since been demolished during slum clearance.

The upstairs half of the home my parents occupied was, as usual, tenanted by others without a water supply, WC, or sink. Also, as usual in most houses of this type, the tenants upstairs had to come down through the kitchen to the back yard for the facilities there.

To help pay the rent, Susan found a part-time cleaning job in a company where the great inventor Marconi was reputed to work. She and my father seemed well on their way to a happy and even prosperous future. However I arrived just eleven months later, so that Mum's blossoming career as an office cleaner came to an end, at least for the time being. So almost did I.

Bethnal Green mums still had their babies at home. That's where I was born in the middle of the First World War, in 1916. It was cheaper and thought to be safer than in hospital.

About the time and place of our coming into this world, we can do nothing, yet these are the forces that, more than any other except one, help shape our destiny. My birthday, 28 October, is shared with Evelyn Waugh and Jonas Salk, microbiologist, discoverer of the anti-poliomyelitis vaccine and the son of Polish-Jewish immigrant parents in New York.

My future was not to be so grand as theirs, nor as poverty-stricken as some. Dad found the atmosphere surrounding my birth so restricting, his fears for my mother so great and his presence so apparently unwelcome to the midwife that he went out and got drunk.

By the time my brother arrived four years later, Dad was older and wiser, but my mother was furious at his absence during my arrival. She did not easily forgive and spoke of his dereliction for years afterwards. Her wrath extended to me as if I were the author of his drunkenness, which, in a manner of speaking, I was.

Soon after my birth, I came down with a lung infection diagnosed as 'croup'. A steam kettle was recommended for my recovery. The vapour from the kettle, smelling strongly of menthol and camphor, helped patients with breathing difficulties. Unfortunately, a roomful of steam creates its own hazards. Mum was not exactly the most deft of women, except in her cooking. She put the kettle, which had a very long spout, on a trivet by the fire.

Temporarily forgetting its existence, she moved across the small room.

'Look out!' yelled Dad as Mum knocked the spout. 'God help us! You've killed her!' he shouted as boiling water poured out over the new baby.

Luckily it was winter. I was wrapped up in so many clothes that only my head and one arm were uncovered. They were badly scalded. My father rushed me to the Queen Elizabeth Hospital for Children in Hackney Road, only a few minutes' walk away, followed by my sobbing mother. I recovered from the lung infection. The accident left its mark in the form of a small bald patch on my head, where the hair never grew again, and a big scar, now so wrinkled it is hardly noticeable, on my arm.

Over in France, avoiding death – not giving life – was the major concern. The war operations had developed into a siege, with opposing armies facing each other in trenches which stretched from the North Sea to the Swiss frontier.

In 1916 came the attack on the Somme. British soldiers bombarded the Germans for six days and nights with six million shells, creating a noise that could be heard even in London.

The English generals assumed that this barrage must have wiped out most of the enemy. The survivors would be too weak to offer resistance. How wrong they were, the 'tommies' soon found out when they were ordered forward across No-Man's Land. The Germans were neither dead nor demoralised. They mowed the British soldiers down in their thousands. The poor devils got bogged down in mud or became entangled on barbed wire, easy targets for enemy fire. The few who lived through this hell were ordered to keep on advancing.

Young men from families rich and poor, miners, farm hands, schoolboys and friends who joined up in 'pals' battalions, were all grist to the mill. The slaughter only stopped when darkness fell.

The British general Henry Rawlinson, 1st Baron Rawlinson, was so horrified by the massacre that he wanted to abandon the suicidal offensive altogether. He was overruled. Sir Douglas Haig reiterated with even more vigour, 'The attack will go on.' And so it did with the loss on 1 July 1916 of 60,000 men, the heaviest day's loss in the whole bloody history of war to that date.

Having recently lost her brother Jack in France, Mum took more interest in what was happening over there than in the suffragettes at home. It angered and saddened her to read of such terrible battle casualties. And they were not to be the last. After the Somme disaster, came another carnage when 6 or 7 miles of ground were gained at a cost of half a million lives . . . a whole generation of young men mown down in their prime for a few miles of land. And that was how the war continued; battle lines never varying by more than 20 miles west or east, until the great offensive of 1918.

Zeppelin raids brought the war closer to home and my mother, along with several other families, took shelter from them in the nearby St Peter's church.

In spite of the war, Mum remembered the promise she made when she married, to bring any children up as Catholics. Like the Watermans, she regarded promises very seriously. Though she never herself became a Catholic, shortly after my birth she took me to the local Catholic church for my baptism.

'And what name would you like the little one to have?' asked the priest.

Having considered the matter of names for her first-born for some time, Mum was well prepared and replied at once, 'Ivy Jennie Rose'. She chose Jennie because of the friend who had kept in touch with her deceased brother Jack; Rose because of the beautiful flower; and Ivy as the first name because she liked it. What Mum did not take into account was that registers, including those at school, entered the surname first and I would become Crawley Ivy, as another girl in my class became Smart Mary. Neither did she anticipate the reaction of the somewhat die-hard priest.

Horrified by the choice, he exclaimed, 'Glory be to God! You can't be giving the poor wee creature only flowers in her name.' Ignoring Rose of Lima, he added in the same shocked tone, 'Not a single saint to watch over her!' He could not understand such a lapse and continued, 'Sure, there must be some saint you'd like for her to have.'

Dad, for whom saints were not part of normal conversation, prompted by my Protestant mother, suggested Helen – possibly thinking of Ellen, the name of Mum's mother, rather than a reference to the Saint Helen credited with having discovered the cross on which Jesus was crucified. He pulled out a further advantage of the name Helen: it was rather posh, and Mum, after her long service with the Watermans, was a soft touch for anything 'posh'.

After some discussion, Rose went out (it didn't go with the Ivy on which my mother had set her heart, priest or no priest). Helen came in . . . or nearly did. Owing to the priest's being Irish, slightly unfamiliar with the local Cockney patois, and thinking, correctly, that he was dealing with some obstinate customer, Ellen instead of Helen went into the records. I thus became the owner of three names, Ivy Ellen Jennie. They proved very useful to me later, for I could always find my name quickly on an examination or other list. Few girls, especially those born in Bethnal Green, were so rich, in initials at least.

When I started my first permanent job in the Civil Service, a supervisor asked my address and name.

'Bethnal Green? I knew you were a country girl. I could tell it from your lovely complexion.'

I didn't dare tell her that if I had a 'lovely complexion' it came from daily washing under a cold water tap in the back yard. When I gave her my three names, she said that she preferred Jennie, and would call me that. It has stuck with me ever since.

5

DIY

Whether it was the strain of his daughter's wedding, the loss of his wife, two sons and a daughter, or the sheer effort of disabled living, my grandfather died not long after his daughter and my father got married. Still in her early twenties, Mum became her family's sole survivor with no relations other than the distant 'cousins'. Two brothers and a sister had died in their youth, her mother in her thirties. Now her father was gone too. He never saw my brother, young Jim, who was born in 1920, four years after me. When he arrived, the question of more rooms came up, as it had done with Mum herself after her birth a quarter of a century before, and with the same problem of a higher rent.

The soon-to-be-vacant rooms were in a house just across the street. The upstairs half was tenanted by just an elderly couple, so the opportunity for a move seemed too good to miss. Perhaps later Mum might eventually get the whole house. What a wonderful dream, to have your own house with nobody to share it except your family!

She hoped she could get another cleaning job to help out with the higher rent. If not, everybody must sleep in the front room. She could then let out the one thereby made vacant. After all these calculations, we moved across the street from number 55 to number 11. It was a grand apartment, a palace of two whole rooms, and a kitchen where we ate. Like most but not all poorer houses of that era, there was no heating other than from the kitchen fire, and lighting was by a gas mantle, or failing that, by candle.

Our new home consisted of a front room facing the street, a middle room and the kitchen. The front room had two functions. The pull-out bed on which my parents sometimes slept doubled up as a sofa, converting the room into a 'parlour'. Two cupboards reached halfway up the walls on either side of the fireplace. One Saturday morning when Mum was out doing her charring, and my father out either at work or looking for it, I ventured into this room, and came upon the most wonderful treasure.

My mother had salted away in this hiding place all her sister Bessie's remaining pieces of material, on which she had worked until her death. There were huge reels of different coloured cottons, yards of net and veiling wrapped round cardboard, lace and ribbons for trimming. Everything was undamaged, in perfect condition. Such a find opened up fascinating possibilities. I dived into it, attired myself in yards of veiling and pranced around, a beautiful, richly attired princess. Then I had a fright. My mother was returning. Too slow to divest myself of my new image, I got a huge berating, not so much for opening the cupboard in my parents' room – after all, it was also a 'parlour' – but for missing out my Saturday morning chores of cleaning up the house.

I hated this job and always stayed in bed until the last possible minute so that I could just manage to clean the place, lay the table and so on, before my mother came in at the door. However, on this occasion, after the telling-off strengthened with a few slaps, the force of which I had long learnt to dodge, Mum softened up sufficiently to tell me a bit about her sister. It was such a sad yet brave tale, I listened avidly.

The material Bessie had never used was used up eventually, though I never became a dressmaker except on sufferance. Today, nearly ninety years later, I still have reels left of that wonderful cotton made in Lancashire looms by some of the skilled, untreasured workers Britain possessed and which, like the Britain of those years, seemed destined to last for ever.

The middle room of our new house became the bedroom for me and my brother. The only furniture other than our bed was a kind of marble-topped table, on which rested a large jug of water standing in a flowered china basin, with a pail underneath. We had few clothes, so there was no need for any other furniture.

We took off our clothes at night and put them at the bottom of the bed. In the morning we were supposed to wash ourselves with the water from the jug, and empty the water into the pail and then into the lavatory in the garden. As my mother was often out doing some early morning charring before we were up, and my father, quite unlike any sergeant major, never checked on his charges' uniform, there were many times when we missed our morning wash.

My parents' bedroom was the largest in the house. When Mum got behind with the rent, as she constantly did in the next few years, she let out, or tried to let out, a spare room. My brother and I then moved into the front room with our parents. The pull-out bed came into use once more. Desperately poor tenants arrived for the vacant middle room. Trying to fight a losing battle against poverty, they shared our lodgings for a short time, then after a few weeks and usually a fight or two, they disappeared into the outer wilderness, invariably owing the rent. Being a landlord was not a job for the faint-hearted.

The kitchen where we ate had three doors. One led straight to the concrete yard and the outdoor tap. Upstairs tenants came into our kitchen by one door, then went out into the paved yard by another. This gave them access to the tap and WC normally used by everybody in a house, irrespective of numbers or age. In our 'new' house there were just the two upstairs tenants, an elderly couple, a quiet and unobtrusive pair named Mr and Mrs Cox. We thought ourselves very lucky indeed not to have a house full of sharers who could come through our kitchen, not merely as often as they needed, but as often as they fancied.

A narrow concrete pathway led from the kitchen door into the yard and outdoor lavatory, a hutlike contrivance which, fortunately, had a watertight roof. You didn't have to sit or stand there with the rain pouring over you, as happened in the old house when you used the WC or collected water from the outdoor tap.

There was also a real garden, a tiny bit of earth bounded by small brick walls and trellis work on either side. Over these walls, we could view neighbours' gardens. Some of them were incredibly beautiful, at least to our ignorant eyes. And best of all, this potential paradise we now inherited had to be 'maintained' by the downstairs tenants, in other words, us.

In some houses, handymen made trellis-work arches leading to the WC as if you were about to visit a faery bower. Inside the lavatory, the wooden seat of the WC extended right across from wall to wall. Even when the trellis was covered with creeping weeds instead of flowers, the seat was quite a nice private place to sit and look out at the garden.

For the moment we had no such bower, but the lavatory seat was still a pleasant place from which to look out and see the garden, bounded at the back not by houses, as were most other properties in the street, but by a large brick wall, the side of a factory building. Covered with Virginia creeper it revealed in the autumn Nature's glorious extravagance. The leaves changed from a limping yellow into a mass of riotous russets, making a glorious backdrop to the black earth and dingy buildings.

When Mum worked for the Watermans, Fred told her the names of the various flowers he and Mrs Waterman tended with loving care. Mum forgot all the Latin names, but remembered the shapes, colours or scents. With a blend of devotion and ignorance, she tried hard to make something of the plot she now 'inherited'. Her tiny patch could never rival the Watermans' long garden, particularly as she was not a bit selective, cherishing anything that grew, even at first, the dandelions. But it was green and colourful.

She knew a little about dahlias from the time she had spent as a young girl working for a Mrs Cohen, and felt a special affection for these flowers. They had helped her indirectly to get her job at the Watermans. She spent hours, or so it seemed to Dad, looking at pictures in the free catalogues she picked up at florists' in the City. Finally she made up her mind what she wanted. The catalogues should have warned her, or maybe they did and she preferred to ignore the fact, that dahlias weren't exactly the best plants for a garden in Bethnal Green.

In the first instance they were very expensive. In the second, dahlia tubers could be destroyed by frost and most species had to be taken inside to avoid the winter. Ignoring these points, and that there was little enough space in the house for humans, let alone dahlia tubers, Mum went ahead and bought her plants: just two from Carter Page in the City.

Dad couldn't understand how anybody could spend so much money on flowers (it was different for a bet or a drink), but put it down to the vagaries of women. Under Mum's watchful eyes, the dahlias blossomed. In autumn, when other blooms were dying, the tiny garden was filled with their colour. Even I eventually learnt to distinguish between the single and double, the cactus, pom-pom and rosette varieties.

As well as the two doors in the kitchen, one leading to the hallway and front door and the other to the yard, there was another one at the opposite side of the room. This opened onto an 'outhouse' which also led into the yard and the garden. The 'outhouse' was a ramshackle extension of the kitchen to increase its space. It was made almost entirely of glass. Rain dripped constantly through the roof, not a happy accompaniment to cooking over the ancient gas stove enshrined there, rooted by rust to the spot.

House repairs were never done by landlords, except under the most dire threats, or possibly, sweeteners. Wives with husbands who could plaster, paint or do odd jobs about the house, etc. were therefore much envied by women lacking such useful helpmates.

My mother began praising up one of these fellows who lived next door. 'I've just seen Mrs Meadows' outhouse,' she said. 'Oh, it's lovely. Her 'Arrie's made a real good job of it. Turned it into a proper kitchen,' she sighed, 'with shelves 'n all. And not a drop of rain comes through.'

Dad kept his eyes glued to the racing results in the paper, several days old, and said nothing.

'Now she can use the kitchen to 'ave a sit down in the evening,' continued my mother. 'Lovely and comfortable it is, with a beautiful Rexine settee.'

'Probably got it off a barrer, second 'and,' retorted Dad. 'You bet the springs will be dropping out any time at all.'

Mum was not to be put off. She continued describing the merits of Florrie Meadows' new outhouse and of her brilliant husband, until Dad decided he'd show his wife he could do as well as any of those fellows, including Harry Meadows.

Borrowing a ladder from Harry, but refusing all his offers of help, he got out the few tools he possessed, and set about repairing the leaking glass roof. His efforts lasted all of five minutes before he fell through it to the concrete floor below. Off he was rushed to Bethnal Green Hospital in Cambridge Heath Road. Neither encouragement nor disparagement could make him tackle any Do-It-Yourself jobs, other than the most minor ones, ever again.

I made a very poor showing when I visited him in hospital. As a child I was a terrible weakling, and the sights in the ward annexe were somehow so overpowering that I fainted. The faint may have had some connection with my first hospital visit as a scalded baby, possibly with my many illnesses thereafter, or with the memory of that never-to-be-forgotten smell that seemed to pervade all hospitals of the time – or it may have been worry about this father I loved so much. Whatever the cause, I fainted, and I have never got over this wretched weakness since: probably the coward's way out of pain.

6

A BRUSH WITH CRIME

My father took some time to recover from his fall. While in hospital, he got a touch of 'bronchitis'. It caused him later to be very vulnerable to chest infections. He smoked Woodbines heavily when he could afford them. When he couldn't, he smoked, like many hard-up men of that generation, the tobacco from fag ends. These were cigarettes smoked almost to the end by other men, then thrown into the gutter or on the pavement, and retrieved by those with no money who were dying for a fag.

Little did any of them know then that this was literally what they were doing – dying for a fag. My father brought the fag ends home, took out the tobacco from inside, and shook it on the table. He picked up a pinch of the tobacco and rolled it inside a tiny tissue tear-out sheet from a packet of Rizla cigarette papers to make himself a 'new' cigarette.

He'd try to avoid doing this when Mum was around. 'Nasty, dirty 'abit,' she'd tell him, but the desire for the weed was usually too strong for him to resist.

And he had too, a real weakness for the poteen. Perhaps that was why my grandfather did not want his daughter to marry him. My father, a darling man, though not always so in my mother's eyes, was in his younger days as strong as a horse, and as pliable as putty. Offer him a drink, and like Oscar Wilde, he could refuse anything except temptation. Down would go the drink, glug, glug, and another . . . and another . . . and if I had not found him in the pub by then, he would stagger home to be met by my mother's wrath, or a locked door which he soon broke open. Yet this gullible, pliable man showed me how even the weakest can prove heroic when emotion and motive coincide.

We were walking to church one Sunday (my father being one of those old-fashioned Irish Catholics who keep up religious traditions as much from habit as belief) when we heard what sounded like furious galloping and steel-shod hoofs on the cobbled street.

We looked behind. A riderless horse was racing madly along Vallance Road. A cart, hitched onto the horse, swayed to and fro with such force it seemed as if any minute it would swing off onto our bit of pavement and dash itself or us to pieces. Beer barrels careered off the dray, vanishing in seconds behind apparently innocent doors.

Not hesitating for a moment, or so it seemed to me, Dad rushed into the road and grabbed the trailing reins of the horse. Hanging on within inches of its charging hoofs, he hauled himself up and onto the animal's back.

Ten years old, I stood on the pavement petrified. My father gradually slowed down the frightened animal's gallop into a trot and climbed into the dickey seat of the cart. I rushed after him. His strong arms lifted me beside him. There was no sign of the driver. He had probably been thrown off and was likely to be lying senseless, far back in the direction of Bethnal Green Road.

Judging by the sign on its side, the dray belonged to a local brewery, not far away, near Brick Lane. My father steered the horse back to base and reported the incident at the factory gates. He left quickly without giving his name and we continued our journey to church as if nothing had happened.

He limped a little as we hurried to St Anne's church in Underwood Street.

'Have you hurt yourself, Dad?'

He shook his head. 'Just a knock,' he said.

I held his hand very tightly. We walked to church as fast as we could from Hanbury Street, not far away. Neither of us said another word about the incident, as if a runaway horse was just an everyday occurrence, like trying to get work at the docks or food tickets at what was known locally as the 'bun 'ouse'. We arrived halfway through the Mass. Coward that I was, I hoped nobody saw me, especially any of my teachers. When we left, we went back to Bethnal Green instead of visiting the aunt who lived nearby in basement rooms at Morrison's Buildings, in Commercial Road, Whitechapel.

Dad said not a word about the incident of the runaway horse when we got home, but my mother was quick off the mark.

'Whatever 'ave you done to that leg of yours?' she asked.

'Nothing much, Sue. Like Oliver Cromwell, it's got knocked about a bit, that's all. It'll be better tomorrow.'

'Well let's 'ope it will. You won't 'ave much luck at the docks with a gammy leg, that's for sure. 'Ere, let's have a look at it.'

Like most men, Dad enjoyed a bit of personal attention. He rolled up his trousers to reveal a calf badly grazed and already turning blue and black with bruising.

'Good Gawd Almighty! Whatever 'ave you been and gone and done to yourself?'

'Like I said, just got knocked about a bit,' he repeated.

In a pitch of excitement I called out breathlessly, 'He stopped a horse, Mum. He jumped up and stopped a horse.'

'Stopped an 'orse, did 'e? Outside the pub, I suppose.'

'No, it was going along Vallance Road. Ever so fast.'

'Soppy thing,' she said, addressing Dad. 'Whatever did you want to go and do a stupid thing like that for? I dunno . . . some people . . . got no sense they ain't. Could lose you a job.'

From a cupboard in the kitchen, she got out one of her patent medicines, a grey sticky ointment called Zam-Buk, a universal cure-all bought in one of the stalls in Brick Lane. She rubbed it gently into his leg, as gently as she could that is, for her long history of charring had not left her with much of a soft touch, as I knew to my cost.

After that she dismissed the tale of the runaway horse as of no consequence other than how it might put paid to Dad's chance of a job. She had this fixed idea of never praising any of the family – my father, brother or me – to our faces. This was due to some old-fashioned Protestant creed, picked up in her youth, that praise makes a person conceited and pride goes before a fall.

She occasionally relented her stance for my brother. There was a strong affinity between them, as there was between me and my father. But my brother was the son of the family, and at the beginning of the twentieth century, sons had value. Girls? Well, they could earn a bit of a living but there was always a big question mark over them except as carers for your old age. Their future depended so much on other people. Boys could make their own way in the world. Mum was not loath, however, to praise up the family, their talents, their accomplishments, such as they were, or anything else she thought worth mentioning to neighbours and any Tom, Dick or Harry who would listen to the exploits of her wonderful family.

'You should just hear my boy, Jim, on that mouth-organ of his. Real clever 'e is. A treat to listen to,' she might say. These reports, which percolated to us second hand, tasted just as sweet as newly minted ones. Praise for the family, especially young Jim, slowly petered out, however, as Big Jim's drinking got worse.

When I was older and we knew Dad had got some wages, I used to go round the pubs at night looking for him, and enticing him out. If Mum was doing her charring she could not go, and when she wasn't working, she was too proud to do so. My brother, born four years after me, was too young to be sent on such missions.

It was almost like a game of chess my father and I played together – dodging across a board of local pubs, using straight, crooked and diagonal moves to achieve checkmate. I loved him so much, yet my heart bled for him and cursed him. He knew there would be, as always, a terrible row when he got home. What made him so weak . . . and to me, so lovable?

Too young to be allowed inside the premises, I opened the 'public' bar door to see if my father was inside. As soon as he caught sight of me, he realised it was 'all up', laughingly tell his mates, 'got to go now', and come out. He never made a fuss, having the same attitude as an old-time criminal who is caught and goes along with his captor, saying, 'It's a fair cop.' But his often staggering gait made it hard for me to get him home. I had too little strength to support him properly. Why did he have to go into the pub?

How could I, as a child, understand the temptations waiting for a man with a little money in his pocket who had to have a drink with his mates . . . and then another . . . and another. Searching for my father, I became almost as well known in the drinking fraternity as the Salvation Army ladies going round with their collection boxes and selling their magazine *War Cry*.

People grumbled that you never got a bit of food from their organisation without having to sing hymns or say prayers. The same could be said of the Mildmay Hospital in Shoreditch. Being taken in there for one of my many childish illnesses, I learnt to sing for my supper any number of 'Protestant' hymns. I have remembered them ever since.

In the pubs, the Salvation Army ladies were greatly respected and admired. Swearing in their presence was considered a heinous offence by customers, some of whom had done 'time' for vicious crimes of violence. And yet such swearing was mild compared with the standard of today's American films, where even educated people are unable to mouth a single sentence without using at least one four-letter word. And not for the sake of 'realism'. The dialogue needed for a book like *The Bonfire of the Vanities* and the throwaway swearing of almost any modern '18' film have nothing in common.

Dad's big weakness, other than his fondness for beer, was being so gullible. He was the most easily led, easily deceived person, possible to find, even more so than I, and I was bad enough. With a childlike innocence, he'd believe almost any tale, the more outlandish the better.

Like me, he never bought any bargain that did not, later on, prove a sheer waste of money. He was full of ideas, none of which ever came to fruition.

He suggested I enrol in his weekly 'diddlum' club, like those run in some pubs. You began by saving one farthing, and increased the amount by one farthing a week. Borrowing was allowed, but you had to pay back double what you borrowed. Poor Dad. I was forever borrowing from his diddlum club, and never paying anything back, until the club was wound up because of lack of funds.

I went to meet him when he came out of hospital. I was deliriously happy to see him, and held his hand tightly as we walked home. He still looked and felt very poorly, but went back to work the next day. Nobody risked being sick too long, for fear their job would go.

Hospitals played a large part in our lives. There was no National Health Service but many hospitals and convalescent homes were helped by charitable institutions or by contributory schemes such as the Hospital Savings Association, to which, I think, it cost threepence a week to belong.

At that time, in the 1920s, vaccination against smallpox was compulsory, and it remained so until 1948. Most people were glad to let their children be vaccinated, for in the sweatshops of the East End, they could see scarred and pock-marked immigrants, including Jews and others from Russia and the Baltic states, who had suffered and recovered from smallpox. The lesson was clear enough. Smallpox was fatal, and even if you recovered, it scarred your face for life.

Most of Mum's 'cousins', the Stokes clan, had gone their various ways, but one of the family who lived in Hackney had a small child. When he was vaccinated something went wrong, and the boy died from the effects of vaccination, not the disease. This tragedy made Mum decide I would not be vaccinated. She had to sign a paper declaring her 'conscientious objection', quite a brave thing to do then, though it would be thought foolish today not to avail oneself of all the preventive medicine around.

The 'cousin' whose son had died in one of those rare mishaps following a jab suffered another stroke of misfortune when the only daughter went down with diphtheria (which, like scarlet fever, was almost as common as measles). Infectious diseases were treated in an isolation hospital in Tottenham, north London. The child was sent there but – such is the burden of sadness some parents have to suffer – the poor little thing died soon after her arrival.

When I, too, caught diphtheria, Mum was terrified. She was sure that God was punishing her. She had promised, as was the practice for people marrying a Catholic, to bring up any children of the marriage in the Catholic faith. But she had sent me, as soon as I was 5 years old, to the pleasant little Church of England primary school, St Peter's, literally a few minutes' walk from our home.

It was far safer for a small child than going to the Catholic school, over a mile away. With only one tiny cul-de-sac road to cross, I was able to go there on my own, and at playtimes could be seen through the railings that surrounded the leafy playground. For a few years I was very happy there, but when I fell prey to diphtheria, Mum, superstitious as ever, thought the illness must be due to a vindictive God chastising her for not keeping her promise.

So now to appease His wrath, I had to go to St Anne's Catholic school, Underwood Street in Whitechapel. Mum was secretly afraid of nuns, with their strange garb, and though it was different for Dad, of course, she did not care for 'Roman' practices either. She went once to Mass, but couldn't understand why you had to keep standing up and kneeling down or why all the service, except the sermon, had to be in Latin. So she never accompanied him when he took me to church on Sunday mornings. Young Jim, much younger, stayed at home with her.

The Catholic school was a very long way to walk from our house. It meant crossing the busy Bethnal Green Road, into Vallance Road on the way to Whitechapel, an area largely inhabited, so my mother believed, by all sorts of strange people – as Nelson Street was not. But she had made up her mind, and as always when she made up her mind, other considerations were disregarded. She steeled herself to meet the nuns and any other teachers at St Anne's and set off, wheeling my brother in an ancient pushchair. Alas! She was not to be so easily absolved by the jealous God. A further disaster lay in store for her and all of us.

Everything went well for a few months, until one day Dad came home looking very worried. Carefree and always ready for a laugh, he never grumbled or moaned about anything, no matter how hard he worked or what pain he might be suffering. Neither did he ever appear downhearted, no matter how bad the present or the future appeared. But now he sat down, silent and morose. Did he feel ill? Surely he had recovered from his accident by now? He finally stumbled out the awful truth.

'I've got to go to court,' he announced with a mixture of despair and defiance.

'Court?' my mother repeated, in a kind of dazed incomprehension.

Oh God! Dad had not done anything that might land him in prison, had he? But it seemed he had.

'I was about 'alf an hour from the depot,' he said, 'when one of my old mates called out to me. I ain't seen 'im for a year or two and 'e's carrying a big case, and looking fair worn out. 'E asks me to give 'im a lift. Course, we're not supposed to give anybody lifts, and I never do, but I used to know 'im, and 'e didn't want to go far. "'Op on mate," I says to 'im, and 'e does. About ten minutes further on, I sees two coppers, and this old mate jumps off my van. The coppers chase after 'im. He drops the case and runs. I can't make out what's it all about . . . and then it turns out this mate 'as not been long out of the nick. The stuff in 'is case is some sparklers 'e's pinched and he's on 'is way to load them off to a fence in Whitechapel.'

'Good Gawd Almighty!' said Mum, in a paroxysm of horror. 'What's going to happen now?'

'Well I've got to go to court, and tell my side of the story.'

'Oh Jim, will you lose your job?'

'Course not,' Dad declared, but with a kind of query in the voice almost as if he wanted confirmation of what he said. 'I ain't done nothing wrong . . . except give a lift to an old pal. I didn't know 'e'd just come out of the nick, or 'ad any stolen stuff on 'im.'

'Why didn't you ask to look in 'is case before you took him on? Then you would 'ave seen what he was carrying.'

'Look in his case!' Her question almost caused him to laugh. 'Look in his case!' he said again and shook his head as if he could not believe what he heard. 'What d'ye think I am, a blimmin' Customs officer?'

'They might say you were 'elping the fellow get away with the stuff he's pinched.'

'Who's going to say a thing like that? Besides 'e never got away did 'e? Let's forget it and 'ave something to eat.'

But the impending court case was not so easy to forget. First and worst, Dad was suspended without pay until the case came up. No wages came in. We could have food tickets from the Board of Guardians to save us from starving (many shops had signs in their windows: Relief Tickets Taken Here), but no money was forthcoming.

How was the rent to be paid? No rent . . . no roof, a lesson that all East Enders and workhouse inmates knew only too well. Mum took me to St Anne's school, pushing young Jim in the old pushchair. Like many toddlers, he wanted to walk everywhere. Hating the indignity of a pram, he cried and struggled all the way to St Anne's.

Mum wondered how she was going to manage. She had given up her job after I was born and would now have to get another. Finding one would not be too hard. She had excellent references and cleaners were always wanted in the City, but wages everywhere were low. And there was young Jim: 3 years old . . . how could she pay for him to be minded? The cost would use up all her wages and we would be no better off.

I was too young to stay at home and permanently look after him. A few days – or even months – might be managed without the School

Board Officer catching up with us . . . but the 'School Board Man' was pretty good at checking on school absentees. He was often used as an ogre by parents to get their kids to school and not stay at home or do a few paying errands when they could get them.

No, me as a young babyminder of my infant brother would not do. Over my crying brother, Mum mentioned the problem to one of the lady teachers at the school, without of course saying a word about any court case. She was far too proud to mention that. The nuns, the teacher told her, were looking for a washerwoman. Mum had never been a washerwoman. She had always felt it to be far harder scrubbing clothes than scrubbing floors. An enticing bait was set for her, however, in the shape of a babyminder.

Compulsory education began at 5 years. Young Jim, who was only 3, could come to school and be looked after in the babies' class while Mum did the washing in the basement. She could take him home with her when she finished, and I too, would be allowed home early on 'washing' days.

It seemed an ideal arrangement. Mum started her new career as a washerwoman. But when she saw the huge boiler underneath the school, where she was to wash the nuns' habits and much else, all her worries about Catholics came to the surface. She had read about sinners being walled up as a punishment. Superstitious as she was, the dark basement, the silence broken only by the entrance of a softly treading, long-gowned nun in black, frightened her stiff.

Her reading, except for newspapers, in which she had a strangely eclectic taste, was mainly of romances allied with the Maria Marten kind of thriller – the Red Barn murder, and such. Mum was sure she was destined for some hideous white slave trade. At the very least she would be carted off somewhere against her will, and nobody, not a soul, would be any the wiser. And what of her poor children?

She lit the fire under the huge boiler, wondering whether her body would be thrown into it, and not even her ashes ever found. Perhaps, she thought, as she carried round the great buckets of water, she might be drowned first. An ancient nun came down with a free dinner and cup of tea. Instead of the new washerwoman showing her appreciation for the food, it started up all her fears. Was this the beginning of the end? Was the food poisoned? Where and how would they get rid of her body? In time Susan's worries seemed to disappear into still waters, but with all the threat of a tidal wave suddenly breaking out through her not quite placid calm.

Though Dad's brush with crime was a minor one, it had a major effect on our lives, for we started to sink to subsistence level. In the East End, crime of any sort, major or minor, was a constant topic of conversation as well as a way of life to take up or discard. The choice was not always in your own power. Social welfare or benefits had not yet arrived. Until the Factory Act of 1901 came in when my mother was 10 years old, children under 12 still worked in factories up to thirty-nine hours a week, while for 12 year olds the limits were forty-four hours until the Factory Act of 1937.

Pensions were introduced in 1908 by the Liberals, at 5s a week (provided your income was under £31 a year, you hadn't been in prison for the past 10 years, or been on poor relief in the previous year).

Until the National Insurance Act of 1911 was passed, there was no sickness benefit and free medical treatment came from hospitals mostly maintained by charity or by voluntary contributions. Even after the Act, families of insured persons were excluded from its provisions. Neither did unemployment benefit exist except for workers in the building, shipbuilding and engineering trades. If you couldn't find work or get poor relief, the only option left was thieving or the workhouse.

Not far away from our house lived a father more often drunk than sober, who cruelly beat up his eldest son if he did not come back with some stolen goods, preferably bicycles or bits of them. Yet the boy was rather religious, as I knew from seeing him at Sunday school, which he attended more regularly than I ever did.

Other children also went to Sunday school, usually for motives quite unconnected with religion. Charity parcels and prizes were occasionally doled out to them, as they were to children attending Christmas celebrations at working men's clubs. But this lad had a genuine interest in the tales of the Bible. In another home and place, he might well have become a priest or missionary or both . . . or if he had joined the Communist party, as many impoverished young Jewish lads did, a politician or a revolutionary.

All the eight children of this family suffered from the 'English' disease, rickets caused by lack of calcium and vitamins. Bow-legged children, like my mother, who similarly suffered from this lack, were a common sight. Like many other diseases, rickets has all but disappeared from the UK today. But nobody bothered about diet or vitamins then. Assuaging hunger was the main concern and a good meal was a blessing.

Everybody in Bethnal Green, and doubtless in other parts of London's East End, especially Whitechapel, had their own attitude to crime. You didn't for example, commit them within your own 'patch'. In some families the foulest of language was the 'norm', in others only a few expletives were allowed. The first group were always referred to by more 'superior' groups as that 'effing and blinding lot'. Infanticide was a capital offence, so getting a girl 'into trouble' could have fatal consequences for the parents as well as the infant. 'A life for a life' was the order of the day.

Sealed lips or lying tongues were expected of a family with criminals in its midst, and necessary for its survival. This unity gave support when times were hard, but woe betide anybody who transgressed the code, often as rigid as that imposed by the Mafia. They would soon feel the vengeance of the 'Godfather' in different, sometimes horrific and terrible ways.

Crime was also a subject for heated debate, especially a murder trial. The merits of the defence were better known and sometimes better argued by local protagonists than, so it seemed, the judge trying the case.

7

CRISIS

Mum stuck at her washerwoman's job until Dad's case came up in court. What would be its outcome? Would he get a prison sentence for aiding and abetting a crook? In court, he heard himself referred to as a 'gullible' young man. Did that mean innocent or guilty? The relief when he got off without, so it was said, a stain on his character, was overwhelming. Now everything would be all right. But stain or no stain, his employers did not take him back. At a time when millions were out of work, who else would employ a man sacked from a safe job for involvement, however innocent, in a crime?

Dad and Mum, though streetwise in some respects, were completely naive in others. Neither of them knew a thing about how to create a good impression with people in authority, or how to 'fudge' a situation in their favour. Florrie Meadows, who lived next door and knew a thing or two, told Mum to get on to one of the societies that helped you out when times were bad.

'There are a few, you know,' said Florrie. 'They take some finding. But you've got to tell the right tale. They visit you, and before they come round, make sure you bring in a few friends down on their luck,' she told Mum.

'They'd fill the whole place up. What do I want that lot in for?'

'It shows how 'ard up you are. Course, everybody's 'ard up these days, but if the 'ouse is packed out, especially with anybody who's got galloping consumption, you'll get a better chance of squeezing something out of the charity geezers, or of them 'elping Jim to find a job. Don't be frightened. You're doing them a favour. That's their job, to hand out a bit of charity.'

Mum was grateful for Florrie's advice, but felt she hadn't sunk that far yet. And she was intrinsically honest, perhaps because her experience of being honest had, so far, been favourable. On one occasion, doing a stint of office cleaning, she found a pound note inadvertently thrown into the wastepaper basket. She put it on her employer's desk with a message written in her round big hand, 'Losers, weepers'.

Next morning, on the desk was an envelope addressed 'To The Cleaner'. Mum picked it up with trembling hands and hoped she wasn't going to lose her job. Had she been too cheeky? She opened the envelope and could hardly believe her luck. Inside the employer had returned the pound note with a memo, 'Finders, keepers'.

She had not yet learnt to lie, to swindle, to cheat, in order to survive. Honesty was not always the best policy for those at the bottom of the human waste pile, as many immigrants knew to their cost. Lies had to be told to evade death. Swindling and cheating might enable you to escape torture. Mum knew the hardships of an untamed capitalist system but had never suffered, as had the Jews and other refugees in the East End, the cruelties of tyranny or the ghettoes. If, for example, she ever had to pay income tax, a situation which never arose in her life, she would have listed the very clothes she wore as income-producing assets.

Now, not a penny came into the house, other than her washerwoman's wages or a day's casual work which Dad managed to pick up somewhere. And that money barely paid the rent. The fear of the workhouse loomed before them. They were completely unable to deal with the situation in which they now found themselves.

Mum kept in touch with the Watermans during her early married life. She wrote in one of her letters, without giving the cause, that Dad had lost his job, and said that she had found work as a washerwoman. Fred replied suggesting she might be better off working as a cleaner in the City. It meant early morning and evening working, but he knew a firm paying better wages than most, and he would put in a word for her if she wanted the job.

Mum's fears of the nuns were receding and she was grateful for the meals they gave her, my brother and me, but she was a small, thin woman. Washing, mangling and ironing clothes in a big steamy basement were a heavy drain on her strength. She wanted to take up Fred Waterman's suggestion, but how to do it? Both my brother and I had to be taken to school . . . we couldn't cross that big Bethnal Green Road ourselves.

She spoke to the teacher who had first suggested the washerwoman's job. The answer relayed back to her was that the nuns would not take it amiss if she tried to better herself, and to help her they would even continue to keep young Jim in the babies' class until he reached the compulsory school starting age of 5 years.

At this crucial point a volunteer now arrived on the scene in the shape of Nellie Hook, the daughter of Mr Hook, the Mayor of Bethnal Green. He was unusual not only in being an Irish Catholic mayor, but in living in a whole house just across the street with his wife and their family of three daughters and two sons. Nellie, the middle daughter, took the youngest girl, Winnie, to the Catholic school. We could go along to school with them. If by any chance Nellie fell ill or couldn't take us, an older daughter, Eileen, would fill the breach,

My mother, always a very independent soul, gave Nellie weekly pocket money for looking after me and my brother, and changed her job to office cleaning. Eventually young Jim became my reluctant 'charge'. Mum left in the mornings soon after 5.30 a.m. My father got our breakfast, and then went out looking for work. I took young Jim to school, and in the evening had to get him home before Mum left at six o'clock for an evening stint of cleaning.

Young Jim was a real devil – always trying to jump on carts, a pastime then much enjoyed by young boys. They ran behind a horse and cart, leapt onto the tailboard of the cart and levered themselves up for a ride.

This could be a dangerous game with the tailboard perhaps broken or loose. Having got onto the cart and risked the driver's wrath, their next move was to jump off. That was the danger point. They often landed, with fatal results, in the path of oncoming traffic, now getting thicker and quicker every day. It was very hard for me to stop my brother playing this dangerous game.

Sometimes he wanted to try a different way home. My opposition to these plans, when it existed at all, was very feeble. We lingered on the bridge over the railway lines running between Liverpool Street, Cambridge Heath, Shoreditch and Bethnal Green stations, and watched the trains speeding below or piling up in a queue waiting to enter one of the stations. Where were they all going? Who was in them? Why were they stopping?

We stretched ourselves flat out on the wooden bridge leading to Brick Lane, the better to see through its many chinks. We looked at every train that came and went, often shifting our positions to get a better view of what was going on below. Lying on the bridge, it was impossible to keep our clothes clean. They got dirtier and dirtier – another reason for delaying our arrival home. Without machines or hot water, washing was no easy chore. The public baths were used mainly for big things like sheets. Getting clothes dirty when there was nothing else to change into except the Sunday best (which might be in pawn), was a major crime.

Getting school uniform dirty was the worst of all; a shirt or blouse that needed washing in the middle of the week (because there was not another to change into) had to be dried overnight so that it could be worn next morning. To do that in winter or during wet weather was almost as difficult as drying clothes on a leaky ship or in a tent. The unpalatable truth not often digested by poor or rich alike is that the poor or handicapped need more brains or brawn than the rich to survive successfully. Even with brains, the state and fate are often against you.

We lay, blissfully ignorant and uncaring, on the bridge, watching the steam hiss out of the trains, happy in our dreams . . . until suddenly I realised that time was passing by as well as the trains. Should I linger longer so that we would arrive home after Mum had gone to work, or should I rush back in time to be told off in her strident voice? Our father was often absent, trying for a casual job, or when he was lucky, working at one. Should I time our arrival just too late for Mum to accompany the telling-off with a few well aimed spanks that she was sure to give me? She would quite often throw things at me when her ire was raised, though I had become expert at dodging missiles such as boot brushes and often retreated into the coal cupboard to avoid them. Jim was always let off or got a comparatively minor reproof. I was the older. I should have known better.

It needed fine judgement to decide when to arrive home. When a choice had to be made, like my father I invariably made the wrong one. I was too young to understand that my mother's fury was due to worry. If her two children did not arrive before she left for work, she would not know what had happened to them. . . . And my father often did not get home until long after she had gone. So unless we arrived home before Mum left for work, we could be missing on the streets, not always the safest of places, even in those days.

Another temptation to delay our homecoming was the quite unusual spectacle of the dairy in Vallance Road, where we watched, in this extraordinary urban venue between Bethnal Green and Whitechapel, cows being milked. Though the smell seemed awful, even to us, so used to smells, we loved watching the beasts in this town yard. There was nowhere else like it.

Looking after young Jim weighed heavily on me. He did not like the situation either and would often punch me up for it. I could not fight back too aggressively because he always got the better of an argument relayed to my mother and when he was older, I still lost out, for he was far stronger than I. Not only had I to get him home safely from school, but also to look after him on Saturday mornings when my mother and father were both usually out. One Saturday, he lost a ball on a shelf in the back yard. He got a pushchair to reach up to it. The pushchair slid away. He went down with a bang, sustaining the most awful gash to his leg. I had never seen such a sight. Muscle and tendons showed through the open wound. It looked terrible. What could I do for him?

I shouted across the brick wall to our next-door neighbours, Mr and Mrs Kelsey. They were related to Florrie and Harry Meadows on the other side of our house and had a business – I was never quite sure what, but it was obviously very successful, judging by all the visitors they had, the lovely carpets and furniture, the tinkling glass chandelier in the hall, and the fact that their elder son was engaged to a girl in Goodmayes, a 'posh' part of Essex. She actually owned and drove a car – a most upmarket sign of wealth no other person in Nelson Street had yet copied.

Somebody was always in at the Kelseys'. Mr Kelsey called out to us to come round the front. He opened the door, sat Jim on one of his beautiful chairs, and put iodine on the wound – can you imagine, iodine? Then he deftly added lint, cotton wool, and bandaged over the lot. My brother did not take the treatment too badly, but I nearly passed out at the thought of the pain he was suffering (rather like my poor father, a long time in the future, who was so distraught with nerves when I was expecting a baby that he couldn't even ring for an ambulance).

There were no antibiotics in the 1920s, so iodine may have been the best thing to use. People in the slums, were tough – those who survived. An earlier calamity was not so easily overcome. In addition to our kitchen with its outhouse, there were two other rooms, used for sleeping. My brother and I shared a bed in the middle room, our parents slept in the front one.

That particular Friday night, young Jim seemed to be very hot. Even stranger, he did not want to hear the stories he used to ask me to tell him at bedtime, about two frogs named Fatima and Eat-a-Lot. Instead of plying me with questions about these two ravishing frogs, as he usually did, he kept talking a lot of rubbish.

In the morning, my mother went out at 5.30 a.m. as usual. My father had got a job for the day, and not sure how ill young Jim was (nobody ever possessed a thermometer), went out at 8.00 a.m. Alone in the house, I got really frightened. My brother seemed to be getting hotter still, and tossing and turning in the bed. I was at my wits' end, wondering what was the matter with him. What could I do? I stroked his forehead with a damp cloth, but he twisted his head and mumbled something that I could not hear. Not appreciating how a high temperature causes delirium, I didn't understand why his ravings made no sense.

Mum returned home from her charring at ten o'clock. She took in the situation at once, and called the doctor. He diagnosed pneumonia. Young Jim had to be taken to hospital immediately. The doctor went to phone for an ambulance, then came back and waited with my mother for it to arrive. My father came in at this point, having explained the situation to his workmates. For once he made the right decision, not to wait for the ambulance, but to call a taxi, an action he had never before taken in his life. The Kelseys lent them the money for the cab which sped them to Bethnal Green Hospital.

In an article in the *Guardian* Dr Arie Bagon, an old-time Sheffield practitioner, recalled treating a patient with pneumonia in 1937, many years after my brother's illness. When Dr Bagon arrived at the hospital he was given two jars, one with salt water, the other containing leeches. The leeches, placed on the back of the patient, were supposed to suck out blood containing toxins. When the doctor removed the swollen leeches and put them in the salt water, it turned a vivid red as they gave out the blood they had ingested. There was no such dramatic change in the patient. He eventually died. Dr Bagon related that the leeches survived.

Bethnal Green Hospital did not use leeches, at least not on my brother. The treatment of pneumonia there at that time – and it did not always succeed – was just good nursing and a reliance on the constitution of the patient. There was no other way: penicillin did not come in until later. The course of the illness was always the same. The patient's temperature went inexorably upwards to what was known as the crisis. If the temperature came down at that point, there was the chance of recovery. If not, the patient would die. It was as simple as that.

Young Jim's temperature kept going up and up . . . from 101 to 102, 3, 4 . . . We knew his chances of survival were almost nil if the thermometer registered higher than that. It touched 105. The nurse keeping such a careful watch at the bedside told my parents not to give up hope. Patients sometimes recovered even after their temperature had soared to unprecedented highs.

Almost as she finished speaking, my brother's began to come down – a barely perceptible fraction – but it was enough to show that he was perhaps turning the corner. Little by little, the mercury fell. Jim came through the crisis, and eventually recovered. He was lucky enough (if suffering from any illness can ever be considered lucky) to have had a most wonderful Irish nurse who, through her devoted care, saved his life.

8

HOSPITALS

My own ins and outs of hospital were not so dramatic as the one childhood illness of my brother. They meant I missed a lot of school, but the lack of reading was more than made up for by the books provided free of charge in the hospital. Tattered and torn, they were nonetheless acceptable. Two hospital visits particularly stand out in my memory. The first was due to an abscess on my bottom, right near the anus. I was always suffering from abscesses of one kind or another, but this was, so far, the worst of the lot.

Whenever I was ill I wanted my father, not my mother, to take me to the doctor's surgery or to the hospital. His touch was so much gentler, his presence so much more comforting than hers. But he hated taking me because in his experience, every time he did so, I was kept in. And so it proved this time. I was operated on, a large incision made in my right buttock, and the abscess was opened up. The wound wasn't stitched. Instead, a piece of gauze was plugged into the hole made by the surgery. When I was discharged from the hospital, part of the gauze was left hanging down for easy retrieval and replugging.

This piece of gauze terrified me. It dangled round my bottom. I could feel but not see it. What would happen if it fell out? I was frightened to walk in case it did, frightened to go to the toilet for the same reason. Then, accidentally or otherwise, I dislodged it. Pus and blood poured out. Mum rushed me to the hospital in spite of my screaming that I wanted my Dad. She gave the surgeons a piece of her mind. I became almost more frightened of what she was saying than I had been of the piece of gauze hanging from my bottom. Once more I was taken into the Queen Elizabeth Hospital for Children, in Hackney Road, and the surgeons went to work again.

Meanwhile, the Duke and Duchess of York (later King George VI and Queen Elizabeth, who subsequently became the Queen Mother), as patrons, were scheduled to visit the hospital. The ward to which I had been sent became a hive of activity. Patients and lockers were tidied up for the occasion. Our beds became models of precision and whiteness. Not a wrinkle, not a pleat, and above all not a book or sweet, blurred the smooth counterpanes. The girls had ribbons tied in their hair. Patients well enough to sit up leaned expectantly against their pillows.

The minutes dragged by with leaden legs. Inside my locker was the most marvellous adventure story with a wonderful hero. Having gone through every imaginable horror, he had come out unscathed from each one of them. But how could he survive the torture that threatened him in the next chapter? Would he be able to escape from his evil captors? The suspense became unbearable.

I looked around the ward. Quietness echoed along the corridor. Sister stood at the ward door, a little knot of nurses crowded around her. Occasionally they glanced back to see that all was well with their charges. With an eagle eye on the group at the door, I quietly eased my book from the locker, propped it up on my stomach, draped the counterpane over the pages and began to read. Life in the ward stopped. I was transported to another world, a world so real that it was some time before I became aware of a hand patting my own. I looked up and saw the important visitors gathered round the bedside and the matron's eyes viewing me grimly through her glinting spectacles.

The visitors seemed to notice nothing amiss. The Duke asked me the title of the book, a few questions about it, and whether it was my own. When I said it wasn't, the Duchess replied before moving on to the next bed, 'We must do something about that.' I forgot all about the visit when I left the hospital for the Little Folks convalescent home at Bexhill. It was supported by, among others, the readers of *Little Folks* magazine.

Many years later, hunting round the bookstalls, I came across a copy of the magazine and it brought back vividly those long-ago Friday afternoons where, with many other children, I spent such happy times. It might have been called a convalescent home, but it gave us all more, so much more, than the chance of better health. I stayed at the Bexhill convalescent home for two weeks. Its inmates came from Shoreditch, Hoxton, Haggerston, Whitechapel and Bethnal Green, and none of us had never seen such beautiful countryside before.

It was such a joy for me to be there that I bore the painful ministrations to my bottom almost cheerfully, judging at least by the kind remarks of the nurses who told me, untruthfully, what a brave girl I was. One stretch of meadow was out of bounds. A stream ran though it, edged by lovely flowers that grow in damp soil, all brilliant mauves and yellows. We named it simply 'Fairyland'. The trees with their branches intertwined overhead made ideal places for playing ghosts. The more knowledgeable among us, however, saw a resemblance in these gloomy bowers with the sun just piercing occasionally through to the formidable institutions known as County Courts, so that's what the dark caverns became.

But the sea and the sands . . . these made Bethnal Green, Haggerston and Hoxton, seem remote worlds, and we could find no parallel for this particular glory. We visited the beach about twice a week, some of us in the long pushchairs known as spinal carriages. I have never since seen these vehicles, which were like wicker beds on wheels. They may have gone out with the horse-drawn bus, but they were certainly useful for taking out children who had spinal diseases or injuries, or who perhaps were temporarily unable to walk.

During one of these outings I met Mr and Mrs Waterman. They were taking a holiday nearby. I was occasionally invited to their home in Seven Kings and for this fearsome journey, all of a few miles, Mum accompanied me to the train at Liverpool Street Station and put me in the charge of the guard. Bertha Waterman, the eldest daughter, a beautiful, dark-haired, very talented girl with the fairest of skins, and who could turn her hand to almost anything, including music and painting, later married a professor at Durham University and went to live in Jesmond Dene. The Watermans told me it was a beauty-spot. I was far more intrigued by the professor. He seemed ages old at 30-something. I just could not understand why anybody, least of all an attractive lady like Bertha Waterman only in her twenties, would wish to marry such an ancient man as the professor.

My mother wrote to the Watermans during my stay in the convalescent home and mentioned where I was. They looked out for me on the beach and contacted the nurse in charge of the party. Their visit uplifted my status. Staff as well as patients saw that I had important friends, and there is no egoism quite so great and quite so vulnerable as that of a child . . . except that of an author reading a criticism of his book or an actress a review of her latest part.

On Friday nights we always lined up outside in the garden of the convalescent home, and sat down on blankets and groundsheets for a picnic tea. At this time, too, all sweets and other goodies sent to patients were shared out among everybody, richer and poorer alike, a practice that might not have endeared itself to the senders but was certainly appreciated by those receivers who otherwise would have had little or nothing.

The biggest surprise of all came when I left Bexhill and arrived home. A book was presented to me, in memory of the visit of their royal highnesses to the Children's Hospital, Hackney Road. I was thrilled, not because of the book itself, but because they had not forgotten. It seemed to me so clever and thoughtful that they should remember such a trifling incident in a hospital and a patient they had met, when they probably had to meet thousands of people every year of their lives.

When my first book, a story for children, was published some thirty years later, I returned the compliment in a very small way by sending a copy to Princess Elizabeth, who had since become Queen, with a mention of her father and mother. From the Palace came back such an interesting and encouraging reply that, had I revealed its contents, the sales of my book would have soared, instead of it merely being mentioned by a reader in the *Schoolgirls' Own Diary* as one of the best children's fiction books of the year.

I wrote to that reader of the *Diary* – now long out of print – thanking him for his kind remarks. He replied that in the twenty years during which he had been writing those lists, not a single author had ever thanked him. Perhaps they assumed it was their right to be so praised . . . to me it was unbelievable, as indeed was getting a book published in the first place.

The second hospital sojourn that had a big effect on me in my childhood was when I had to go in for inflammation of the middle ear and a possible mastoid operation. My pain was as nothing compared to the sorrows around me. Phoebe, aged 15, occupied the opposite bed. She was suffering from emphysema, a disease which destroys the air sacs in the lungs and makes breathing very difficult. It is often caused by smoking.

This was not the case with Phoebe – her illness was probably due to working or living in smog-filled surroundings, or a similarly polluted environment. It used to be common among miners. Phoebe was obviously much loved, for she was surrounded constantly by family and friends. 'Get Well' cards covered her locker. It was understandable: she was such a lovely girl, so sweet natured and so brave. As soon as I was allowed up out of my bed I used to go across the ward to hers.

She looked very frail, with her head of fair hair nestling limply against the pillows. I gathered that every so often she had to have fluid drained from her lungs. It sounded horrible. I was so glad when she appeared to be getting better. She would be home before me, I told her. Then my ear trouble took a turn for the worse, and I was wheeled off for inspection and surgery.

I came back unconscious. When I awoke, I saw screens round Phoebe's bed. Poor Phoebe, I thought, she's got to have the treatment again. No sound came from behind the screens. The dope or whatever I had been given sent me off once more. When I next came round, I saw that Phoebe's bed was empty and newly made. With the innocence of the ignorant I asked a nurse what had happened. 'Phoebe contracted pleurisy a day or two ago. Poor girl wasn't strong enough to cope with another illness. She died during the night.'

I could not believe it. To see somebody sitting opposite you one day, and then to realise they have gone for ever seemed so unreal, harder to envisage and even more incredible than the possibility, hardly ever contemplated except by the pious of one faith or another, of one's own death. But the idea of human mortality was soon swallowed up by the routine of living.

A commotion disturbed the ward. The nurse looked round. A stretcher was wheeled in with a woman who had tried to take her own life. She looked already dead. The staff worked like mad to save her. Though they had failed with Phoebe, they succeeded in bringing this woman back from the brink of the grave. She was only in the hospital for two days, but told me she was married to a Jewish fellow, a wonderful chap, but she had to live with her in-laws and they were making life so terrible for her, she could take no more.

9

IN THE CARE OF MY FATHER

St Anne's, the school to which Mum sent me as her tribute to a punitive God after my bout of diphtheria, was tucked away in Whitechapel. It adjoined the Gothic church, designed by Pugin's disciple Gilbert Blount, but due to insufficient funds, lacked his originally planned transept and spire.

Built in 1855 for the priests of the Society of Mary, it served the needs of thousands of Irish immigrants who settled in London's East End after the terrible Irish famine. Two years after the church was opened by Cardinal Wiseman, the London firm of Bishop and Storr installed an organ. It cost £600 and remains one of the few surviving Victorian organs still in its original position.

After the Irish, came a variety of other immigrants, fleeing from poverty or from persecution in Europe. They, too, settled in the district, so the church and school were attended by a real ethnic mix, except for the Jews who had their own school and synagogue.

Jews were the largest group of immigrants (though the Irish arrived first), and in the 1920s numbered some 125,000 – down from 300,000 a decade earlier. Many worked in and some set up sweatshops, mostly in Whitechapel. Cockneys imitated the customs and humour of their Jewish neighbours or integrated their own slang with a more strident tone. The mix made the area a hotbed of talent, nurturing painters such as Mark Gertler and Isaac Rosenberg, and writers such as Arnold Wesker, Emmanuel Litvinoff and Wolf Mankowitz.

Politicians also imprinted their mark on the district: men like Labour Prime Minister Clement Attlee, and in an earlier generation Will Crook, who, with the explorer Stanley, were the only MPs who ever 'graduated' to Parliament from a workhouse. Outside that august assembly there was Canon Bartlett, founder of Toynbee Hall, as well as entrepreneurs like Sir Gerald Broakes, who early saw what the derelict docklands might become.

At school in the 1920s, I swam happily in the sea of immigrants that flooded into our non-welfare state from less friendly shores. In my class were Irish, Poles, Italians, Lithuanians, Russians. There was hardly an 'English' name among us: Wanda Matchansky, Victoria Toubkin, Ada Mikonis, Annie Spurgaitis, Janina Grenkowicz, Annie Dzvonkus, Maggie Manilus, Rose Ferrari and Maggie Sinunas. Bringing up the Irish rearguard were Winnie Hook, Annie Hurley, Lizzie Whitehorn and me, Ivy Crawley. As one of the few girls with an English name, I felt quite ashamed to have been born in such an ordinary place as Bethnal Green. My aunts or uncles, for all their Irish blarney, could never match the fascinating histories of these girls and their relatives from foreign parts.

The waving of flags on Empire Day, or the doling out of shamrock on St Patrick's Day to people without the slightest connection with the saint, welded us into a homogenous whole. But apart from the rigours of the Catechism, we had a fairly liberal education: as well as learning papist hymns like 'Full in the panting heart of Rome', we could also sing the Welsh national anthem in Welsh, a few Scottish songs, and numerous Irish ones with a melancholy flavour.

Teaching was mainly by the nuns, who ate and slept in a cold, subterranean dungeon below the school. Did they ever wonder what odd fate had taken them from the green fields of Ireland to this alien land? Like our home-grown boxing fraternity, the nuns were tough, brave fighters, full of a religious fervour that overcame all doubts. Antonia White (*Frost in May*) tells of the cruelties suffered at the hands of evil or ignorant religious. No such horrors lay in wait for us at St Anne's school in Whitechapel.

The patience and learning of Miss O'Farrell, Miss Maher and Miss Read were incredible. We were all in love with the beautiful, dark-haired, blue-eyed Miss O'Farrell and her wonderful poetry readings.

I longed to see the Isle of Innisfree and what a 'cabin of clay and wattles made' looked like. As for Masefield's 'Cargoes' (with its glorious tongue-twisting opening: 'Quinquireme of Nineveh from distant Ophir'), she made the contrast between the 'stately Spanish galleon' and the 'dirty British coaster' and their cargoes as real as if we were actually viewing them across the width of a great ocean.

All the teachers, save headmistress Sister Hedwig and her coterie of nuns, were of course entitled 'Miss'. No woman stayed on after marriage. There was little equality in the workplace, though after the carnage of the First World War the 1920s were a decade of improvement for women. Oxford University opened its degrees to them in 1920, the United States of America gave women the vote in the same year, and the Matrimonial Causes Act of 1923 allowed them to sue for divorce on the grounds of a husband's adultery. Various professions, including teaching and the Civil Service, however, would not employ married women. If you married, you had to resign. As economic conditions worsened the same caveat was adopted in 1932 by the BBC. A few women might manage to stay on in their jobs through some helpful contact. Others doubtless did too, until nature revealed the dreadful truth. They then had to retreat to *Küche, Kirche, Kinder*.

When school ended we went home through the mainly Jewish streets. On Friday winter's evenings, when the sun set very early, Jewish mommas stood at their street doors waiting for us Catholic children to come home from school. We knew what they wanted. Going into the Jewish houses was one of the highlights of the week, almost as good as the Saturday cinema show where Mum enjoyed recounting, until 'shut down' by Dad, the life story of every hero and heroine appearing on the screen.

In the Jewish houses money was left out by the *bubbe* for small jobs forbidden to them on the Sabbath day – but we did not miss the chance to peek at the beautiful white cloth on the kitchen table, the decorative candles, or to try to discover whether the mommas wore wigs. The rumour was that they shaved the hair from their heads when they got married.

A halfpenny for the Gentiles was always left on the top of the stove. I never bothered about the ethics of getting others to do what your religion does not allow you to do yourself; just made my thanks as nicely as I could and fervently prayed to my own God that I would be invited into more than one house.

Our school was in the real East End, not like Waltham Forest or Wanstead or Stratford or those other places far out where it was almost country. Our bit of country was Victoria Park; our bit of green, London Fields. To improve my status in our class with its mongrel mix, whenever I mentioned my aunts or uncles and even my father to my friends, I always gave them the most fascinating start in life I could think of, though I never properly explained how they had arrived in Whitechapel. I couldn't do much about my mother either, for she was born in Bethnal Green, as was her mother before her.

I did my best: on St Patrick's Day, I cadged a big spray of shamrock and strutted proudly round wearing it, so that nobody could take me for a naked Londoner. I felt a bit like St Peter (though not, of course, so saintly) when he asserted three times that he knew not the Lord. The crowing of a cock reminded him of his infidelity, as I too was reminded of mine on St George's Day. To make up for the defection, I waved my Union Jack even more wildly than the Poles and the Irish and the Italians . . . and the rest (but still played for the Irish team in school games).

Until I started at the school, I had never visited the church nor seen the stained glass window featuring St Anne. She ought, as the mother of Mary, to be considered the patron saint of grandmothers. Such degrees of consanguinity were delicately not mentioned in our Christian instruction. Nor had I seen the brilliantly coloured decorations by Joseph Aloysius Pippet which adorned the chancel.

My mother, being a nominal Protestant, did not particularly care for 'popish' customs. My father took me to Mass in the French church, so called not because of any worrying French vagaries in the practice of the Christian faith, but because it was served by priests who were reputed to be of French origin. Situated near the Bethnal Green Museum Gardens, it was the nearest to our home.

Dad also took me occasionally to the Church of the English Martyrs in Prescot Street. I knew nothing about martyrs of any kind, but loved seeing the soldiers who, Dad told me, were Irish Guardsmen, get into formation outside the church. After the service, they marched off to their barracks, or maybe the Tower if they were serving there.

One of the tales Dad told me, whether true or not, I never found out, was that on Sundays the commanding officers at parade grounds throughout the country used to give the order, 'Catholics and Jews, fall out'. To avoid parade duty, so many soldiers declared they were Catholics that they were asked to say the 'Hail Mary' prayer to prove their faith. Many, at least initially, fell by the wayside at this unexpected hurdle.

He also told me of one of the men who, declaring he was a Catholic, was told to turn up for Mass with a platoon of other 'nonconformists'. As soon as he got inside, the Sergeant in charge waiting for him yelled in a voice that could be heard all over the church and as far as the Tower itself, 'For God's sake, soldier! Ain't you got no respect? Take your bloody 'at off inside the effing church.'

We sometimes went to St Boniface's church in Adler Street, often called the German church because of its name, and the nationality of some of the priests and congregation.

Katy, wife of a policeman, and one of Dad's three elder sisters, lived in official quarters not far away from the church. She had a huge brood, or so it seemed to me, and a 'kitchen' to match. It looked so big, in spite of its many occupants, that it could have served as a training ground for runners. Judging by the activity whenever we arrived, it was often used for this purpose. Katy sat immune from the noise, complacently feeding the newest arrival, chatting as she did so.

I was so embarrassed and intrigued by this domestic picture of my aunt (perhaps a trait inherited from my mother with her odd mixture of prudery and Rabelaisian humour) that I always tried to join the boys' games, though I was hardly a welcome visitor to the team.

Dad had another sister, Nellie, who lived nearby in Morrison's Buildings, Commercial Road, so visiting the German church on a Sunday gave him the chance of a chat, and often a drink, with his relations.

Nellie's tiny basement kitchen was in complete contrast to Katy's large living room. In the front, it faced the noisy high street and gave a wonderful view of people's legs as they walked by. The room was filled with Irish and religious relics, often under a glass case. A portrait of Robert Emmet, one of Nellie's Irish heroes, hung from one wall.

Under this picture was a small table at which she and her husband Bill had their meals. Even with so few chairs in the room, there seemed hardly enough space to sit down. Everywhere one looked there were statues – the Sacred Heart, the Blessed Virgin in one guise or another and pictures of less holy beings like Roger Casement and Parnell (without Kitty O'Shea) as well as scenes of Ireland and one of the Easter Rising, with another picture of de Valera underneath.

Unlike Dad, both his sisters were born in Ireland, but they shared with him lovely talking and singing voices. I could listen to them for hours. As is the way with exiles, real or imagined, they put so much depth of feeling into songs connected with their 'native' land, that it surpassed even a Welsh choir singing 'Land of My Fathers' for bringing tears to my eyes.

Later on, at high school, I heard Inez Pearn, the beautiful first wife of poet Stephen Spender (and who was painted in such a lifelike fashion by William Coldstream, RA), sing 'Ave Maria' with the same degree of emotion.

But the only person to sing 'Danny Boy' with even more pathos than my Irish aunts was a lady from Ceylon (now Sri Lanka), Mrs Padmanahba, one-time housekeeper at Plater College, Oxford. When I saw her – an exile from her homeland – and she got to the lines, 'Oh come ye back, when all the vale's in shadow . . . Oh Danny boy, I love you so,' her voice was so moving that I have remembered it ever since.

Dad could not sing quite as well as his sisters, but he beat them hollow with his fund of London lore. On our way to church he would point out the door to the Jewish cemetery in Brady Street, and tell me that if I knocked, a keeper like St Peter at the pearly gates would let me in. I never tried, and so missed seeing the mausoleums of Nathan Rothschild, founder of the London branch of the famous bank, and of Miriam Levy, who opened the first soup kitchen for the poor in Whitechapel.

As we walked down Vallance Road we passed the Dew Drop Inn, created by Miss Hughes, an eccentric but well-known dispenser of local charity, and the sister of Thomas Hughes, author of *Tom Brown's Schooldays*. Gossip had it that further along the road was the home of the Kray family, later to harbour the notorious Kray twins. I never knocked at the door to find out.

One of the stories Dad told me, again with little truth I imagine, was that the statue of a horse with rider outside the Mansion House had no stirrups and the sculptor was so upset at seeing it thus unveiled that he committed suicide. It was fascinating to hear, on the way to church, these tales – true or false – about long ago events, of monuments and people.

Dad had political opinions too, and when I was about 8 years old told me how the French were venting their revenge on the Germans in the Ruhr for starting the dreadful 1914 war and killing off a whole generation of young men. From where Dad got his knowledge, who knows? His reading consisted mainly of old newspapers, racing stories by Nat Gould, and detective fiction by Edgar Wallace . . . but oh, how he could tell a story!

To attend midnight Mass in the German church was for me a treat of utter enchantment. There were Christmas carols sung by a wonderful choir, the rhythm of the Latin chant, the decorated Christmas firs, the sanctuary lamp burning bright, and the candles shining on the high altar where three priests served in gold vestments. What a feast it was for my young eyes – and ears. We might possibly have a drink afterwards of cocoa – at least I had cocoa – at Auntie Nellie's. Dad and his sister took something stronger and longer.

I stared at the pictures of Irish patriots on the walls. Robert Emmet was the best. He looked so young and handsome. Auntie Nellie told me he was very brave too, and that after leading an unsuccessful revolt in Dublin, he was hanged in 1803 when he was only 25.

'Brave, like Joan of Arc,' I said. 'But it's worse to die in a fire. Burning somebody! Weren't they cruel? Horrible!'

'Never change,' said Auntie Nellie, finishing her glass.

After cocoa and more tales of Ireland's heroes, came the adventure of walking home in the dark, late at night, often through snow-covered streets, holding my father's strong and loving hand.

Yet going home from Mass was the first time that I learnt personally, though obliquely, that there was a darker, seamier side of life than I had noticed in Bethnal Green. Street-wise in many respects, I was, unlike my far more sensible brother, also very naive – and remained so for a long time after the age when most girls are going out with boys.

Coming home from midnight Mass at the German church as usual, we arrived at the junction of Whitechapel Road. Dad had imbibed too many drinks at Auntie Nellie's to get home without feeling the call of nature. He seemed sober enough though, when he said he had to pop away for a moment. He stationed me outside a brightly lit sweet-shop, still open even at that late hour, and gave me the strictest instructions not to move.

'Stay there,' he said. 'And whatever you do, don't go away. I'll be back in a jiffy.'

I promised to stay outside the shop. He moved off. I kept my eyes firmly on the goodies flickering brightly under the Christmas lights in the shop window. My eyes became glued to the tempting array before me. The minutes ticked by. Dad did not return. I was staring at some gob-stoppers in a shining glass container, and a beautiful box of chocolates, when a stranger approached. He stood looking in the window for a few minutes and then asked me, in a pleasant, friendly tone, 'Which do you like the best?'

I didn't know how to answer him. Did my father mean me to stay silent as well as immobile?

'They're all nice,' I replied, without even looking at the man beside me.

'Tell me which you like and I'll get you some . . . a Christmas present.'

What an offer! I loved sweets, on the rare occasions when I could get them. Though I knew generosity often sprang from the most unlikely quarters, there was something about this fellow that didn't seem quite right.

'I'll get something nice,' he said, going into the shop. Should I move away while he was inside? But I had promised my father to stay there.

The stranger came out of the shop and showed me the sweets he had bought. How good they looked. My mouth watered. 'Go on, take a few,' he urged as I hesitated. Where was Dad? If only he were here, he could tell me what to do. And then, like a shining knight out of the darkness, he came. How glad I was to see him – but not for long.

He looked at the sweets. He looked at me. He looked at the man. 'What d'ye mean by getting sweets for my girl?' he said. 'She don't want no strangers buying 'er anything.'

'I just thought I'd get the kid a few sweets for Christmas. Nothing wrong in that, is there?'

'Go and buy your own blimmin' kids some sweets,' shouted my father. He swung out a fist at the man, who staggered back, looking amazed and fell to the ground, his hand to his jaw.

I was terrified. The police would arrive and my father be taken to jail. The man lay on the pavement, not daring to get up. My father looked very threatening. He continued shouting and sounded quite violent. A crowd collected. A policeman arrived. What would happen now? I grew more frightened than ever while, perversely, Dad seemed to become more pacified by the presence of the law.

'I won't charge him,' Dad said with an air of extreme generosity, though he was probably more guilty of an actual offence than the man now rising from the floor. 'Seeing as 'ow it's Christmas,' he continued. 'But you look out,' he said, pointing an accusing finger at the stranger he had felled with no mean punch, 'and make blimmin' sure you don't go accosting my girl again . . . or any others.' He raised an aggressive fist.

Hearing my father use such a strange word as 'accosting', I forgot for a second what the quarrel was about. Perhaps he'd picked up the word from his previous court appearance, perhaps from his reading of Edgar Wallace? What did 'accosting' mean?

The policeman was speaking. 'That's enough of that,' he said to my father and then added a few conciliatory words. The crowd began shuffling away and Dad and I were allowed on our way.

'Don't you ever go off with no strangers,' said my father sternly as we walked home. 'You never know what they're after.'

I couldn't surmise what any strangers, least of all a male stranger, could want with a 10-year-old girl, but nodded obediently. I could look up 'accosting' later on.

'He was only going to buy me some sweets for Christmas. They give you sweets in the Working Men's Club parties at Christmas time and you don't say anything about that.' I felt aggrieved.

'That's different. Different altogether. Just remember what I've said. I don't want no arguments. . . . Don't talk to no strangers.' His voice was firmer than ever. 'And don't take no sweets from them either.'

'Dad, what does "accosting" mean?'

'It means talking to strangers and offering them sweets and no good comes of it.'

He was quiet for a little while, as we ploughed back through the streets and then he said in a much softer voice, 'There's no need to tell your Mum about all this. She'll only get worried. No need to worry 'er.' I nodded again. 'All right, Dad.'

We often had secrets of this kind. I knew he didn't want my mother to hear of this fracas, not so much because he wanted to spare her worry, but because he was afraid of her criticism: that he had drunk too much and, for however short a while, left me on my own.

10

SISTER HEDWIG

Walking to St Anne's school with conscripted Nellie Hook and her sister Winnie was not a bit like skipping around the corner on my way to St Peter's. We crossed Bethnal Green Road, becoming daily thicker with traffic, went down Vallance Road, past bagel bakeries and philanthropist/politician Margaret Hughes's Dew Drop Inn, and then through long streets of terraced houses.

Strange-looking people stood by open doors, 'Jews,' whispered Nellie, several years older and several centuries wiser than me, as if that one word explained everything instead of nothing. On a very hot day, occupants leaned out of, or sat by the open upstairs windows, a habit greatly frowned upon by certain more 'upmarket' citizens of the East End.

Finally we reached St Anne's, ugly and frightening as it then seemed. A long narrow basement led, via stone steps, to the first floor entrance hall with its adjoining classroom for the bigger children. The hall was large and almost empty save for a circular row of benches.

Almost empty too, was the new Honours Board on the wall. It boasted one name: Janina Grenkowicz. She had won a London County Council scholarship to a high school. In the farthest corner of the hall away from the entrance door sat headmistress Sister Hedwig at a large desk. She looked a bit like an ogre to me. Almost all her face was covered. She had very rosy cheeks, like an autumn pippin, and her blue eyes glinted fiercely from steel-framed spectacles.

'New girl?' she asked of Nellie dragging me in unwillingly by the hand. Nellie gave my name and address, and my new career as schoolgirl at St Anne's began.

Before I left for the classroom I stared at the painting on the wall behind Sister Hedwig showing a young boy being questioned by obviously evil men. It was called 'When Did you Last See your Father?' How sorry I felt for the boy. Most of us children had at least heard of our fathers. We were luckier in this regard than some twentieth-century children who do not know who or where their fathers are, and may have been born not by the usual route, but chosen from some genetic store. If our fathers were not around, they were dead, in the nick, in the pub, in a job, or – more likely – seeking one. Sometimes, like the boy in the painting, we didn't want to reveal what we knew.

Near to Sister Hedwig's desk was a door opening onto classrooms for smaller children at the back of the school. Little trays of sand to trace out letters of the alphabet were provided for these 'baby' classes. How anybody ever cleaned up after the children, I don't know, but the lessons did not last long. Through this primitive system, everybody learnt to read and write. Exercise books we had, but no other kind, other than borrowed ones. These were passed on to the next class after we left.

Two flights of stone steps led upstairs to the eldest children's classrooms and cloakrooms. St Anne's had no churchyard with trees and ancient graves, as did my old school St Peter's, only a big shelter with a corrugated tin roof and a row of lavatories, always spotlessly clean, in the playground.

The shelter was a useful place to congregate at playtime in wet weather. We played under the tin roof. The most popular game was throwing a ball up above the roof to the boundary of the high wall beyond. To catch the ball, if our aim was short, we had to gauge its path as it bounced or rolled downwards along the roof. If the ball got stuck in the guttering we retrieved it, when no teacher was looking, by shinning up the poles that supported the roof.

Through a gate near to the row of lavatories another yard, much wider and bigger, was fenced off except on feast days, when processions took place. Sited in this large yard was the church hall where whist drives, dances and meetings took place. A wooden door in Deal Street, opening onto a long concrete path, provided the entrance to the hall for these events when the school was closed.

At around noon, the hall was open for the St Anne's schoolchildren who took midday dinners there. The aroma of stale soup which hung around both inside and outside the hall was harder to dispel than a November fog, but the mess of potage was hot and it was free.

To describe St Anne's school in the 1920s without mentioning Sister Hedwig is like trying to describe the House of Commons without the Prime Minister. But the feats the other teachers also performed for those under their care were almost as praiseworthy. To give them their due needs the imagination and descriptive powers of a Tolstoy.

Miss Maher and Miss Read showed us the fun of words like 'the fleas that tease in the High Pyrenees' in Belloc's 'Tarantella', and Masefield's 'Firewood, iron-ware, and cheap tin trays'.

Miss O'Farrell taught some of the bigger girls. How beautiful she was . . . the most beautiful lady I had ever seen in my whole life, with her dark curly hair, her blue eyes, and rosy cheeks. How beautifully she dressed, and how wonderfully she spoke. Her Irish accent gave something extra to Yeats's lines, 'I will arise and go now, and go to Innisfree', in the same way that a Scots accent heightens the beauty of Burns's 'My love is like a red, red rose that's newly sprung in June'.

Seeing the lovely Miss O'Farrell made me want always to remain a Miss and never become a Mrs. What a different being she was from the harassed mums in our street and other places! They spent their whole lives looking after everybody, getting nothing or precious little, it seemed, either in thanks or money. Who would want to be like them? I determined I would never get married and have babies even if all the girls at school seemed to dream of nothing else. For all I then knew,

Miss O'Farrell herself might have been secretly married . . . secretly because once women married they had to resign their posts in teaching or in the Civil Service.

Sister Hedwig was different again. With whom could she compare? How did she and the other Irish nuns bring themselves to leave the leafy fields of their birth, and come over to an alien land? But at least the nuns had the chance of becoming the head of a school, an opportunity rarely available elsewhere except for brilliant single ladies in girls' schools.

She had a faith that moved more than mountains. It moved hearts and minds, and shook cash from seemingly empty coffers. For children who went to school barefoot, as many did, Sister Hedwig first cudgelled the heavens and then beat the earthly bodies. The required boots eventually appeared from some mysterious source. It was she, too, who organised the school dinners and childrens' holidays.

The holidays came through a country holiday fund. They were offered in seaside and country areas by supposedly kindly folk. Some of these kindly folk, however, were poorer than those they took in. Child lodgers often spelt much-needed extra cash. After one of my stints in hospital and following another of our family's hard-up spells, I was designated for such a holiday. This year it was to be spent at the seaside.

Mum and Dad were thrilled for me. It seemed ideal: free transport to the seaside and back home, with food and lodging provided for a whole week . . . in theory wonderful, in practice, unforgettable . . . for all the wrong reasons. What a week that was!

The bedroom that had been destined for us and shown to whoever had checked up on the arrangements was now occupied by adult holiday-makers of whom we saw very little. Two of us from St Anne's, with three of the landlady's own children, slept in the other bedroom, five in a bed. As the thinnest and smallest person, I had to take the outside place at the edge of the bed. From this tenuous position I was nightly kicked and pushed out onto the floor. I made numerous attempts to get back. All failed.

Sometimes I squeezed in at the bottom of the bed, hoping nobody would notice me. But the kicks I got there were worse than being pushed out of the bed. I dared not cry out. What would be the use? If I did, the landlady would come in, furious at being disturbed by a troublemaker that could only be me. How could it possibly be the other St Anne's girl, big, strong, loud mouthed? Nor could it be her own dear children. No, if I woke up the landlady, I would certainly be called a trouble-maker – and worse, a wicked liar – and sent home in disgrace.

Finally, I gave up and tried to sleep where I landed. Curling up as best as I could on the wooden floor, I put my clothes over me for a bit of warmth. The bare boards were so cold and hard, I rarely managed to close my eyes. Straggling down late for breakfast I would be told off by the landlady and faced with an empty plate, my worm's ration having been eaten by the early birds. Exhausted, I used to fall asleep in the daytime on the stony beach, while livelier companions paddled in the sea. How I longed to get home to my own bed in Bethnal Green. The only other sharer there was my brother, young Jim. And he, being then smaller than me, gave me ample room.

When I got home, I never said a word to my mother about being five in a bed, or being pushed out of it every night. As for having no breakfast, that was my own fault for being late. Whingeing about trifles was never allowed in our family, nor in most others in the East End. Had I dared to complain about the holiday, I would have been accused of being a moaner and told that I should never have given in.

'Why didn't you kick back?' would have been the question levelled at me. I should have had a go, kicked back at my aggressors in the bed harder still and given them something to remember me by, even if the odds were four against one. But though I said nothing about the holiday and remained a 'stummer lolly', as our patois had it, word got around. Children talk and 'country holidays' soon lost ground to hop-picking.

'You're not very brown,' was the only greeting I got. My mother's idea of a holiday was a place from which you returned with a skin the colour of tan shoe polish. No matter what the destination, how short the stay, how much or how little you paid for it, if you didn't look tanned, it was no holiday. Besides, how else could anybody know you'd been away – a real sign of prosperity and hence that you had a job? No matter how far down we fell, Mum always liked to keep her end up.

Another task Sister Hedwig took on was getting clothes for our First Communion. In a locked cupboard downstairs she kept a secret hoard of white frocks, veils and blouses, shirts and shorts. They were brought out for the dressing up trials that preceded the First Communion day, an event in the Catholic calendar comparable with a Jewish boy's Bar Mitzvah, or an Anglican's Confirmation.

It stood out like a peak in the valley of our lives, for we could not forget the material banquet which followed the spiritual feast. In the school hall, tables were set out with jellies, cakes and other delectables, as well as books, rosaries and medals, donated by charitable bodies. Squeals of joy accompanied the laughter as we tried on our borrowed First Communion garments . . . but not from everybody.

Winnie Hook looked lovely in her cotton frock edged with broderie anglaise, but the only dress to fit my skinny form was of muslin covered with frills, tucks and lace. Today a girl would rave about it. Then it filled me with horror. I could almost have bartered my soul for a plain dress. I even told my mother about the dress I fancied, describing it in great detail, but I knew there was no way of getting it.

Mum believed money, when it came, had to be spent in a good way, not wasted. Drinking and gambling wasted money. So did buying silk frocks. My mother wasn't a Catholic, but I knew Sister Hedwig would agree with her.

I looked at her hands, red and worn with charring. Never at the best of times good for sewing anything but big strong stitches, how could they ever earn, or sew, white silk?

11

FIRST COMMUNION

Nineteen twenty-six was hardly a good year for St Anne's big annual event, its First Communion day. In the spring, miners refused to accept the lower rates of pay forced on them by coal owners and on 30 April they were locked out of the pits. The General Strike ensued. Although conditions in the mines had improved over the years, safety was still woefully inadequate. Only thirteen years earlier, a mine disaster at Sengenydd in south Wales, resulting from the negligence of owners and agent, cost 439 lives.

With low wages and dangerous work, the miners thought they had an unbeatable case in refusing to accept lower pay; so did all the workers who joined them – bus drivers, railwaymen, dockers, and general labourers – but in November, they were forced to give in to the greater power and ruthlessness of the mine owners and the incompetence of politicians.

Against this wider world, our Communion day seemed hardly worth a mention, especially now that an ex shoe-shine boy called John Logie Baird had just invented a miracle gadget. It showed, on a screen, moving images sent from a camera nearby. Scientists thought that soon there would be a 'TV' in every home, receiving moving pictures from all over the world. And women of 21 and over would soon get the vote for the first time.

Nobody in Bethnal Green cared overmuch about the TV or the vote. With a general strike in progress, more people seemed out of work than in. The queues at the labour exchanges and for relief tickets grew longer and longer. With the tickets, you could make sure of a bit of food at least.

Women with tuberculosis (rampant in London's back streets) were still gluing cardboard to make boxes. Stronger sisters hand-stitched coats, basted trousers or pressed suits with huge hand irons. Nobody labelled them 'scabs' or 'blacklegs' – the epithet which men, including miners themselves from other pits, got for grabbing a job in such desperate times. Some women wired flowers, mostly for funerals, of which there seemed more than ever. Diphtheria, smallpox, consumption were the killers. Rheumatic fever merely crippled.

During school time in St Anne's we were partly insulated from the troubles of the outside world. Excitement mounted as the day approached for the reverential walk to the altar. In the school hall, tables would be set out with all manner of good things for the white-clad children filing from the Church. And white clad everybody would be.

Sister Hedwig made sure of that. No shoes, no socks? She opened her big cupboard and out they rolled. First Communion outfit? No problem. From her magic stock, lent out each year, tumbled shirts, frocks and veils, white and gleaming as a washing ad. The squeals of joy when trying-on day arrived didn't only come from the girls.

The boys enjoyed their dress rehearsal every bit as much, and swaggered round in their shirts like turkey cocks. But I hated that awful muslin frock, the only one that fitted my skinny body, and longed desperately for a plain silk one.

Sister Hedwig said prayer was always answered. I prayed. Nobody heard my plea. She said faith was often tested. I promised bribes, holy bribes, to any saint who would put a quiet word for me into the good Lord's ear. Heaven proved not only deaf but also dumb.

Whatever our backgrounds, the First Communion day united us all. The day for the reverential walk to the altar drew near. Yet uppermost in my mind was the utterly unattainable objective of a plain silk frock.

There was no one I could confide in. My poor father was in hospital with another infection of his lungs. To my mother, buying silk frocks was a waste of money.

Perhaps the playing cards or tea-leaves would help? My superstitious mother and the friends who came in occasionally, saw signs and wonders in all manner of odd places. They drank their tea, swished the dregs round the cups, and from the pattern of the leaves deduced all manner of future happenings.

'Dots,' came their excited cry. 'Ah, Susie, you'll be getting some money soon.' My mother, hoping, believing, fearing, replied, 'Not in the bottom of the cup, thank you. I can do without that.'

Though dots were usually a good sign – for they meant a financial gain or reward – the bottom of the cup was an area of ill omen. Who would want to see the two together? Leaves at the top were better. They predicted a happening quite close in time. Leaves at the handle of the cup foretold an event near to home.

When Mum haggled with a street trader, he always came off worst. No *spiel* in Brick Lane, however brilliant, ever took her in. But the cards or the tea-leaves . . . that was different altogether. So superstitious was she that any tale the tea-leaves or other signs and omens told her, she believed as implicitly as a convert absorbing the teachings of a new religion.

I stared at the dregs in my cup day after day. They never told me a thing, and not once did they form the pattern of a frock.

Mum set out early every morning and after five in the evening to her charring job in the City. Midway on the pavement at the top of our street stood the bookmaker who took bets on the horses and the dogs. He hovered there like a bird of prey. As soon as a cop came on the scene, the whisper spread more quickly than a bush telegraph. The 'bookie' disappeared with a speed and dexterity that beat anything that the incredible Houdini (just dead from a punch in the stomach), ever pulled off. In and out of the neighbours' open doors he darted, through their little back yards and away, usually coming out in Mansford Street. He might look like a vulture in the street, but in the back yards he was quicksilver.

I knew my mother never gambled. Indeed I had seen her crossing the road to avoid passing the bookmaker on her way to or from work or to go shopping in Brick Lane or Bethnal Green Road. Alone in the house on this occasion, I made a last desperate prayer. Please, couldn't anybody up there please send me a plain silk frock? But nobody did and nobody would.

As if to prove heaven was shut for the season, Sister Hedwig chose that moment when I was at my lowest to make her terrible announcement. If the weather looked fine, we should have a procession through the streets surrounding the school. I thought I should die. To wear that hideous frock in church was bad enough, but to parade round the streets, stared at by everybody! In that awful dress!!! My cup of bitterness was complete.

The district of E1 wasn't like N1, where so many Catholic Poles and Lithuanians were congregated, or like EC1, verging on Little Italy whose processions were really something to be seen and wondered at. Our school was in Whitechapel, in the middle of Jewish 'territory'. It may seem strange that a school like ours, so full of children who had been born or whose parents had been born in other countries, should have thought of Jewish neighbours as different, but we did. Childish cruelty? More likely envy – envy of their family life, their ability to make jokes and to laugh in a different way from the native Cockney. What we envied most of all was their togetherness, the way they helped each other.

We of another faith watched through the windows the celebration of their religious feasts. We knew the taste of matzos, bagels and Kosher food. We knew Jews ate chicken and fish, but not pork or bacon, the poorest ones put sand, not oilcloth, on their floors, sat by their windows, and sometimes even slept outside the house on hot nights. We had heard the rumour that Jewish ladies shaved their heads and wore wigs so they shouldn't appear beautiful to any men other than their husbands. We knew the dates of their Passover, New Year (Rosh Hashanah), and Day of Atonement (Yom Kippur) – when, as in our Lent, they fasted – but understanding . . . that was a different thing.

I had met Mr and Mrs Cohen when my mother worked for them, and played with their children, Hetty and Isadore. There were few other Jews I knew, other than having passed them by in the street. Mrs Silverman was an exception. She stopped me once as I came out of school on Friday. I knew why. Jewish women often asked us Gentile schoolchildren to turn out the gas taps on this day. After Friday sunset was a holy time for the Jews. It was not to be used for even the most menial of servile works such as turning off a gas tap, but in preparation for the holy Sabbath.

When Mrs Silverman paid me she did not touch the coin, but left it on the gas stove for me to pick up when my work was done. I came a second time, and again . . . and again. *Shabbas goy* I might have been, but how impressed I was by the Sabbath ritual: the table covered by a white cloth, the gleaming candlesticks, the family prayers. Like Mum, I wanted to hold my head up too, so I told Mrs Silverman of my First Communion day, and then – how are we so easily led into temptation? – described the white silk frock I was going to wear: plain, white, beautiful, its only trimming pearl buttons at wrist and neck, and a v-shaped pocket edged with white braid.

I knew that she would never venture into a Catholic church and discover me, liar that I was, in all my trumpery. Now Sister Hedwig, with her plan for an outdoor procession, had ruined everything. If we walked through Whitechapel not even my veil would hide the muslin frock with its hideous frills and furbelows. Mrs Silverman would see, as we passed her street door, that I, a Christian, had lied to her, a Jew.

Why had Sister Hedwig dreamt up this martyr's walk? I thought of praying for rain. The words stuck in my throat. Courage was what I ought to ask for, courage to acknowledge my lie. Perversely, the strength came unsought. The truth seeped out one day, encouraged by Mrs Silverman talking about the wonderful dress her sister had ordered for her wedding.

'I haven't really got a white silk frock,' I said, almost enviously. 'Not really. It's not really silk. It's more . . . well . . . thin . . . and rough, and it's got frills.' Trying to end on an upbeat, I added, 'Still, it's only a lend. I don't have to keep it.'

'Silk frock, cotton frock, black frock, white frock,' Mrs Silverman replied, waving her hands. '*Nisht geferlekh*. It's what's here that counts.' She put her large hands on her ample bosom.

'Sure, everybody talks big sometimes. But when you're poor or little, you gotta be brave. Brave you've gotta be, my little *kinderlekh*. That makes you big. When you're brave, you're big.' She stretched out her arms as if to embrace the world.

I didn't understand. Being big or brave had nothing to do with a white silk frock. Yet somehow, when Mrs Silverman patted my head, it felt as if she had lifted a great weight from it. I had made my first confession, not the one to the priest, timed to go before the first Communion, when innocence lies upon us like an untouched garment, but the far harder confession when one has become aware of sin and guilt and their pain. My conscience was clear. I ran all the way home.

If I looked happy, my mother certainly didn't. Though she laid down the law about gambling and booze (the aunts always said it was the drink that brought down my father), she was always such a fighter, never short of a bit of quick Cockney wit. Now all the troubles of the world seemed to lie on her shoulders. What had happened to upset her?

That night her friends came in for a session with the cards. 'A crown,' I heard them say. My mother's reply was inaudible. She did not sound like her usual interested self. Perhaps they had told her I was going to marry a prince. Easier that was, than getting a white silk frock.

Next morning, before going to school, I laid the table with one of the out-of-date newspapers Mum brought home from the waste baskets in her City office or Liverpool Street Station. Sometimes I got so interested in the papers, however old, that I was almost late for school. There seemed nothing in this issue to catch the eye – only the dull old sports section with no crimes of passion, just pages of football results and the names of the greyhounds and horses running in big races that week.

It looked as if bookmakers were going to make a rich haul as usual.

When I got to school, I learnt how wrong I was. At the mere sight of a cop 'our' small and wizened bookie, with legs as fast as his brain, slipped in and out of the houses, over the back yards and away. It seemed impossible for him to be caught. Yet the impossible had happened. He'd been picked up by the cops and thrown on remand in the nick. Caught he was, and probably all the big race winnings with him. Until his friends bailed him out, in the nick he'd have to stay, and hard luck on those who were waiting to be paid any winnings on their bets.

I rushed home that evening and just managed to catch my mother before she went out for her evening charring stint. Hoping to cheer her up, I blurted out the news about the bookmaker. She wouldn't be hurt by his departure.

'Good job you don't bet,' I said.

'Yes, it's a good job I don't,' she replied. 'Gamblers always lose. And they lose most when they can afford it least.' Her voice was strangely bitter.

'Never mind, Mum,' I said, unusually sympathetic. 'You'll win something one day.'

The words had a strange effect on her. The truth broke out. She too had a confession to make. She knew how much I wanted the dress. And so she had placed a bet on the outsider of the week, hoping in this way to get the money to buy the frock of my dreams. Of course she hated gambling. She hated the bookie too, but how could she not follow the signs when they were so clear, almost like a message?

There was the horse and crown in her cup, the dots at the top spelling a money windfall quite close in time, and the handle, an event near to home. There was the newspaper headline 'WILL THE KING OF HEARTS RUN?' How could she resist a horse with that name and those signs, especially when it was running in a race at 20 to 1? When her game of patience ended with the playing card the King of Hearts, she had to take a chance.

And the omens were right. Her outsider had come romping home. What had not come romping home were the winnings and the bookmaker. Worse, my mother had ordered the dress from a little paralysed dressmaker living round the corner who had bought the material and now could not be paid. I was full of contrition for the trouble I'd caused my mother.

'I'll find a job,' I said, hugging her. In spite of all the favourable omens and signs, it still could not have been easy for her to place her bet. She never would have done so, had it not been for me.

'And pay Annie for making the dress,' I added. What a hope. I was not quite 10 years old.

Because of me, my mother had used the sacrosanct rent money, always to be put by before any other spending. Now we would have to pawn something – dead soldier Uncle Jack's medals, or the little chest of drawers that her other brother Dick had made. It was all my fault. The bookie got out from prison. It was rumoured that there had been a street collection for his bail. He paid the winners and there, when I came home from school before the Big Day, was the Communion dress, exactly as I had dreamed about it. White silk, long-sleeved, unadorned save for the v-shaped pocket trimmed with white braid, and the pearl buttons at wrist and neck. And wonder of wonders! There too, was a pair of white boots.

What a luxury that was. Charities might provide food and shelter and sometimes even holidays. None in their maddest moments would think of supplying white boots. Yet now that the longed-for gift had arrived, I tasted little of the pleasure anticipated for so long. It was like dust in the mouth. Perhaps I sensed how very much the gift had cost.

'It's lovely, Mum.' I hugged her again. 'One day I'll get you a beautiful present. Whatever you want. You see if I don't.'

The Communion day turned out fine. A motley collection of children, led by Irish nuns, walked through the Whitechapel streets. What brought our Jewish neighbours to their doors? Curiosity, or the sight of the innocence and wonder that is a child's loveliest possession?

As we passed Mrs Silverman's house, she came out and pressed into my hands a necklace.

'A little present for you. It's all right with no cross?' she whispered anxiously, walking by my side. I understood what she meant for she was very *fromm*. Like many other Jews she would not even use the word God or write it down except by way of initials. It was emotionally impossible for a woman of her faith to buy a crucifix, icon of another faith. But she had given me something better in her own eyes.

'It's good? Yes? *Goyisher nokhes I bin*.' She shook her head.

'It's lovely,' I murmured. 'Thank you.'

I fingered the tiny charms hanging on the thin gold-plated necklace and noticed that they each had a letter on them. She saw my puzzlement.

'*Lekhayim*, To Life. That's what they mean. I ask Morry Isaacs to get them, put them on. He knows everybody. "What is this" he asks me. "Am I a *shtik goy* to be writing Yiddish to a Catholic girl?" "Why you mahken a *tzimmis*?" I ask him. "It's for my *shabbas goy*. It's her communion. Like a bar mitzvah." "*Tzimmis*!" Morry says. "You think by me it's nothing? I'll be out of the *mizrakh* and into the back row if anybody finds out this foolishness." But he gets them on for me, just the same.'

'It's lovely. I'll keep it for ever,' I said again as Mrs Silverman ran back to her house. She looked different from the woman whose gas taps I turned off on Fridays. I was older now. I knew the cost of courage. I was too young even to assess the courage of Sister Hedwig, to guess how often she had faltered, wondering whether a procession might provoke our neighbours, how she had prayed for strength to go on with her plans, because she had learnt as an Irish exile that knowledge precedes love . . . and hate too.

I've never quite made up my mind who showed the most courage on my Communion day – my non-Catholic mother who overcame her scruples in the hope of getting a Communion frock for her child; the Irish nun leading a procession of Christian children through the Jewish streets; the Jewish woman, religious as she was, buying a token of love for a child not of her faith. And I never learnt how the bookie managed to pay my mother her winnings when the money for his bail was so high.

I've never found out either whether it was proper for me to turn up at the altar rails in a frock bought with a winning bet. What I am sure of is that mothers know more of their daughters' yearnings than daughters ever guess, and I have long since learnt that somebody, somewhere, has the most peculiar ways of answering prayer.

The longings of children, so intense, are so quickly evaporated. I never even remember what happened to the white silk frock, or the boots, and little enough about the First Communion day too. I grieved too much at the thought of having led my mother astray into the wicked ways of gamblers. My Dad was different. I knew he gambled, from the tiffs he had with my mother about the money he spent on his 'sure fire winners' that always limped home last.

He was now out of hospital, and a few weeks after the Communion day he said casually to me, 'Real lucky, your Mum is. Every time she 'as a bet on a big race, she seems to pick the right 'orse. I don't know 'ow she does it.'

'Every time?' I asked, unable to credit that my mother actually gambled on the horses, though I had seen her run out sometimes with a slip in her hand. Dad, of course, didn't mind placing a 'tanner' on something he fancied and made no secret of it – if he won.

'Well, not every time,' he said. 'She only goes in for the big races like the Cesarewitch or the Derby. But she certainly knows 'ow to pick 'em. There's no getting away from it.'

I could not believe it. My mother did sometimes gamble! The Communion dress was not her first winnings on the horses. I should have been relieved. The guilt I felt for leading her astray into the wicked path of gambling should have been washed away. But it wasn't.

The Catechism answer, Nine Ways of Being Accessory to Another's Sin, rang in my ears: by counsel, command, consent, provocation, praise or flattery, concealment, by partaking, silence, or defence of the ill done.

In what way did I share the sin? I worried about it and then thought that perhaps gambling wasn't a sin after all. Dad never seemed to think so. He would know. 'Is gambling a sin?' I asked him.

'Only if you lose,' he said, laughing.

I must have looked bewildered for he added, 'You're too young to be worrying about sin. You sin if you 'urt somebody . . . like I do to your Mum sometimes.'

He shook his head. 'I'm glad she touched lucky this week. We could do with a bit of luck for a change.' Relieved and a little wiser, I said to him, 'Never mind, Dad. You'll be lucky soon any time now.'

'Do you know what, my girl, I bet you're right.' And this bet at least was right for a change. He was lucky enough shortly after, not with a win on the horses, but in getting a job.

It was only casual work, but to a hungry man a crust in the hand is worth more than pie in the sky. The job might not last for more than a few days or weeks. But it meant money coming in, and at a particularly good time, for the couple upstairs suddenly decided to move. This meant a big decision for Dad and Mum.

Anyone might now become tenants upstairs – gangsters, or crooks on the run – depending on the landlord's whim. My parents were never a pair for taking risks, but they now did so, perhaps because they both had jobs: Mum's charring and Dad with his stint of casual labour. They asked to take over the tenancy of the whole house. In spite of their constant ups and downs, the rent was always paid (eventually), so the landlord agreed, and they moved into their first house.

12

WHEN SOFT VOICES DIE . . .

Revelling in the remains of a winning bet, the wonderful sensation of renting a whole house, and remembering her musical evenings at the Watermans, Mum went completely overboard. She had a tendency to save and scrimp for days on end and then suddenly, perhaps as a relief from the daily grind, to splash out on some extraordinary, luxurious and quite unessential purchase, or even a bet on the horses.

Now a piano came into our house to transform the front room into a sitting room, though we rarely ever sat there. Mum bought it on 'hire purchase'. We called this method of payment the 'never-never' or the 'Kathleen Mavourneen' because of the line in the Irish song: 'it may be for years or it may be for ever'. For ever was what hire purchase in the 1920s invariably was, for the item never, never became yours until the last payment was made, and could be taken away at any time, with no refund, if payments weren't kept up to date. However, Mum did not want to delay the purchase of a piano until her two children were grown up. They would be too old then to learn.

Not content with buying the piano which nobody could play, she arranged for a teacher to give me lessons. Alas! I proved the worst of all possible pupils with no ear for music at all. Even today, after years of listening to classical music, if I do remember the name of an opera I cannot say who wrote it or reproduce a note of an aria. If I were asked in my teenage years who married whom in *The Marriage of Figaro* I would probably have answered 'Figaro? Can't seem to remember the name. Is she from Bethnal Green?'

Hymns were different. Singing for my supper in so many charitable hospitals and institutions, including those of my own faith, I soon learnt to rattle off 'Onward, Christian soldiers' as tunelessly as 'Full in the panting heart of Rome' or 'Yoi yoi mazal tov'. As for playing the piano, or getting a tune from it, the only way I could memorise any piece of music was by the alphabetical names of the keys, for example, 'ggbcd gcde gdef . . . (high) g gagf fgfe efed cc'. To give a touch of bravura to the performance I finished on a chord that took me ages to learn and never came out quite right, yet I continued to play it at the end of any piece, no matter how much it clashed.

My poor brother suffered as a result, or so it seemed, because after my dismal performance nobody was going to waste any more money on piano lessons. However, who knows what experiences shape our future? Sometimes an initial failure or inability to achieve a dream acts as a spur. For young Jim, maybe the sound of music became an inspiration – or the sight of another's failure, a challenge.

He taught himself to play by sight, with a keyboard of black and white notes which he fixed to the piano, and, without ever having had a tutor, could soon sight-read a difficult piece like Brahms's Second Piano Concerto. After the piano he learnt the guitar and accordion. Soon he was proficient and confident enough (still only in his teens) to go out with a friend, and later by himself, busking on an accordion outside London theatres and cinemas. He didn't regard this as begging: it was more in the nature of a performance paid for by those he entertained. If you liked it, you paid for it. If you didn't, he got nothing. He often came home with hundreds of coins, more than the combined earnings of our parents for a week.

Leicester Square was his favourite 'stand'. Sometimes he would put a foot inside a pub and say 'Excuse me guv. All right if I come in and play a tune?' He was always invited in because, unlike his sister, he had such a wonderful aural memory, and had mastered several chords, so could accompany any song or take up any request. Soon he had scores of invitations for private engagements, most of which he refused.

He bought endless records with his loot, playing them in the kitchen where I did my homework. I got fed up with Verdi, *Pagliacci* and anything else of that ilk, although no matter how often they were played, I never managed to recognise any of them. The only advantages of all this classical stuff, as far as I could see, were the loads of coppers young Jim brought home and an excellent excuse for rarely finishing my homework.

Much later on, a chance meeting with an antique dealer from Morden in Surrey helped Jim to change his hobby into a career. The dealer said he had some spare records and wanted 5*s* each for them. Jim asked for a list. Most of the items listed were junk but there were two Marie Tempest 1900 Berliner recordings for which he offered £10 each, saying they were probably worth more. He sold them for double the price.

The dealer was quite happy with the transaction: he had bought them for sixpence each. Soon afterwards Jim acquired some more records, about which he knew absolutely nothing. After playing them, he realised that the language was Russian. With the aid of a dictionary he translated a few of the words. The records turned out to be speeches made by Lenin and Trotsky and he eventually sold them to the BBC.

There were three factors that made these and other records of the time so valuable. First, there was the rarity value, as in the case of the two Marie Tempest records which the dealer sold to my brother, or the speeches of Lenin and Trotsky. As another example of this rarity, there were only two pressings of Dame Nellie Melba singing in *La Boheme* (1926).

The second factor that sends the value of a record skyward is the musicianship, that is, the quality of the singer, song, or composer. Finally, there is the record's historic significance, as, for example, a singer's early connection with a composer. The vocal interpretation then takes on a particular importance.

Jim soon learnt how to tell the age of a pre-1940 record from its label, which also revealed the singer's sex and the language of the song. As an instance, The Gramophone Typewriter Company, one of the earliest recording companies in the UK, had black or red labels from 1900, the red indicating a celebrity.

Changing tastes made this clue no longer reliable, particularly for artistes of international status like Butt, Melba, Patti. Like today's film stars, they demanded and got what they asked for, namely individual labels. These were coloured blue, pink and lilac respectively. Germans had a black label no matter what their status, while Maurice Renaud, the French baritone, got a black or red label depending where his records were to be sold.

The years of the Gramophone Typewriter's pressings were easily recognised from their labels: flat in 1900–2, raised in 1903–4, sunk in a dip and often in a 'rubbed' condition, over the next 4 years. Around 1910 a dog was added and the word 'Typewriter' deleted. In 1920 the records became double-sided, as the Continental pressings had been since 1907.

Jim told me, though I was not a very good listener, that a female singer got the prefix 3, male 2, and an ensemble 4. Countries were also numbered, for example, 5 for Italian, 6 for Spanish, 3 for French, and 4 for German. From 1900 to 1910 all the Company's records began with the figure 0. When he picked up a record labelled 052000 for example, he knew that it was of an Italian (5) male (2) singer, with the date 1900–10 being made more specific by other clues such as dog, dipped, raised or flat labels.

'But whatever you do,' said Jim, warning me of a possibility that I never even contemplated, 'only buy a record if you like it'.

He eventually amassed a collection of some 30,000 records, all recording the sounds of piano, guitar, cello, orchestras, solo singers and the spoken voice. When he met a girl called Bella, he took her out on his busking proceeds to as many first nights in the cinema and theatre as they could fit in, and (except for our mother, whom he adored with a love reciprocated in equal measure) no other woman entered his life from that time on. Jim and Bella eventually married and set up a business called Vocal Art in Edmonton, North London.

He became a famous figure in the vocal record business, possessing the second largest collection in the world. Sometimes he lent rare recordings such as Oscar Wilde reading a poem, to organisations like the BBC for programmes they wanted to make. He started up a magazine called *Vocal Art*. It brought him letters and requests for records from all over the world, including Japan and Stalinist Russia.

The front room of his house and the insulated shed at the back, housed the most fascinating selection of musical 'trophies' that Jim had searched for and finally found. Any stranger (for Bella and his sons were well prepared) entering either of his Aladdin's caves could be in grave danger of knocking down or falling over a mountain of memorabilia: piano and violin records from 1900 to 1960, records of Enrico Caruso, John McCormack, Richard Tauber, Beniamino Gigli, Nellie Melba, Theodore Chaliapine, Giovanni Martinelli, Tito Schipa, Emmy Destinn and many more. You might unearth a couple of Puccini scores signed by the composer, or documents bearing the signatures of Dumas, Victor Hugo, Sarah Siddons, Landseer, Cowper, Millais and Constable. Jim later branched out into selling historic photographs, and autographs not only of musical and literary figures, but of religious, medical, military or royal personages who had made their mark on paper and on the world.

Unable to remember any tune, let alone sing anything even faintly resembling it unless there are words attached, I found my brother's aural musical memory incredible, absolutely fantastic, and certainly impossible for me to emulate. If you rang him to ask the name of some music heard on the radio, he would name its exact title, composer, current and past conductors, where the song/opera/music was first played, and anything else about it you wanted to know. He could name an opera's cast, where and when it was last performed. You only had to sing even in the most tuneless way or play him a line of vocal music, and he would give you any statistic about it that you wanted to know.

Active service in the Second World War brought all Jim's activity to a temporary halt. Encouraged by my mother, who had a penchant for picking winners (some), he resurrected his music business after the war. It prospered enough for him to raise a family of twin sons and a daughter, the sons eventually going to university. Unfortunately, as with my father before him, cancer caught up with Jim's smoking. He died in his early fifties. One of his graduate sons then tried, with Bella's help, to carry on the business, but though knowledgeable, efficient, and real aficionados of music, they lacked Jim's genius, and eventually decided to sell his entire collection. I have one of his old records, but nothing else.

Fate plays some strange tricks. From such a culturally impoverished East End home, would Jim have become so interested in music, so famous in the musical world, had his sister not been such a failure?

13

THE MYSTERIOUS LODGER

The changeover from three downstairs rooms to a whole house, and the consequent introduction to the piano, changed the pattern of my brother's life. It changed mine too, but much more quickly and dramatically.

Determined not to be outdone by Mum's purchase of a piano, during this period when wages were coming in my father bought a second-hand bed.

'Marvellous value,' he said, bringing it to the door in a borrowed barrow.

'Full of dry rot, I bet,' Mum replied, always distrustful of his bargains.

The bed passed her inspection, however, and she helped him unload it. Together they began moving the parts to the front room upstairs, now to be their new bedroom. When they got to the middle of the stairs they began arguing about the best way to carry the load.

Unable to get her own way, Mum clumped down the stairs in a fury. She had barely reached the bottom before Dad accidentally let the bed-head slip. Tread by tread it gathered speed until it landed on the bottom step with a most ponderous 'plop'.

'Now see what you've gawn and done,' Mum yelled, more in fright than in anger. Still cross from her removal as helper in the bed-carrying operations, she added extravagantly, 'You've been and ruined all the banisters.'

Dad ignored the invitation to view the damage, and carried on taking the rest of the bed into the upstairs front room. When he came down, he looked at the damaged edge of the banisters.

'Don't worry, old girl,' he said. 'It's just got chipped a bit, that's all.'

He put his finger on the splintered banister. Giving her one of those lovely smiles she could resist only when he was drunk, and appealing to her superstitious nature, he added, 'There you are, you see. Touch wood, and we'll all be lucky.'

He picked up the bedhead, took it upstairs, and assembled the various pieces without further incident. We all trotted upstairs, like a visiting party to a museum, to view the finished product. A heavy piece of furniture, the bed stood aloof against the wall, in magnificent and splendid isolation. There was nothing else in the room, not even a chair or a piece of lino for the floor. Dad started singing a line he had heard somewhere, 'I dreamt that I dwelt in marble halls . . .' The tension that had built up melted away.

Neither Dad nor Mum minded that their possessions were few. Everybody had to start somewhere. First things first: rent must be paid, otherwise there would be no roof over their heads – and a roof was even more important than food. Somebody would always provide you with a crust. A roof was far more difficult. Other things would come in time, they hoped. Meanwhile they kept their old bed-settee and the piano to make a sitting room downstairs.

I was promoted to the upstairs end room which overlooked the outdoor lavatory and the garden. It had neither gas nor electricity and was the only room in the house without any kind of light. The weather was bitterly cold, so my father borrowed a cheap paraffin stove from the ever-obliging Harry Meadows.

Mum was not slow to point out that the Meadowses could spare the stove because Harry was modernising his home with new wiring.

'I hope 'e electrocutes 'is blimmin' self,' muttered Dad uncharitably, as he carried the stove up to my new bedroom. After lighting the wick, he told me he'd turn it off in half an hour because of the cost of paraffin. Meanwhile, I basked in the delicious heat coming from the old stove, watched the red and white dancing patterns it made on the ceiling, and read anything I could get hold of.

A week later, Dad came home absolutely knackered. He had managed to get a day's overtime labour in the docks. Piecework was being offered: a ship had to make a fast turn around with a cargo of pig-iron. Piecework meant higher pay. But first you had to fight your way through the hundreds of men clambering outside the gates for the privilege of getting work, any work, especially piecework.

And if you got the job, it meant carrying heavy, inflexible loads biting into your shoulders for nearly fifteen hours, almost without rest or respite. Mindful how he was able to buy the second-hand bed with his last pay, Dad felt himself one of the lucky ones to have work, until he finished it and had to walk home.

He sank into a chair, completely exhausted. His lean long frame shook with fatigue. Mum went to the stove where she was keeping a meal ready over a saucepan of hot water. I unlaced one of my father's heavy boots and prised it off his foot. 'That's all right, girl,' he said. He took the boot from me and wearily put it on the table by his side. Mum looked round, saw the boot, and screamed, nearly dropping the steaming plate she was carrying.

'Cor luv us! 'Oo ever's done that!' she screamed. 'Now we'll have bad luck for years and years.'

Dad was too tired to speak, and almost too tired to eat. I grabbed the boot in my hand, and put it by his feet.

'Why, what's wrong, Mum?' I asked.

'Don't you know that? I always thought you was clever. Boots on the table means bad luck, of course.'

'I thought the bad luck came if you broke a looking-glass.'

'No – that's just seven years' bad luck.'

'Seems an awful lot of things give you bad luck, putting up an umbrella in the house, boots on the table, knives crossed on a plate . . .'

'Crossed knives are not for bad luck. They mean a quarrel – and you must never give a knife as a present unless you put a coin with it,' Mum continued, less excited now that she was onto one of her favourite themes of good and bad luck.

As I could not see myself giving a knife as a present, still less a coin with it, I ignored her remark. Dad drank some tea and looked a little brighter. Mum's superstitions always amused him. He began pecking, and then gobbling his meal.

But the bad luck did come – as it would have in any case – with one of the worst depressions of the century. Dad could get no more casual labour on the docks or anywhere else. He rejoined the ranks of the two million unemployed. Unskilled as he was, he tried, with no luck, for any kind of work that might be around. Conditions at home became worse. The piano on hire purchase had to be paid for. And there was the new, higher rent.

Too little money was left for necessities, let alone furnishing any of the extra rooms we now had. Mum decided that she must take in some lodgers. There was already a bed upstairs. She added some chairs and other oddments from downstairs, and she and Dad moved back into their former sleeping quarters on the bed-settee in the downstairs front room. Young Jim also stayed downstairs, in the bedroom that I had previously shared with him.

I kept the small back room upstairs. Mum reckoned nobody would want that tiny room without electricity or gas. You might be a bit suspicious of them if they did. The weather was still freezing, so Harry Meadows let us keep the paraffin stove a little longer.

Hours after Dad turned off its wick, I kept on reading by candlelight. Mum did not encourage reading. Like most women of that period and that area, she thought books for girls were a waste of time, though birthdays and Christmas might merit the purchase of an annual at a second-hand stall. Learning to use a sewing machine, or even better, a typewriter; to cook a meal or clean a room: there was some sense in these pursuits. They had to be done – and they could earn you a living. And playing a piano, though not quite a necessity like other skills, might introduce a girl into the right kind of company – but reading?

So I early and secretly acquired a taste for short stories, diaries, letters, essays, anthologies: anything that promised quick reading and long remembrance: a Coventry Patmore poem, an essay of Lamb or Hazlitt, the letters of the Brownings, or of Frieda to D.H. Lawrence. Memorised in minutes, hidden in seconds, their presence was never discovered. But long did their fragrance linger.

The tiny light heightened my desire for pathos in a phrase, passion in a paragraph, and all life's emotions in a few pages of print. I throve on O. Henry's tales with their end twists, the sly humour of Saki and his portrayal of the hemmed-in child, backgrounds remote from my own, but real. Nothing, as long as it was short, seemed too old, too young, too strange. 'The Necklace' of Maupassant, Alphonse Daudet's 'The Last Lesson', 'Our Lady's Juggler' by Anatole France, came – like the Russian short stories – in translation. All were equally moving.

Dialogue akin to Cockney presented no difficulty, though I had no taste for Dickens. Ring Lardner's baseball and fighting champions with their droll turn of speech, his men and women with their so-human weaknesses, so cruelly portrayed, preceded Damon Runyon's toughs with the (occasional) heart of gold. But savouring a whole book, watching through 80,000 words or more the unravelling of a plot, the building up of tension or character, Proust in one volume, let alone twelve? These were not yet for me.

I hated blowing the candle out, and would let it dwindle until almost the last bit of tallow. My brother had nearly always been near me when I went off to sleep. Now alone in the dark, I felt afraid, imagining all kinds of spooks and spectres coming in. There was no lock on the door.

But I gradually got used to the new regime as different lodgers came and went – usually after a scuffle or a night-time flit. Then a fellow purporting to be an American turned up. A real charmer he was, with lots of tiny little books of poetry in his soft leather travelling bag.

He showed them to me and read some verse from Kipling. With captive eyes, I gazed at him as we sat drinking a cup of tea. I was absolutely enthralled by his looks, his exciting background from that fabulous land across the sea, and of course his fascinating American accent, so attractive to an East Ender.

What a wonderful way he had of reciting . . . almost as wonderful as Miss O'Farrell's renderings in the classroom, but different. He said he was staying in London before rejoining a ship to Canada.

'Don't sound like an American to me,' Dad said later that evening. 'I bet 'e's a blimmin' con man.'

If anybody ought to have been able to recognise a con man, it should have been my father. He never could. He'd been 'conned' more often than any person I knew. And he resented Mum and himself being relegated to the bed-settee downstairs, while the American got the best bed in the new room upstairs.

'Well, he's paid a fortnight's rent in advance,' Mum retorted, 'so he's welcome to stay.'

A few days later my parents had a fearsome row. Dad picked up a bag and said he'd had enough. He was leaving. He sometimes made this threat. My mother never took it seriously, for he always came back shortly afterwards saying he'd forgotten something. He left, banging the door after him. The American lodger, too, was out, but had his own key. The night drew on. Dad did not return. My mother did not want to be left in the house on her own while she had lodgers, so I did not go out and look for him, as I so often did, and help to get him home.

'Your father will come back when the pubs are shut,' Mum said to me, pursing her lips. How would he pay for his drinks, I wondered. The hours passed with no sign of him. My brother and I went our separate ways to bed, he down, me up.

Some time later, I heard Mum open the door of the sitting room downstairs on her way to bed. My father did not come back. No father . . . no warm stove . . . I had no heart for reading. The candle was almost burnt out. Hours passed.

A key turned softly in the front door lock. Then came the sound of footsteps up the stairs. They weren't Dad's. His heavy plod was very distinctive. Who then was coming up . . . and not going to the middle room, but by the steps that led to mine? There was no light to turn on.

The candle had burnt itself out. The door handle swivelled softly round. I knew without any doubt that the person outside must be the 'American'.

I wanted desperately to scream . . . but couldn't. My throat tightened so much I felt suffocated. I could not even manage a whisper. To try to call for help and find yourself so paralysed by fear that you are struck dumb, unable to utter even the tiniest sound, is absolutely terrifying. My heart began pumping like a piston engine. I have never been so frightened in my life as when I tried to scream and nothing, but nothing came from my throat.

During London's bombing in the Second World War I was in a street that got blown to bits, with many killed in the house next door. The survivors were screaming for help. We could not help them for we had to be dug out ourselves. That experience was as nothing compared with the night when my bedroom door handle slowly swivelled round and I was literally struck dumb.

Suddenly, through the darkness, I heard my father. Stumbling into the hall, he was very loudly and very obviously drunk, singing in his rich dark voice:

> She was lovely and fair as the rose of the summer,
> Yet 'twas not her beauty alone that won me;
> Oh no 'twas the truth in her eyes ever dawning,
> That made me love Mary, the Rose of Tralee.

I imagined him standing downstairs inside the front door, wobbly on his feet, singing those romantic lines from one of his favourite love songs. Suddenly he stopped.

'Where is everybody?' he called out. 'Not a soul waiting up for the old man?'

The handle of my door stopped turning. Quick soft steps hastened to the middle bedroom.

'Hush, you'll wake everybody up,' came the voice of my mother.

Dad started going up the stairs. 'Where are you going?' Mum whispered sharply, adding, 'Gawd luv us, 'es forgotten we're down here, now.'

'Oh yes, the blimmin' American, or so 'e says. Let's all bow to Swank, the Yank.'

'Come in, for goodness sake,' Mum said. She was sure her lodger would disappear by morning if Dad continued in this way. And disappear he did.

Worse was to come. The old lady in a corner house nearby was murdered in her bed that night. Who knows, but for the sound of an Irish song, it could have been me. The murderer was never caught. For years afterwards I had the most terrible nightmares, and would wake up terrified to find myself singing 'The Rose of Tralee'.

14

THE STREET

Richer citizens viewed the East End before and after the two world wars as a depressed area. For most of the people who lived there, it certainly was. But as children, what we never had, we never missed . . . much. And if we did miss anything we knew there was little chance of getting it – unless we 'pinched' it.

My mother regarded 'pinching' anything other than what you needed to survive as a crime. 'Pinching' did not include the items that, with man's assistance, fell off a van. They were like apples or plums dropping from a tree into the hands of anyone lucky enough to catch them.

If you had to go round 'pinching' (the word 'stealing' was never used) it showed, according to Mum, that you had no guts or, to use the local idiom, weren't much 'cop'. It was worse than playing games on Sundays or swearing. Adults might be permitted a 'bloody' or 'sod' in our house, never young Jim or me. As for using any four-letter words, my mother was scathing of anybody with such a limited vocabulary who was 'always effing and blinding.'

She had very rigid ideas of right and wrong. Most came from her upbringing by a somewhat bigoted Protestant father, and what she learnt from her days as a housemaid with the Watermans, a family of no specific faith but who held firm noncomformist beliefs with Methodist overtones. If asked, the Watermans would probably have described themselves as Church of England.

The only contribution made by my Catholic father to Mum's spiritual uplift, if so it can be called, was that time had to be spared for prayer via the Mass. As she had promised to bring up as Catholics any children she might have from her marriage to him, she took this idea on board. Also taken on board was the reverence for the Sabbath day assimilated from the Jewish families where she worked.

This meant in our house that my brother and I went to church on Sundays with our father, though young Jim sloped off a bit as he grew older. It also meant Sunday was not for street games, nor sewing, nor anything that could be construed as manual labour, or any jollification which we might otherwise have enjoyed.

So much for the rules – all there to be broken of course. At the back of our minds as children was what we had heard about a young boy who had stolen something he needed in order to survive. When asked in court, 'Didn't you know that what you were doing was wrong?' he is supposed to have said (a tale doubtless dreamt up by a clever lawyer), 'I knew it was against the law, but I didn't know it was wrong.'

Our attitude to 'pinching' was somewhat similar – but not to attendance at Sunday Mass, any foregoing of which led to a Hell even worse than Mum's wrath.

In spite of the dirt and poverty prevalent in Bethnal Green and its surrounds – and the dirt was sometimes worse than the poverty because buildings could not be jacked up, nor the fleas, lice, cockroaches and mice exterminated – and in spite of our somewhat rigid Sunday regimen (which, apart from the holy Mass, lessened in severity with each passing year), we still had dreams.

We read books that told us how some youngster, slightly older than ourselves, always male of course, swept through hurricanes, climbed mountain peaks in raging blizzards, or swam through whirlpools and treacherous currents.

In this triumphant manner the intrepid hero continued for several hundred pages, conquering every disaster that nature and a creative author could invent. Having destroyed all his opponents (in the bravest but fairest possible way), he saved all his comrades, even the unworthy ones; fought injustice; helped the weak to survive; and then at last, having reached the end of the rainbow, he always found a crock of gold and a long lost relative, welcoming and rich. Sometimes he discovered a beautiful new love, equally rich but otherwise strangely like the young female at that moment reading all about his wonderful exploits.

There were other books too, that told us how, for practically no effort and (even more important) no money, we could make cupboards or bedside tables and other wonderful pieces of furniture from wooden vegetable or fruit crates. They showed us how to lay a table – illustrated by cups and saucers that actually matched and never had a single crack. But no matter how hard I tried, the vegetable or fruit crates (when I could prise them from a street trader) obstinately refused to look like anything other than the crates they were, and nothing at all like a cupboard or bedside table.

Sometimes the effort of making things appear better made you feel worse – but as children of Nelson Street, not far from the scenes of Arthur Morrison's *Tales of Mean Streets* and *Child of the Jago*, we knew we were lucky in at least one thing: we had the best playground for miles, right on our doorstep.

We didn't want to go marching off to Victoria Park to kick a ball around, though the park had lots of grass ('Please keep off'), a lovely big lake, and later on an outdoor swimming pool. We never knew or cared that it was created over 150 years ago at a cost of £50,000, or that the money to pay for it came from the Duke of Sutherland's £70,000 sale of Lancaster House, St James's. And even if we noticed the two stone dogs over the entrance, our classical education was not quite upmarket enough to tell us that they were the Dogs of Alcibiades, friend of Socrates.

When we drank from the fountain in the park, none of us realised that the intriguing Baroness (Angela) Burdett-Coutts had built it. Her name lingers on in several Bethnal Green streets, for example Angela Street near Brick Lane, Virginia Street in Columbia Road flower market and Burdett Road in Bow.

Another much smaller drinking fountain in nearby Lauriston Road had a little inscription which similarly meant nothing to us: 'From LS and BS 1881. To commemorate 25 years of happy married life.' Now, from a distance, I can thank LS and BS for their thoughtful and happy legacy, which quenched the thirst of so many kids.

We knew everybody, and everybody knew us, in our street. Shaped like the letter H, our particular bit formed the vertical bar, so it was a very safe place in which to play. Practically no traffic ever entered except for a rare delivery. Woe betide any luckless van driver who left his van unattended, or inadvertently let goods slip from his cart. The speed with which any trifle was picked up would have won an Olympic gold medal.

Nobody in the street owned a car except the 'young lady' of Frankie Kelsey next door. But she lived in Goodmayes. They were a 'posher' lot there, so though she possessed and even drove a car, she didn't really count. When my Dad had a dray, it was about the only moving vehicle we ever saw come in or out of the street.

Mr Pinchin, builder and decorator, lived in a corner house. On the other side were the Rixons. Their daughter, Gladys, was a lovely looking blonde, who, according to my mother – with a despairing look at me – 'knew how to dress'. Her looks made it almost inevitable that she should marry the manager of a thriving nearby public house.

Frank Kelsey, the elder of two boys who lived next door to us, set up a printing business with Gladys's brother. The more the firm prospered, the worse the relationship grew. Finally, the partnership broke up, leaving much bitterness behind.

I sometimes heard Leslie, younger brother of Frank, singing in the back garden of his house a line from a then fashionable song, 'Why not take all of me?' Leslie was not exactly the skinniest of young men, so I rushed indoors with a fit of the giggles every time I heard him sing that line. It was all too much.

The Kelseys had several relations living nearby. They included Harry and Florrie Meadows, who lived in the house on the other side of our own. The Meadows were wonderful managers. Harry Meadows could do anything in and out of the home: plastering, carpentry, plumbing, wiring. Nothing seemed beyond him – except getting a job where he could profitably use his skills.

His wife, Florrie, sister of Mrs Kelsey, was an even better manager than her husband. If only she could find the ingredients, she could make anything: pickles, jams, bottled fruit. She darned, sewed, upholstered, and made her own clothes and even her sons' suits. You name it . . . she could do it. She was the only person I ever met who, with a tin of salmon and half a loaf, rivalled the Biblical miracle of feeding the five thousand with five loaves and two fishes.

When economic conditions improved, Harry became taken up with the idea of buying a plot in Romford, Essex. Our family all went with him to see the piece of land he was sure would one day be worth a fortune. Standing on that isolated windswept spot, he spoke about it with all the love for the soil of a Scarlett O'Hara.

'Be worth a fortune one day,' he kept repeating, like a magic formula. Dad and Mum, temporarily well off, had taken the journey to Romford on this bank holiday because it meant a pleasant country outing, nothing more. They nodded pleasantly at everything Harry said. His sales talk left them unmoved. There were better *spiel*s to be heard in Brick or Petticoat Lane.

'We could go halves,' Harry the salesman addressed his silent listeners. 'Or we could get some others to go in with us. Only cost us a few quid.'

At this, his audience looked up. There might be something in what Harry said.

'Twenty-five quid – that's all it will cost us for this marvellous bit of land. And you can bet your bottom dollar, it's going to be worth a fortune in a few years' time,' he went on. 'Take it from me: somebody's sure to build a road along here, when things improve.'

When Harry mentioned £25, my parents nearly died with horror.

'Twenty-five quid!' exclaimed Dad, hardly able to contain himself in the face of such a figure.

'Yes, but you only have to pay five pounds down and you can get a mortgage for the rest.'

That did it. The mere mention of 'mortgage' alarmed Dad and Mum even more than the twenty-five quid. The only time they had ever heard the word 'mortgage' was in American films, where it always meant the collapse of a bank or a farm, and the loss of some poor hard-working person's money. No mortgages for them. Harry's idea had to be seen as nothing more than a pleasant dream, and so it became . . . almost.

Dad and Mum agreed politely with everything Harry said, but left him to get on with it, which he did. Not only did he buy the plot (perhaps on mortgage or perhaps with money borrowed from relations), he even managed to build on it a kind of immobile caravan.

It served the Meadows well. They moved from Bethnal Green and settled in Romford, growing their own produce and becoming almost like country folk. Later on they sold their £25 plot for a fat figure. With the proceeds they bought themselves a most 'desirable residence' in Romford.

Florrie's skills might seem everyday ones in country districts, but they weren't much practised in Bethnal Green. Rotten vegetables were the diet of the poorest, with a bit of sheep's head or pig's trotters for an occasional feast.

When there were jobs around, the daily fare improved. It could hardly get worse. Boiled salt beef with pease pudding and carrots was absolutely delicious and Mum could make a real treat out of a sheep's head or pig's trotters. When the rare chance came up for cockles, winkles or whelks, we gobbled up these delicacies from the tiny plate provided by the stallholder, and never gave a thought to the hunger of the black babies the nuns told us about on Mondays.

If we were lucky, Jewish food like latkes and gefilte fish, bought or given, might come our way. But nothing in the Jewish dessert menu could compare with spotted dick. If the chance ever arose I would eat and eat of that pudding until I could hardly move from the table. Nobody picked or fiddled with their food. We ate everything put before us.

Living in our street was hardly a bed of roses and the Meadows, like many others of that time and place, were always trying for something better. Their elder son, young Harry, was a marvellous looking boy – tall and nearly as blonde as his beautiful long-haired mother. He blossomed out into a handsome young man, much sought after by all the women around. He was madly interested in sports, swimming, body-building, and excelled in any he took up.

At the other end of our street, was another related family of Meadows, all just as good looking, especially Willie, the eldest son, another blonde bombshell. He passed the scholarship examination for Parmiters School and later became a librarian at Bethnal Green Library.

Librarians were awesome creatures: beings from a different planet. They lived in a world inhabited by books. Our library in Cambridge Heath Road, endowed, like many others, by the Scottish–American philanthropist Andrew Carnegie, boasted a marvellous reference library, complete with individual desks and lamps. If you were so moved, you could study anything under the sun there until 9.00 p.m. when the library closed.

No matter what the condition of your home, no matter how noisy, damp or pest infested it was, the library provided a marvellous retreat in which to hide, read or study. And librarians knew Absolutely Everything . . . even more than teachers. No matter what the query, they could always find an answer.

When a librarian also had the looks of Willie Meadows, any number of young ladies suddenly discovered an irresistible urge to study. If Will Meadows was on duty in the reference library, there wouldn't be a vacant seat. Sadly for love's young dream, Willie Meadows emigrated to America, where he joined the US Air Force at the outbreak of the Second World War. I don't know whether he survived that holocaust.

For him, as for many others, the East End was a jumping-off point from which many boxers, writers, entertainers and some politicians soared to fame. Others, less talented, less blessed with good health, good looks or good fortune, sank into a morass from which it was difficult, and sometimes impossible, to emerge unscathed.

Our street was inhabited by grafters, a street where, even in the Great Depression, people were always striving, always trying to improve their lot. You had to struggle . . . and win. Because if you didn't win, you went under, perhaps for ever.

The strong tried everything to help in the unremitting fight to make ends meet; the weak . . . anything for solace when the battle went against them. The ends of cigarettes, thrown away by other men after their smoke, as in postwar Germany, were scrounged from the gutters, unfurled and stuffed with the luxury of dirty tobacco, rolled up to make a smoke. Hardier souls, not addicted to the weed, picked up newspapers discarded by travellers at railway stations and elsewhere.

Paper served many needs. You could cut it into squares and leave it in the 'lav' – very high class that was. Paper fuelled a fire, or filled out holes in shoes . . . if you had shoes. Soaked newspapers could be moulded into flowerpots or containers and sold near to the Virginia Street flower market. When there were enough clean papers to make a parcel, the fish shop would always pay you a penny or even more for them. With a penny you were a millionaire indeed, a world of choice resting, but not for long, in your hot, grubby hand. A cheap or discarded wheel – better still, two or more – fixed onto an orange box could serve as a pram for a baby, or for carting around anything that might prove saleable.

If your home became almost too unbearable because of damp, overcrowding or far worse ills, you could try for a council house – a hard job indeed because, unknown to the applicants, allocations for the houses went not to the local Metropolitan Borough of Bethnal Green but to the owners of the homes, the London County Council.

You did not tidy up your rooms, as the inexperienced applicant might do, when the Housing Officer, who assessed your needs, came round . . . oh no . . . You kept them as shabby as possible; and filled them with every relation you could drag in, with their old mattresses or anything else to serve as a bed.

Everything was tried to make a living, but with unemployment figures so high, what hope was there of getting a job? And if you were disabled, as was Susan's father, the chances were slimmer still.

The workhouse was always there, its baleful presence glowering in the distance, threatening anybody who gave up the fight to keep body and soul together. When I was taken to see an ageing relative of my mother, I remember the atmosphere of despair and desolation, the dreary clothes, the compulsive wandering of inmates round the bit of grey yard, like trained but captive animals who had given up all hope of release.

There was the occasional poignant moment when husband and wife, who might have lived together for a lifetime, caught a glimpse of each other through the grille that separated the sexes.

But that was the situation. When all the efforts to improve your lot failed, including even illegal ones, most people in the street realised that what couldn't be cured had to be endured . . . until better times came along. For some, these better times were too far ahead. If relations, neighbours or friends couldn't help, the outlook might be bleak indeed.

In the small street of around sixty houses where I grew up, there were four suicides and one murder.

One man hanged himself from a scaffolding in Bethnal Green Road; a mother drowned herself in the Victoria Park lake. The two saddest cases, however, were those of poor Mrs Thomas, reputedly heavily in debt. She gassed herself, and left her 12-year-old daughter, coming home from school, to discover her body. The second sad case that I remember happened just round the corner in the house of Mr and Mrs Cohen. They were a quiet, respectable couple, thought to be comparatively well off. When their beloved only daughter died of diphtheria, her Jewish father could not come to terms with her death. Distracted beyond reason, he committed suicide and left his poor wife to suffer the tragedy of the two deaths.

For Jews or Catholics, suicide was a particularly sad end. Neither religion appeared to look very sympathetically on those who found life's misfortunes too great to bear. Most of the Catholic hierarchy regarded suicide as the sin of final despair and such 'law-breakers' were not 'entitled' to a Christian burial. Most magistrates mitigated the suffering of those left behind as best they could, by adding to suicide as the cause of death the ameliorating phrase, 'while of unsound mind'.

No such troubles bothered us kids as we played in the street. Our biggest disaster was a ball going through somebody's window. Not all children played in the street as I did. It was not considered 'nice' by some families. But for those of us not doing odd jobs or with mothers at work, and who were let out to play in the evening or on Saturday afternoons (on Sunday it was forbidden), the street had all its own entertainment, and an occasional visiting barrel organ, too.

We skipped with the rope used to tie up orange boxes. If they lived in 'buildings', the more adventurous boys used the same rope twisted round washing-line poles. Those who lived in a house looped the rope onto the street lamp-post and swung themselves round and round, first one way and then back again.

We enjoyed hopscotch on the pavement, threw a diabolo in the air and caught it, played ball games against the house walls, wheeled a hoop, or kicked a football about in the road until we broke a window or otherwise aroused the ire of a householder. If we didn't escape in time, she would come running out, shaking her arms at us in fury.

'Bugger off outside your own door,' she shouted. 'And I'll tell your Mum what you've done to my b . . . window. You'll have to pay for it, yer know.'

If my Mum's window were broken by any of my pals, it was always me that got a 'good hiding'. She had never read the Catechism describing the ways in which you can share in another's sin. All she knew was that if I was out in the street, then it must be my fault that the window was broken. She was probably right most of the time. At mending windows, she was a real dab hand, buying the putty and the pane, and having everything fixed up before nightfall.

In the winter we played with conkers from the chestnut trees that grew in St Peter's churchyard at the top of the street. The best conker thrower had a thirty conker. Most of us could only manage ten at most, and only because we had soaked our conker with vinegar or put it in the oven so that it was very hard and could easily smash any other.

Sometimes we sang electioneering songs. Sir Percy Harris, originally a Liberal Party member and later Labour, was our MP. We had a lot of unflattering songs about everybody who stood for election. 'Vote, vote, vote for —. Kick old — down the stairs . . . If he goes to kingdom come, we'll kick him up the bum, and we won't vote for — any more.' Names could be inserted to suit your fancy or your party.

In the summer we cut small numbered holes into old shoe boxes retrieved from shop dustbins and rolled cherry stones or 'ogs', as we called them, into the holes. If your cherry 'og' rolled into a hole numbered 2, you got two 'ogs', and so on, but if it didn't roll into the shoe box, or rolled into one numbered 0, you lost your cherry 'og'. What good the 'ogs' were to anybody, I can't think, but they were as greatly sought after as conker-battle winners.

We called a kind of hide-and-seek 'Black Man's Dark Scenery', though we'd never seen or noticed a black man except that nice Dr Jelly who lived round the corner. And a game which surprisingly broke nobody's back was when one person began it by stretching out their arms and resting their hands on the wall.

The next person put their arms round the waist of the person in front and so on. Then a volunteer jumped as far as he could onto somebody's back. If he landed on the back of the person nearest to the wall, he won the game. We all took turns, and screamed 'Om Bom Bee And Away' when we landed on anybody, though what the words meant, nobody knew.

For a change from street games, I wandered down to Bethnal Green Museum in Cambridge Heath Gardens. How fascinating were its contents, especially the beautiful doll's house and all its wonderful items of furniture. Somebody told me it was a long-ago raffle prize that had never been claimed. I was almost as interested in why the prize wasn't claimed as the prize itself.

When the museum first opened in 1872, the Marquis of Hereford filled it with art treasures. They included works by Hobbema, Rembrandt, Rubens and Vandyck; Andrea del Sarto, Leonardo da Vinci, Canaletto, Murillo and Velasquez; Watteau, Fragonard and Delacroix. Portraits by Reynolds, Gainsborough and Bonington represented the British school. Perhaps because of Bethnal Green's not-quite-spotless reputation, the pictures did not remain in the museum for long. They soon went off to become part of a collection in a more prestigious part of town.

But there were plenty of other things to see. I loved the miniature butcher's, sweet and hat shops and went home to make my own.

Sometimes I wandered off to nearby Brick or Petticoat Lanes, but hardly ever dared buy anything even when I had the cash, for fear that there was a catch in what was being sold.

In our street kingdom we forgot about parents' rows, somebody being ill or dying; about being cold or hungry though never starving – as were the 'black babies' for whom the nuns collected tiny sums from us when we possessed both cash and generosity: a combination that rarely go together.

We forgot about having to go to the cleansing station because the nurse who came round to the school had found nits, or worse, lice, in our heads; about the bodies in rags that came alive as we passed them under the arches. We forgot about the mice that scampered out when you opened a cupboard door; about the everlasting battle against poverty and pests and damp; about not having this, that or the other . . . and concentrated on the games we played until the first call came for bed.

'Or-ris . . . Or-ris,' a mother yelled out, not for Horace as the uninitiated might think, but for Iris. Iris drifted dutifully indoors. Then one by one, not quite so dutifully, so did the rest of us. Another day had ended in Nelson Street.

15

LAST DAYS

The school-leaving age in the 1920s was 14 years. Though I didn't know it at the time, I was getting near the end of my days at St Anne's and going on to a whole new world. But first there was classwork to get through.

This Tuesday morning was scheduled for religious instruction. There were only two more classes to go before we reached the top class, so we were already supposed to know the Catechism, including the Ten Commandments, the seven sacraments, the seven gifts of the Holy Ghost, the eight beatitudes, the spiritual and corporal works of mercy, the seven deadly sins, and much else. I wrote as much as I could in an exercise book because the virtues which I hoped for were even easier to forget than the sins.

The eight beatitudes were particularly hard to swallow. So were the spiritual works of mercy. The sins crying out for heavenly vengeance, especially the oppression of the poor and defrauding labourers of their wages were OK by me, but I didn't dare ask anybody, lest it looked unnaturally stupid, what was this intriguing sin of Sodom? My trusted friend the dictionary, with its definition of 'the town of Sodom' and 'unnatural sexual intercourse' enlightened me not at all. I left this particular sin of Sodom for the moment and concentrated on the one of sloth, about which I knew a bit more.

The teachers of religious instruction varied, sometimes a nun, sometimes a priest, sometimes the class teacher. Father Sullivan, due in today, was an Irish priest given to the fire and brimstone type of sermon so vividly described by James Joyce in his book *Portrait of the Artist as a Young Man*. Big and fat, with a very red face and thinning hair, he was not a bit like the handsome young Father Butterly, who served the early Masses on Sundays and holidays of obligation.

Father Sullivan's far reaching voice was like that of a sergeant major instructing a group of rookies. It sent shivers down the spines of church-going sinners, though they kept coming in their hundreds to hear him give his thunderous sermons.

Slightly gentler with schoolchildren, he was still frightening enough. Would we be able to answer his questions? They were always very difficult. He sat down heavily and began to read out the register: Crawley, Dzvonkus, Ferrari, Grenkowicz, Hook, Hurley, Manilus, Matchansky, Mikonis, Norwick, Pellici, Spurgaitis, Toubkin, Whitehorn, Vip.

I missed hearing some of the names he called out, but Maggie Vip, Annie Hurley and Winnie Hook were friends of mine. Maggie's real name was Sinunas. When her Lithuanian widowed mother remarried, her new name was anglicised to Webb. Mrs Webb wasn't such a good speaker of English as Maggie, and so the name of Webb which she gave when enrolling her daughter at the school went down as Vip. Maggie remained Vip for years afterwards.

You could tell by her pock-marked face that Maggie's mother had once had smallpox. She was lucky to recover. Though the illness was slowing dying out, and recovery more certain, its unkind traces were always left behind. Maggie herself had a lovely clear skin, short fair hair, blue eyes, and gorgeous dimples when she smiled.

Winnie Hook also had dimples, and the cheeriest grin you could see for miles. It spread all across her face and lightened up the spirit of everybody around her. Her mother was one of those women to whom you can truly apply the adjective 'good'. Without a vestige of fuss or condescension, she was always ready to help anybody who needed it.

When I was ill with some childish complaint and Mum out charring, my father often ran across the street to ask Mrs Hook to look after me for an hour or two until my mother got back. Never did Mrs Hook refuse. Too busy, no time, got to do this, that or the other, were phrases not in her vocabulary. Yet as the mayor's wife, and with a large family of her own, her days must have been full enough without the nuisance of me.

Annie Hurley, another friend, had a rather frail appearance, an impression heightened by a pale, almost anaemic complexion. Her two golden plaits hung down to her waist. She looked so like the blonde German maidens featured in story books that you could easily imagine her name to be Gretchen. Not a chatterbox like Maggie or me, Annie moved silently and sinuously, almost like a trained model, and spoke in a most fascinating way, riveting her eyes to the ground and never once looking at you until she came to the end of a sentence.

Then the sudden flash upwards of the eyelids and the penetrating look of her blue eyes staring into yours was quite electrifying. Perhaps she had learnt this mannerism from the films which we saw during periods of affluence.

Father Sullivan finished his exposition of the sacrament of marriage, in which I had no interest whatsoever. In my usual trance, a way of escaping from boredom without actually falling asleep, I hardly took in a word of what he said. He looked round the class searching for a suitable candidate for the question trembling on his lips. I hoped he wouldn't look at me. Fortunately, he pointed to Lizzie Whitehorn at the back of the class.

'And can you tell me what sacrament', he asked her, 'sanctifies the contract of a Christian marriage?'

Lizzie had the most beautiful head of hair, a lovely dark red colour, thick, curly and long. I had pulled it in a recent playground fight with her and was glad she got the question. I couldn't answer it.

Lizzie hesitated, thinking on her feet.

'Come on girl . . . marriage,' repeated Father Sullivan. 'You've been to a wedding, surely, or seen one, haven't you?'

Lizzie nodded.

'Right. Then can you tell me what is needed for a Christian marriage?'

Lizzie thought for a while, then finally came out with her answer. 'Please, Father,' she said, 'a feller. For a Christian marriage, you've got to 'ave a feller.'

With her handsome head of hair, Lizzie was never going to be short of a feller, and might even now have one or two in tow.

'A fellow, hmm, hmm. True, true . . .' Father Sullivan said, and paused.

At that moment somebody came in to say that the headmistress, Sister Hedwig, wanted to see me. How relieved I was to escape from the religious class, though I loved some of the prophecies we had to learn, like 'Rachel bewailing her children because they are not.'

How fitting the words were, how well they illustrated the massacre of the innocents by Herod and the suffering of mothers bewailing their children, 'because they are not'. And there was that wonderful description of Jesus in Isaiah, 'A man of sorrows, acquainted with grief'. As for the sins crying to heaven for vengeance, they were a joy to read. The one about defrauding the labourer of his wages seemed to be just right for where we lived.

I learnt by heart the seven deadly sins, and wondered which would be my downfall – pride, covetousness, lust, anger, gluttony, envy, or sloth? In case it was sloth again, I rushed to the stairs and learnt something more. A downfall does not depend on sin and it is not only pride that goes before a fall. Haste does too. I missed my footing at the top of the stone steps, and was saved from serious injury only by the presence of body, not mind, of plump, slow-moving, slow-talking Agnes.

Had she tried to save me, we both might have been badly injured. As it was, my escape from catastrophe wasn't due to any heroism on her part. It was her total inaction that saved me from crashing on the stone floor below.

Standing at the foot of the stairs, she was horrified by the sight of a girl toppling down from the top, a descent that took all of three seconds.

Not knowing what to do about an event as unusual as a meteor coming out of the sky, she moved not an inch from her position. I crashed against her fleshy form, probably hurting poor Agnes more than myself, though afterwards neither of us seemed the worse for the mishap. We picked ourselves up, dusted our clothes and, a bit hazily, went our various ways.

East Enders rarely mentioned to parents or teachers accidents or misadventures unseen by others. Teachers held too lofty positions to be involved with our minor calamities. Parents would only tell us off for being such clumsy idiots – or worse – always in trouble, etc., etc. It was best to hide sprains and minor injuries as best you could.

Somewhat shakily I went into the hall. Sister Hedwig told me to sit down, and said that there was a scholarship exam shortly. I was too young to enter. I must have still looked a bit dazed for she said, 'I know this has come as a surprise, but I'm going to put your name down for it. You won't pass, but taking the exam will give you the sort of practice you need.'

I nodded, only vaguely understanding that if I took this exam, Sister Hedwig thought the experience would be good for me. When the London County Council scholarship came up I wouldn't then be as nervous and so spoil my chance of passing this important milestone. How she managed to enter me for the exam without altering my date of birth and so disqualifying me at the start, I have never enquired.

From now on, Sister Hedwig continued, I was to miss the needlework classes and come down to the hall to do arithmetic and English. Mum was furious. She did not approve of such a change at all. Even ten years later in the 1930s, marriage was the usual destiny of women. And whether married or single, needlework was always useful. You only had to look around at Whitechapel to see how the Jews had used their talent with the needle to climb up through the human jungle of London's East End.

'Ridiculous! Arithmetic might be all right,' stormed Mum. 'But what does she think she's doing to stop the needlework classes? Only useful bit of learning you'll get at school. Taking English instead! As if you can't speak your own language!'

'Lots of people can't, Mum.'

'Well, let them learn. There's these evening classes all over the place. Why don't they go there? No matter where you come from, if you're here, you gotta speak English. Of course the Jews speak Yiddish but they make sure they can speak English too. How would they get on if they had to go round everywhere speaking Yiddish? Tell me that?' Not waiting for an answer, she continued, 'If their mothers and fathers can't speak English, the kids soon teach them. But teaching English to English kids instead of sewing or something useful like that!' She was too indignant to continue.

Though Mum grumbled so much at home about this change in the syllabus, I was glad that she never went to the school and argued about it. Strong as her emotions were, and usually victorious as she was in any battle that she took on, in this one of mother versus teacher, I felt and hoped the teacher would win.

Sister Hedwig, God bless her, had higher aspirations for me. At every needlework class, I slipped away. Arithmetic wasn't all that much better than needlework, but occasionally I also had to write an essay.

And she widened the curriculum for everybody by introducing swimming lessons, a really modern innovation, especially by nuns. Maggie and I enjoyed our swimming so much at Goulston Street baths, near the school in Whitechapel, that later we went off to the baths at Haggerston, nearer to our homes.

By practising breast stroke on a stool left over from my 'piano experience', we learnt the strokes. We went off to the baths together, sharing our water wings. When I realised that my wings had floated away while I was trying out the strokes, I was so astonished that I just carried on swimming. Another 'thank you' to Sister Hedwig for all the pleasure swimming has given me since.

She called me in some months after I had taken this first scholarship exam. More excited than I had ever seen her, she told me that I had passed the exam with very high marks, but I was too young to take it up.

I wasn't bothered at all. I had my eye on the London County Council scholarship. If you passed that you got free books and tuition at a school of your choice, including, for boys, public schools.

There were nearly fifty schools on the list, situated all over London, but what was so good about the scholarship was that a grant went with it; unlike the 'free places' also offered at that time and which gave to 'elementary' school children who passed the exam free tuition at high schools. That was what I wanted: a grant to cover the cost of uniform, fares, dinners, and all the rest.

My mother fought for anything she thought right, just as she did against anything she thought wrong, but I didn't want either her or my father to skimp on food and other essentials to give me a pricey education.

A few weeks before I was due to take the scholarship examination, Maggie told me in an unusual bout of confession, that she was really jealous of me.

'You're so lucky,' she said. 'You're sure to get the scholarship. Then you'll go off to high school, and with your looks, you'll marry some rich fellow and we won't see each other again.'

I was absolutely mystified and simply couldn't understand anybody being jealous of me. I was getting on for 11, still as skinny as ever, though I had, so many people told me, a pretty face. But my hair was far too thin and straight for me ever to be a raving beauty. So what did Maggie mean? Lucky? Perhaps I was, with a mother who never gave up the struggle to do better for her family, and a father who, without his drop of drink, was the kindest and most interesting man I knew.

If that was luck, I had it, yet never noticed it. As for marriage . . . not me. I compared the single teachers in our school with the mothers in our street. No, marriage seemed like slavery. It was not for me. I didn't want it – though lots of girls, including Maggie, apparently did. And what had I got that she thought so desirable? Looks? A nuisance, a trap for the unwary, a noose for the naive. I had already discovered even a modicum of good looks could attract attention you would rather do without.

Maggie replied that I had brains. One day I would get to a high school, like our librarian Willie Meadows, while she would have to stay at St Anne's and probably become a dressmaker, or help her mother baste trousers at home in Teesdale Street. I told her not to be so silly, and especially to pray. God would hear her prayers. Sister Hedwig believed fervently in prayer, and kept on at me to remember my quota.

A fortnight before the London County Council scholarship exam, I went over to see Auntie Nellie in Morrison's Buildings. I liked all my father's relations. Nellie had no children, though she would dearly have loved some and would have made a marvellous mother. Auntie Katy, the other sister, had a huge brood. They ran around the huge police quarters where they lived as if it were a playground.

Katy's first child, Davy, though as nice looking as the rest, was backward. Today, he would be regarded as a savant, for he could tell you the bus numbers, train times and fares for almost every service travelling to and from London. Apparently there was no class which he could profitably attend or which would take him in, so he never went to school, though he learnt to read and write and could do simple sums. Auntie Nellie with Bill, her husband, more or less adopted Davy and he was oftener in their house than in his own.

I used to go over there sometimes by myself. I enjoyed Davy's company but didn't see Bill very often. He seemed a cheery soul, very patient and always ready for a joke or a laugh. He acted as a security guard for a car company nearby and was home this Sunday. I was interested in the cars he described in his garage. He offered to take me there to see them on my way home. We crossed Commercial Road, and I walked with him to the big entrance door of what looked like a huge warehouse. I went inside. There was a great array of cars. Bill followed behind and locked the door.

This worried me a little, but not unduly. After all, he was a security guard. Perhaps locking doors was the custom. I pretended not to notice that he had turned the key in the lock. He came across to where I was standing by one of the car doors, and put his arm round me, as if to escort me around. Instead he began kissing me. He was not drunk, but breathing heavily.

I could not understand what was happening, and made inept excuses about having to leave. He got more excited and appeared deaf to what I was saying. I wanted to escape from the horrible fondling of his hands about my body. Whatever possessed him to act like this?

By some stratagem, I managed to reach the garage door, unlock it with trembling hands and get away. I ran and ran from Whitechapel to Bethnal Green without once stopping for breath. All the way home, I wondered whatever had happened. What had I done wrong? Should I tell my parents? Mum's temper was as hot as Dad's, but exploded mainly in the house, whereas Dad could let off steam anywhere, indoors or out.

By the time I got home, I'd cooled down a bit, but didn't understand why Dad and Mum kept asking me such odd questions. Were my clothes pulled up . . . or down . . . did he do this, that or the other? No, it was only kissing, I said. I began to play the incident down, as I sensed it could make a lot of trouble if relayed to the relations.

Maybe I had exaggerated the whole thing, though naive as I always was (for sex was never mentioned even obliquely in our household) I knew the kissing was not quite that of an affectionate uncle showing his regard for a niece . . . nor did an innocent kiss need a locked door. Dad went straight round and confronted Nellie and Bill. He wanted me to go too, but I just couldn't face them. That incident almost spelt the end of Dad's relationship with his sister, yet he loved her and I did, too.

A week later, I went down with such a severe attack of tonsillitis that I could not go to school. My illness also meant, far worse, that I could not take the London County Council scholarship examination.

I cannot describe my disappointment at being unable to sit for the scholarship. It was like a physical pain. There was no guarantee that I would ever pass, but without taking it there was not even the chance to do so. I felt let down by heaven and all its inmates, especially as I had besieged them night and day with the most fervent appeals. How could they not respond? Was God punishing me for the garage incident, telling me that I should not have gone in there? Well, I wouldn't in the future, but what good was that going to do now? Everything was going wrong. Disappointment, anger, misery, a whole welter of emotions overwhelmed me, leaving me almost sick with frustration.

Still, Maggie at least could sit the exam. I was so glad for her when she was awarded a free place. I told her she was the lucky one now. Her prayers had been answered. Mine couldn't have been as good. My chance was gone.

'Pray,' said Sister Hedwig, using the old watchword. 'Pray,' she said again. 'God is just testing you.'

She must have seen from my face that I thought this testing a bit unfair. 'Try St Jude,' she urged, like a salesman offering you another brand because the first doesn't quite suit. When I heard that St Jude was the patron saint of despairing cases, and his feast day was on my birthday, I thought I might as well give him a chance. After all, I had tried all the rest up there, and they hadn't been much good.

Something must have worked for we heard that the London County Council had an exam for anybody who, through illness, was absent from the original scholarship test. I was able to do my bit.

Fail or win, I had my chance. One question needed a description of the River Thames. I went hell for leather on that, concluding the 'training ship on the mouth of the River Thames, where boys are taught to follow in the footsteps of Nelson, the father of the British Navy, and fight for king and country as every citizen ought to do'. Phew! What a sentence: such an awfully long one I can remember it seventy years later. But I got the scholarship.

'Go south of the river,' advised Sister Hedwig, as if a school on the south of the river was on the other side of the world. Perhaps, from the viewpoint of Bethnal Green, it was. And it might have been too, for a nun who had left Ireland to find her own niche in Whitechapel.

On my way home, I imagined how my parents would take the news of my success. The post must have arrived by now. Mum would say, 'That's nice. But how will we afford it? All those books, and uniform and fares,' and I would tell her there was a grant of £12 a year, not a fortune, but it could buy something.

She would be secretly proud, her only regret that it was her daughter who had won a scholarship, and not yet her son. My father would just say, 'Must be clever like your Dad,' and send me to the seventh heaven of delight.

I reached the house of old Mrs Shea, who lived not far away from us, at the end of our street. Her son wrote to her from America once a month and I went into her home to read his letters. She had very poor sight – or so she said. I thought perhaps she had never learnt to read, though a glass-fronted bookcase full of old classics was in her kitchen.

After I read a letter with far more expression than it merited, I put it on the table. She would pick it up and look at it with so much love, that I wondered how on earth he could ever have left his mother. But like many East End sons, he never really did.

It was about time for his latest letter. I knocked at the door. She opened it, invited me in. Before we began the ritual letter reading, I burst out the news of my scholarship. She laid a knobbly hand on my arm. 'Lovely to be a scholar,' she said. I couldn't understand why her eyes filled with tears. Two years later, she died. The bookcase and all the books came to me. Her son said she wanted me to have them.

Alas! The bookcase and books, like almost all our other possessions, were destroyed in the first bombing wave of the war. I do not remember us ever getting any compensation, but my parents managed to get half a house in the same street.

Just before Maggie and I started in the new school together at Notre Dame, Southwark, in 1928, the River Thames overflowed its banks. My uncle Bill was in the danger zone at the time, but missed the disaster, in which several people were drowned.

Another caught up with him, however, in the Second World War, and in some strange way, gave him back the respect he had lost in the garage incident. He was an Air Raid Precautions (ARP) warden and his garage and the nearby streets were heavily bombed. Bravely helping to evacuate people from the area, with complete disregard for his own safety, he went back once too often and was killed.

Maggie and I kept in touch briefly in later years. An article of mine in the *Daily Telegraph* brought in a response from somebody who had been, like me, a bridesmaid at her wedding in Canning Town when the church and everybody inside it had been almost blown to smithereens. I learnt then that Maggie had seven children, all doing extremely well, with one daughter studying for a medical degree at Southampton University.

But the youngest daughter had taken a far more unusual path. Doing some vacation work in a seamen's hostel in the summer, she fell in love with an Iranian working for his master's ticket, married him and went to live in Iran. She has three children and still, I understand, practises the Catholic faith. What a family journey . . . beginning with her grandmother's move from Lithuania to England, and then her own to Iran via Bethnal Green and Canning Town.

In my last days at St Anne's, how could I guess that my own future wanderings from Bethnal Green were to be nearly as strange?

16

NOTRE DAME

In 1928 Maggie and I left St Anne's and began as pupils at Notre Dame High School in south London, 'across the water', as Sister Hedwig advised. The water was the Thames, the daily crossing point, London Bridge.

Maggie got on the bus near the police station; I boarded it further up Bethnal Green Road where it was just possible to see the spire of St Paul's over the warehouse buildings of Shoreditch. The bus began its magical journey . . . first to Liverpool Street, then through the City, teeming with people on their way to work. Round the sweep of Gracechurch Street we sailed towards the river. Cranes stretched their tentacles far up into the sky, ships hooted or whistled their departure to faraway places. Tower Bridge raised its arms and big boats passed under them to unload or to export their cargo.

How fascinating the grey waters looked, so busy, and encased by all the river's friendly sidewalks, so safe. Yet disaster could happen here as anywhere . . . accidents to seamen and dock workers, to people on pleasure cruises, even to people living nearby, as when the Thames overflowed its banks soon after we started school, and drowned four sisters and ten others in their basement homes.

After London Bridge we went through the Borough and the Elephant and Castle; nothing interesting about that dreary stretch except theories as to how the Elephant and Castle got its name. We walked along St George's Road until we came to the big convent of Notre Dame, then situated opposite Bedlam Asylum where a few poor inmates still remained.

When we crossed the road to the yard of the asylum for our lunch-hour playtime, I often used to see high up at the top window a person waving to us as we passed by. Poor soul I thought, waving back. It never occurred to me that she might be a nurse or an administrator of some kind – for it surely was a lady – though it was difficult to make out from our vantage point so far below. I learnt a very different lesson in the Bedlam playground from those taught in school – and one forgotten even more quickly – that there were always people worse off than oneself.

At Notre Dame I learnt other things, the most memorable being the lessons of division . . . not arithmetical division, but social and physical division. The first division came with Maggie. We somehow drifted away from each other among the mêlée of new girls and only renewed the closeness of our friendship after we left school.

Maggie had one of the free places at Notre Dame. These provided tuition only, no other financial help. Books, uniform and fares all had to be paid for. The very poorest children could not always take up the free places. In 1928 some parts of England were just recovering from the effects of the General Strike. Mining districts suffered for years afterwards, with miners drifting to other areas and vying with 'locals' for any work going.

The bitterness between the so called 'scabs' who found jobs in other pits and those who remained workless in their own, continued long after the strike was over. Not all trade unionists, especially those of the far left, accepted the dictum mouthed by Berthold Brecht, that 'food comes first, then morals'.

After the strike, the 'better' times did not last long. The terrible depression of the 1930s soon showed its teeth. Maggie's parents kept her going until she reached the then school-leaving age of 14, when she had to leave. She could be earning a living instead of reading books.

With a London County Council grant I was luckier, though feeling no richer than anybody else and poorer than most. Several times having carelessly left my indoor shoes or other items on the bus, I tried in vain to retrieve them. Not daring to tell my mother of the loss, I walked to and from school every day until I saved enough money to pay for the missing item.

Pocket money and a bit more for the family coffers came by working in the evenings for a local doctor, carefully transcribing into a book some of the prescriptions made up in the surgery. Like so many doctors of that time Dr Z. Roodyn was a most caring man, too caring for his own strength.

He had his surgery in Bethnal Green Road, and might have been part of the wave of Jewish immigrants of the period. I knew only that he was a great diagnostician, and however dark a future he foresaw for his patients, he always found something uplifting to say to them. With more flattery than truth he once praised my handwriting. That made me take even more care about entering 'mist.expect.stim' and similar abbreviations for everyday remedies in his medicines book, though he always checked what I had done. In later years, any young person helping him in such a minor capacity might possibly have thought of a medical career. Such aspirations never even entered my head.

On the very rare occasions when my mother was not well enough to get to the City office for her night-time charring job, I deputised for her. She did not want to lose the work, though the pay was only sixpence an hour. Well briefed on how to go about it (Mum was rightly suspicious of my cleaning skills) I used to walk to Finsbury Pavement, go heavily covered up into the offices so that the doorman would not unduly notice my entry, enter the lift as to the manner born, and eventually land safely in the empty but still sacred chambers of the 'City gents'. Coming home after ten o'clock was no problem . . . plenty of buses, and if I walked, as usual . . . not a single rapist, paedophile or other threatening presence crossed my path, though there might be the occasional 'flasher'.

The lives of those who came to the surgery and those who worked in the City made a huge contrast. At Notre Dame there were further differences. Some girls seemed so much cleverer, better endowed than others. In childhood, these differences can dissolve in a bout of tears; sometimes into blows of frustration. The moment departs, and with luck is lost for ever.

Previously a boarding and day school for young ladies, a different kind of student was now entering Notre Dame's portals. We would have to be taught etiquette; first, table manners: nothing should ever be removed from our mouths without a spoon. On the school dining tables a little bin was therefore provided. We used the spoons dutifully to put into it any stones, pips or peel left over from our packed lunches. We were also told never to run anywhere inside the school, to let nuns and teachers precede us, especially on the stairs, and to bow to the nuns whenever they walked by. Breaking any of these rules was a crime on a par with treason, though nobody had yet been imprisoned in the Tower.

Like their pupils, some nuns found it hard to adapt to the new situation in which they found themselves. Sister Mary Austin was one. Known as Gus, she was short and squat, square-faced with a strong jawbone that matched her forthright speech and manner. Her eyes were a penetrating, almost glinting blue, her cheeks of an unusually high colour due, so the informed gossips said, to some mysterious illness. She often lost patience with our behaviour or our work, but lessons with her were always exciting, and bequeathed to us all at least a vestige of a foreign tongue.

Flinging open the door, she would burst into the classroom – never entering quietly like other nuns – and yell 'Amo, amas, amat' as she covered the few steps across the floor to her desk. We were just beginning to learn Latin. Few of us had any idea of what she was saying. We fell into a fit of hopeless but barely hidden giggles and tried to keep our cool by staring fixedly at 'Gus'. We did not dare glance at anybody else lest the giggles started up again. Seeing our look of incomprehension, she called out to nobody in particular, 'That's what we've got here now, the scum of the elementary schools.'

To make sure we heard her mantra, she said it again, in a slightly lower voice but with a derogatory movement of her arms that embraced the whole class, 'The scum of the elementary schools, that's what we have here now.' She repeated this phrase, 'the scum of the elementary schools', regularly throughout our school career.

Another day her entry, as rushed and dramatic as ever, might be accompanied by the phrase 'hic, haec, hoc'. Sounding like an attack of hiccups, these words brought us to the verge of hysterics. Only her command for us all to make the sign of the Cross and begin, 'Au nom du père, et du fils, et du saint esprit, ainsi soît-il,' followed by the Hail Mary, also in French: 'Je vous salue Marie, pleine de grâce, le Seigneur est avec vous,' brought a degree of equanimity to the class.

We had of course to have religious instruction, not merely the Catechism and the Commandments. To these Gus added her own asides, concentrating on chastity – in which she was patently an expert. Better still if she had also been an expert in communication skills.

'Always remember', she enjoined us, 'that you are like crystal vases.'

Not quite sure of what was to follow, we waited eagerly for her next line.

'If any man should come up to you,' she continued, 'you must say to him, "My crystal vase is not yet broken."'

Hearing this advice was almost more than some of us could take. We imagined trying it out and wondered what reaction we would get.

A fit of infectious choking permeated the class. Gus would probably think this was due to our sensitive natures and continue with her wonderful exposition of men and the crystal vase relationship. No such luck. Before long it was the scum of the elementary schools again.

We thought of ourselves not as the scum but the cream, and some of the class surely were. Kathleen Kenny and Rita, her elder sister, were boarders, as they had been before our influx. 'Scholarship' girl Norah Hurley, the daughter of a former pupil at the school had beautiful manners and a lovely posture; Dora Head, also a 'scholarship' girl, was the daughter of a headmaster; Kathleen Mackay, quite brilliant; Eileen Taylor, so proud of her Scottish heritage among us Sassenachs, proved a talented humorist and mimic; Minette Moan, daughter of a French mother, was as good a French-speaker as any of our teachers; and Kathleen Seglias a mathematical genius. Furthermore, most of the girls came from far more 'wholesome' districts, south of the river, than Whitechapel or Bethnal Green.

Gus became used to us in time, we to her, and we were devastated when she died. It seemed impossible for such a character, bigger than life, with all her unconscious humour, to be struck down in middle age. She was surely indestructible. But God had called her. Like His earlier call to a religious vocation, and in spite of all other pulls, she had to answer it. Her response showed the same courage but far more humility and grace than she was able to summon up in her lifetime.

Never afraid to speak her mind, Gus left a great gap in our lives, some wonderful memories of not unkind laughter and – no matter how far we later strayed from the paths of righteousness – the facility she passed on to us of being able to pray in French. Whether God takes more notice of one language than another is not revealed in any holy book, but the French were certainly impressed.

Among the lay teachers and girls, there were often close relationships: 'crushes', as we called them. We never heard or used the term lesbian. Perhaps having seen such wonderful films as *Mädchen in Uniform* there seemed nothing unnatural about such friendships. Nobody assumed there was anything sexual in them, or if they did they never commented about them unkindly – more inquisitorially as if such obvious mutual devotion was unusual.

It was rumoured that Miss Saltmarsh the English teacher had a crush, or vice versa, for the head girl, yet if it existed at all, it was probably due to extra solicitude on the teacher's part for a most talented girl, who died of tuberculosis before she left the sixth form and whose sister, in a lower form, would also fall a victim to what was still a killer disease.

'Crushes' did not trouble us. We took them in our stride. All I cared about Miss Saltmarsh was how brilliant a teacher she was, although not in the same way as the teachers at St Anne's. They recited poetry so beautifully that it remained in your memory for ever. The expertise of Miss Saltmarsh, apart from her highly perspicacious and helpful marking of our work, was in the technical points of the English language. She taught us précis, so often despised, but vital for journalists and lawyers. We learnt grammar and syntax, so that everybody knew when 'who', not 'whom', was the right word to use in a sentence, and whether or not a comma should be put in after the 'who'. These were never boring, but challenging exercises which left us all better speakers and writers than we might otherwise have been. All the teachers were brilliant in their own way and as far as we knew all, of course, unmarried. Miss Leblanc might have been an exception, but then she came from France and what little we knew about that country was that there they were 'different'.

An unusual star in our south London firmament was sixth-former Inez Pearn, quite unlike the common meteors that fell to earth. It is easy to understand why her virtues were so constantly extolled to the scum of the elementary schools. Coming from a home in Spain, Inez brought with her an intriguing past and the possibility of an even more intriguing future.

As well as her beauty, regal manner and reputedly formidable intellect, she had the most wonderful voice. When she sang 'Ave Maria' with such clear bell-like notes in the school hall at the end of term, some of us who had never before heard Gounod's melody were mopping up hidden tears. Then to crown everything we heard that she had won a scholarship to Oxford University. Oxford! The word itself was magic. University was far enough beyond our reach. I had not heard of a single soul, other than our teachers, who had gone to one, though I knew there was a university in London because we had to take their exams in the fifth form. But Oxford!

Most of us dared not even think of following her example – though the bravest in the class allowed themselves the luxury of contemplating London. Then Inez – how could she do it? – let the whole side down . . .

by marrying before she finished her course. Fortunately she redeemed her tarnished reputation a little by choosing or being chosen by the poet Stephen Spender, later Sir Stephen Spender, but Inez never regained the place in our hearts that she won with her singing of 'Ave Maria'.

At Notre Dame we were like horses entered for a race, some with heavy handicaps, some well groomed odds-on favourites. As bookmakers and gamblers know, front-runners do not all last the course and few retain their early placing by the end of the race. At school, I was one of the losers. Among the top three students in my first year, I soon went down the ladder to nestle among the next half-dozen or so, and never again went up.

Rose Ferrari moved in the opposite direction, from near bottom to near top. She had a sister, Beatie, in a lower form, a brother in a boys' high school, and numerous other brothers and sisters. She asked me over to meet her family, who lived in a church housing estate. Her father seemed to me so very old, about 80 at least, so unlike my handsome Dad, that I kept rudely staring at him when I thought he wasn't looking, wondering how he could be the father and not the grandfather of this huge brood.

It was impossible not to admire Rosie's mother, the aspirations she had for all her family – girls and boys – and her determination to let them get on as far as they could go. She had no false pride. Every source of help she could find, she got. Rose did too. Starting at the bottom half of the class, she absorbed all the lessons, accepted happily the hot dinners daily provided by the nuns for her at the boarders' table, while richer girls like Maggie and me sat at the day girls' table, eating whatever we managed to bring in and sharing any bit of fruit or other rare luxury with each other or whoever sat next to us.

Rose even worked hard in needlework classes, which the rest of us thought quite irrelevant to our wonderful futures. At the end of a term, she could make beautifully embroidered handkerchief and nightdress cases which were sold at sales of work and jumbles, raising funds for many good causes. The techniques of twisting yarns also proved useful as an introduction to other crafts.

She never lazed about, and helped by her parents (for a girl at school after 14 meant the loss of a wage earner), matriculated and reached the sixth form, having notched up higher marks every year since entering the school.

Moya, another pupil who became a lifelong friend, also asked me over to her house. Her mother had died when Moya was only 11. Her brother Eddie, three years older, stayed with his father in the family home, while she went to live with a maiden aunt some distance away. The loss of a mother and the splitting up of the family was a dreadful blow to aunt, father and children, from which they all suffered for many years afterwards. Moya was hit the hardest, for having already lost her mother, she also lost the daily contact she previously had with two other people she dearly loved.

This whole new life began with tears and grew only slightly happier with the passing years. Moya never complained about anything, however, not even the terrible chilblains which affected her fingers and toes so severely every winter. She never even revealed her sad background to me until many years later. I knew she lived with an aunt, but coming from Bethnal Green I learnt early not to ask personal questions of friends or relations. You might not like the answers. One day Moya asked me over to tea.

The neat Upper Tooting house in which she lived looked very impressive. Its little front garden, gleaming white curtains, painted front door and shining brass door-knocker made me feel as 'umble as Uriah Heep. I did my best to hide my feelings, not wanting the educated aunt to know how unused I was to such surroundings. I certainly did not know how hard Moya had struggled to get me over to tea.

'This girl comes from Bethnal Green?' asked her aunt. 'Be careful. Nasty district over there. Lots of thieves and other villains live in Bethnal Green. However did your friend get into a nice school like Notre Dame?'

Knowing nothing of this background, I was so touched by the aunt's hospitality, the tea, sandwiches and delicious cake she provided, that I determined to ask Moya back to our house.

'Over 'ere?' said my mother. 'You can't ask her over 'ere. Not to this place. Whatever will she think of us?'

'Why shouldn't she come over here? If my friends don't like it, then I don't want them as my friends.'

Secretly I was terrified lest a mouse appear suddenly out of a cupboard, or an insect that had missed my mother's culling session drop from the ceiling into Moya's cup of tea. I steered her strategically to the safest part of the kitchen.

Such worries did not bother my father. Home was where the heart was. Anything south of the river he regarded with deep suspicion. Once when we were going on a school outing to a play at the Old Vic, he said, 'The Waterloo Road? Good God Almighty! You don't want to go over there my girl. The Waterloo Road? Real den of thieves that is. You be careful if you're going over there. Watch your pockets and look behind you.'

By contrast, north of the river at Bethnal Green, or at least our street, was a haven for saints. After the biggest tidying up the house had ever seen, the whitening of the front door step, and the purchase of two extra cups with matching saucers, the ultimate in 'poshness', Moya came to our home for tea. She and my mother warmed to each other the moment they met.

Dad had ideas of polite conduct that must always be scrupulously met. When not drunk himself, he believed friends, relations, visitors should be escorted and in certain cases helped (mostly from the pub) to their homes or to the appropriate bus. This evening it was his duty, he believed, to take his daughter's friend back to the bus stop at Bethnal Green Road.

Much as I loved my father, I didn't want him to come with us. With the best intentions he would not shine as an escort. He was a really clumsy fellow except at work, very strong physically but not a bit deft, always dropping things from his pocket or missing his step when he crossed the road.

After a fond farewell to my mother, Moya left, with my father as escort to the bus stop. I joined them. On the way, Dad fiddled about in his trouser pocket for the bus fare and brought out a flurry of coins. They rolled across the pavement. At least he was still upright. A few yards further on, he took out his cash again with the same result. We helped him gather it up.

'Leave it Dad,' I said. 'We've got the money for the fare.'

I hoped Moya had. I hadn't. We got to the bus stop. Dad told Moya to go inside. He would pay. Again he dropped the coins, this time scattering them all over the bus.

Fortunately the bus conductor was a patient man, and Moya went safely on her way. She did very well at school, showing her grit and staying power at matriculation. In those days in order to matriculate you had to pass science, an arts subject, maths, a language and an optional subject in the same examination. The first time Moya failed in maths and got distinction in French. She took the exam again, got distinction in maths and failed in French. Third time lucky; she went on to the sixth form but couldn't proceed to university: money and her aunt's patience ran out. Like many other people who early missed out on a higher education, she bitterly regretted the lost opportunity.

After later study and the usual perseverance, Moya rose to the position of a headmistress in a huge multi-ethnic school where more than twenty languages were spoken. She acted like an unpaid counsellor to parents and children alike. Able to mix so sympathetically with different creeds and cultures, she nevertheless hung on doggedly to her Catholic faith. Even in her eighties, wherever she happened to be and though one of her daughters, after a spell in Egypt, became interested in Islam, Moya never missed a Sunday Mass.

Different abilities become more noticeable the higher up a particular ladder you try to climb. You meet people on their way up. On the higher rungs there is space only for the best, so you also see those falling down. I learnt this not only in school but also later, in a more dramatic way. Urged on by an enthusiastic friend, in my teens I joined a famous athletics club, the London Olympiades. It boasted several women such as high jumper Dorothy Odam, who later became good enough to represent England in the Olympics. I had no such aspirations, but was a fairly good runner, or so I thought, having won every race I entered. Persuaded by the same enthusiastic friend, I even went in for the Women's Athletic Association's Southern Counties cross-country championship. Never having raced more than half a mile, I came second in this event after cycling 50 miles to the venue, the only time I have ever (to my knowledge) been featured in the *News of the World*.

In spite of these little 'triumphs' under my belt, I was very nervous when the coach asked me to run 100 yards against some of the members of the club. What a revelation! How are the mighty fallen . . . fortunately not literally. The sensation of running as hard as I could and not being able to pass the front runner was absolutely unforgettable. Straining every nerve and using every muscle in my body, I could not, just could not, pass her. It seemed impossible, unbelievable, but is probably an experience well known to athletes in any field. The truth had to be faced: I was not naturally good enough.

In longer races – 220 yards and half-mile – I did better than in my initial sprint, but my swimming for another club drove the coach to distraction.

'For God's sake, give up the swimming,' he said as I arrived at the track one evening on my bike, hair wet, face red. 'You'll come to nothing if you don't concentrate. If you want to get to the top in sports or anything else, you've got to concentrate on that and nothing else.'

But I liked my swimming, for which I won a few cups; I liked my running, for which I won a motley collection of objects including a few salad bowls, one of which turned out to be rather valuable. I liked my hockey and the call-up for the Southern Counties team; and I found cycling a marvellously enjoyable, cheap and, as it then was, safe way of moving around. So I never concentrated on any one thing as he advised, and never came to anything in sport – and for a long time not in much else.

* * *

At Notre Dame school, I was still very thin and under-sized, as well as being extremely naive, much younger in almost every respect than my schoolmates. This was in part due to my mother, the oddest mixture of Puritanism, prudery, superstition and Cockney wit that you could ever meet. Add to that a degree of superstition so great that she would go under the table when hearing thunder, and read all manner of messages in tea-leaves left in the cup, as well as signs and wonders unseen by anybody else, and you may understand why sex was never mentioned in our household.

Mum had lost all her family except her father at a very young age, and spent her teens as a maid with the Watermans. They kept up a strict but compassionate Church of England regime, taught her to be a wonderful cook, rules of etiquette above her 'station', how to manage money if she ever got any spare, together with a rigorous sense of honesty and nothing at all about sex, a somewhat unusual learning curve for a Bethnal Green citizen.

What little reading Mum managed was mostly pre-Barbara Cartland/Mills and Boon. Ethel M. Dell was her favourite author. Lawrence's book would soon break upon the world outside, but *Lady Chatterley's Lover* never impinged upon us. Many East End women were beginning to learn a lot about sex and contraception from birth control crusader Marie Stopes. What they learnt they kept private, not as yet for passing on to children.

My naivety was due not only to my mother, but to myself. I did not want ever to marry – the examples of married women in Bethnal Green certainly didn't inspire me to join their ranks. Just the opposite. Single women were better looking, richer and apparently happier than the harried mothers in our streets. Some were burdened with an unemployed or ill-paid husband and hordes of kids badly clothed and fed, in spite of all their mothers' efforts to keep up with the standards of smaller families. Married women worked too hard for too little return. So I kept as far as I could out of harm's way, which meant men.

My mother mentioned the topic of sex twice in my life, the first time even more obliquely than the second. Unlike 'menopause' or its derivatives, the word 'menstruation' hardly ever appears in fiction except in euphemistic terms, such as 'the time of the month'. Yet other than childbirth, the menarche, when girls first cast off the inner lining of the womb and become fertile, is the most fundamental physical change in a woman's life. All other words relating to bodily functions are OK in the politest of society, and the most erotic descriptions, down to the last panting detail, are given full rein in today's books and magazines. TV movies barely start (and the adverb is precise) before some couple fling off their clothes and begin 'snogging'. And it seems quite in order for men and women, after the briefest acquaintance, to share a bed – and not for the sake of cheapness either.

I was not only very naive, but also undeveloped for my age, quite flat-chested, and I remained so until I was well into my teens. One morning, nearly 14 years old and still not knowing much about the facts of life as they are called, I got up from bed and found I was leaking blood from the area around my bottom. I had a very faint idea of its cause only because certain girls at school sometimes opted out of gym and I heard that this was the 'time of the month' for them.

An operation when I was young, just alongside my back passage, had left a long scar. Now I thought this might have opened up. If so, I would have to go through all the agonies of the repeatedly inserted and extracted gauze that were the remedies for the original abscess. Penicillin had just been discovered by Alexander Fleming but there would be a long wait before the miracle drug became readily available.

It was Saturday morning and my mother was home. I called out, 'Mum, can you come in here a minute.'

She came in with a puzzled expression on her face, for I rarely called her. There was never any need. The rooms we rented meant we lived almost on top of one another. Looking down at the stained sheet, she said, 'Oh don't worry about that. It's all right so long as you don't wash your feet.'

Wash my feet? What had feet to do with this strange and unwanted flow? I stared blankly at her.

'Why mustn't I wash my feet?'

'I just 'eard it wasn't very good to wash your feet at this time of the month.'

'What do you mean, Mum, at this time of the month?'

'Well, it lasts for a few days and you'll 'ave it 'appening every month now.'

Every month? Surely she must be joking. A few days? Every month? Never.

'How long for?'

'For a long time. Till you're about fifty. Though it stops when you have a baby.'

I could not believe this . . . this awful monthly manifestation, every month for the best part of my life and the only relief to have a baby? Some relief that would be. Worse than ever. And what about my running and swimming and cycling? This was a real curse. Why should women have to suffer it in order to have babies they didn't want?

How lucky men were not to have this burden thrust upon them. For years, I did not think of boys' voices breaking, choristers losing their high notes and perhaps the high wages that went with them. I ignored the fact that boys changing into men might have to start the routine of daily shaving . . . unless they belonged to some religion that appeared to reverence bodily hair to such an extent that believers were forbidden to get rid of it or had to hide it. Or even that men were cursed with an organ that when functioning did not allow them to use their brains at the same time.

Somehow I eventually became reconciled – what other option? – to being a woman without washing my feet at a certain time in the month. But the only way out from this awful 'time of the month' was having a baby? What a Scylla and Charybdis of a choice!

I knew vaguely how babies were born and where they came from, but had no idea – and this may seem impossible for young people of today to realise – how the babies managed to get there in the first place. The penalties of finding out could be drastic and bitter.

About this time, Maggie and I met on our way home from school a couple of lads from a nearby school. I rather fancied John, but he fancied Maggie, so any romance there was out. The other boy fancied me, but I did not fancy him, mainly because (how could I be so unkind?) his voice was breaking and had not totally reached the pitch of a grown man. 'Squeaker', as I cruelly spoke of him to Maggie, eventually became a pilot in the RAF and got the Victoria Cross for bravery.

It was from him I got my first kiss, and very passionate it was. Going home I was worried sick. Had I done whatever led up to having a baby? For weeks afterwards I looked at my stomach to see if it had grown at all. That was the end of burgeoning love . . . a few more meetings and then, absolutely determined to avoid the trap of marriage, with or without babies, I said goodbye for ever to young romance.

17

WORLD OF WORK

Two years after Maggie left Notre Dame, I followed her. There was a barrier to my leaving at the same time. The parents of scholarship pupils had to sign a 'guarantee' that their children would stay on at school until at least 16 years or they would repay the grant received from the age of 14. Not daring to risk imposing this penalty on my family I stayed on, longing for the time when I could get out and earn something.

The London County Council did its best to defer the wastage of early leavers. It gave a higher grant to 16 year olds who passed the General Schools (matriculation) examination. Less creditably than most of my classmates, I passed this exam, but going home for the summer holidays, felt the sense of dependence quite overwhelming. Had my brother gone to high school instead of me, I am sure my mother would have moved hell and high water to let him stay on to university. (He later did brilliantly without any push, except my own failure in that direction, in the field he liked best – music.)

Letting girls stay on at school after the leaving-age of 14 was bad enough; longer, a complete waste of time – a view then commonly held. I decided then and there to start work anywhere that I could get in. I had not said goodbye to anybody, not to teachers, nuns, or friends, including Moya.

I wrote several job applications and turned down an offer of an interview at Allen & Hanburys in Bethnal Green, maker of medical instruments and much else, passing it on to my brother Jim, who was leaving school that summer. He took it up for a few months, but hated it and left.

The best job that I could get was in a jeweller's shop for a wage of 15*s* a week, not much more than the London County Council grant. Still, it was another world. What a world, and what a sad end!

I shared a downstairs office where, into an unnumbered daybook, I entered articles such as watches, rings or small clocks brought in by customers for upgrading or repair. The owners' names were attached by labels to these items which were then taken upstairs to the repair department.

In this big room men sat behind long benches mending, cleaning or polishing articles handed in at the shop below and which I gave out on a loose rota system. A man on the rota for the next bit of jewellery might say he was too busy to take on more work and it would go to somebody else. Wages were based on length of service, not on productivity, so quarrels might break out between the quick workers and the slower ones, and might even be continued outside.

Whoever received the article acknowledged its receipt by signing his name against the date in the daybook. In the afternoon, before the shop closed, I went upstairs, collected the work that had been done, and handed it to a supervisor who put it away in a safe until the customer called for it.

I had been in the job nearly three months when one morning I arrived to find a notice at the entrance: CLOSED. Through the glass frontage I saw three men talking. One was the boss. The others appeared to be wearing police uniforms. What had happened? Had there been a robbery? I rang the bell. The boss, whom I rarely ever saw, came to the door. As he opened it, he glanced up and down the street.

'Good morning, Miss Crawley,' he said as I came in. His voice and greeting were as cold as ice to the skin. 'We'd like to have a word with you.'

Was the 'sack' in store? So soon . . . after barely three months? How could I tell the family? Worse was to come.

'I'm afraid, Miss Crawley, a problem has arisen with your books. A customer has lost a valuable heirloom.'

Were they trying to blame me for the loss? Trying to keep up my end in this threatening situation, I asked 'Heirloom? What kind of heirloom?'

'A very old engagement ring. The customer wanted it polished and the diamond surrounds strengthened. We've ascertained the ring has been lost here. I have called in the police, and they want to question you. They think you may be able to help.'

My mouth felt dry. The police . . . question me? It sounded so sinister that for a moment I could hardly speak. This was surely far worse than losing a job.

'Me? Why me?'

'You will doubtless find that out when you speak to the police.'

Saying this he led me over to the two officers standing by the counter.

'Good morning, Miss,' the senior man of the duo began. 'We'd just like you to give us an idea of what you do here.'

It sounded an innocuous request. I felt happier and described the work I did.

He held out the daybook in which were entered the articles for repair received from customers.

'Can you account for this?'

He opened the book out flat, placing it carefully on the counter surface and continued, 'Anything odd, for example, about these left and right pages?'

I stared long and hard. Then a disparity in the sequence struck me as forcibly as a blow.

'The dates don't run on. I take stuff up to the men every day. There's always an entry. There shouldn't be a missing gap of dates like this.'

'How do you account for it?'

'I don't know. I can't understand it.'

Suddenly I remembered a school exercise book where I had removed an essay I did not like. To cover its disappearance I tore out a balancing page from a later part of the book.

Now I picked up a wedge of pages in the daybook before me and saw a tiny offsetting looseness from the missing page. I did not check back pages unless there was some problem, which was rare. Normally missing dates in the margins and the loss of a counterbalancing page would only be noticed at the quarterly audits.

In a kind of trance, I said, 'The book was perfectly all right when I last saw it.'

'Oh? And when was that?'

'Yesterday. I hand out the work and enter it every day.'

'Can you give us any idea when this page was torn out?'

Pulling myself together, I answered in my 'best' voice, not the Bethnal Green one, 'I've no idea, no idea at all.'

'Does work come in here every day?'

'I've never known a day when it doesn't. It's a very well-known shop, you see, with a very good reputation.' I glanced at the boss.

'Who are the men you give work to?'

'All of them. At different times. Look. You can see their names in this column.'

My finger slewed down the pages of the book pointing out names entered and the dates when watches, clocks or rings were received and handed out.

'Can you remember giving out a gold and diamond ring inset with emeralds to anybody in particular?'

This was the crunch question, one the police had surely been leading up to. Even if I remembered the man who received the heirloom, no grassing would come from my lips.

'Pinching' was never countenanced by my mother. Nor was it my particular temptation. 'Pinching' was only OK for the desperately hungry, though I had never quite analysed what should be the limit of the 'pinching'. Burglary and violence were taboo. We knew all about violence in the pubs and streets of Whitechapel and Bethnal Green. My lips tightened.

'All dressed up and nowhere to go!' Jennie at 18 months, 1917.

Winnie Hook and Jennie at their First Communion, 1926.

My mother, brother Jim and father on a holiday at Hastings, 1925.

A country holiday in Limpsfield, Surrey, 1927. Maggie Gorgious and Jennie are seen here with the Crane children.

In the back garden with Dad and brother Jim, 1929.

Beginners at Notre Dame: Jennie with Maggie Webb (Sinunas), 1929.

Some of the teaching staff at Notre Dame High School, 1929. Back row, left to right: science technician, Miss Sherratt (geography), Miss Bineham (gym), Miss McLoughlin (maths), Miss Smythe (Latin), Miss Butler (English). Front row: Miss Fitzpatrick (maths), Miss Leblanc (French), Miss Murphy (botany) and Miss Saltmarsh (English).

Schoolfriends at Notre Dame, 1929. Moya Ring, Eileen Taylor, Madeleine Bottone and Jennie.

Jennie in her teenage years photographed in the back garden of 11 Nelson Street, *c.* 1933.

A typical East End outing of the 1930s. Mother is second from right on the first standing row.

Mother and friends pose before embarking on the coach for another trip, date unknown.

Jennie (standing in the back row with a hankie in her belt) at a residential summer school in August 1938.

Jennie's husband-to-be, Frank Hawthorne, as an aircraftman. He is seen here second right in the back row.

Frank and Jennie's wedding, 1940.

Above: Jennie with baby Francine, 1941.
Right: Francine dressed in a coat sent from the USA during wartime.

Francine with her grandfather in a Nelson Street neighbour's back garden, 1942.

'I can never remember any of the stuff we get. It's all so lovely, watches and jewellery, it's like a jumble. And there are lots of men working upstairs, too. I can't remember who gets what. I'm not very good at faces. I just enter the articles in the book, label them and give them out.'

'Lovely jewels. Don't you ever wonder who they belong to and maybe fancy one or two yourself?' asked the junior constable in this inquisitory partnership.

'Jewellery's not much use to me. I'm interested in other things.'

'Such as?' continued Number Two.

'You know, swimming and running and stuff like that.'

'I see you have given quite a number of items to —.' The senior man resumed his questioning and pointed to the book. 'This man Dave —.'

'Oh Dave,' I interrupted. 'Yes, he works very hard and is quicker than the other men, so he often takes on work when a customer needs a job done urgently. He's very helpful and has been here a long time, one of the oldest, I think. None of the men work on piece rates, so it doesn't matter if one man gets more work than another.'

'Do they ever quarrel about who gets what?'

'Sometimes. Not for long.' I was tempted to mention the quarrels outside the premises, but kept my mouth shut.

'Thank you, miss. That will do for now.'

Breathing a sigh of relief, I turned to go. And then I heard the ominous words:

'We'll get back to you later.'

I moved quickly towards the haven of the office.

The boss blocked the door. 'We are closing the office today, Miss Crawley,' he said, even more icily than before. 'Come in as usual tomorrow. The police will probably want another word with you.'

A veiled threat? He led me to the exit door and closed it behind me. I didn't dare ask whether I would lose any pay, nor could I go home so early in the day. Questions would surely be raised at home in Bethnal Green. I hung about in the area until I thought it safe to start for home.

My mother as always was out doing her evening cleaning stint. My father had got some piecework cutting iron bars into smaller pieces for a steel merchant. Only my brother Jim was in, playing his mouth organ. There was always music when he was around.

'Have you had anything to eat?'

'No. Only what I've taken out of the cupboard. I was waiting till you or Mum got back.'

By which he meant the son's privilege of other people cooking for him. I was too hungry to bother about this at the moment, for my mother was a lovely cook and, I too, preferred, if there was a chance, lazily to wait for her meals rather than cook my own. This time, however, I was very hungry, having eaten nothing since breakfast time, so cut a big potato into letter 'O' chips and halved an egg between us.

Next morning, when I went into the office, I learnt that Dave, such a cheerful fellow, never short of a quip or two, and who had been so kind to me when I arrived, was 'helping the police with their enquiries'. Did this mean he was under suspicion? What would happen to him? I wished I had an idea of the real crook, for I knew in my heart it could not be Dave. He was getting on for 50 and had been with the firm so long. Why should he steal the ring? What would be the point? He would lose his job and find it very hard indeed to get another. Then a nagging thought struck me. I heard he was going through a bit of financial trouble. In the 1930s, with unemployment nearing two million, who wasn't? And then came disaster: the book's torn page was found, stuffed far back in his drawer.

An even worse blow was to follow. Further investigation revealed that Dave had a prison sentence for burglary in his younger days. He had not mentioned it when applying for his job. Who would? What did a boss expect? Would anybody in their right mind ever mention a prison stint when trying for a job? And Dave had worked hard and honestly for over thirty years, more than ten of them with this firm.

'It can't be Dave,' I protested.

'We must let the police do their job,' the boss replied. When I saw the police, I repeated that Dave could not possibly be the culprit, the thief who had taken the heirloom ring. There was no softening of their approach, either.

Nothing was proved against Dave, but he was dismissed and bundled out of the firm without a reference and not even a chance to say goodbye to his mates.

A few weeks later, investigating another robbery and questioning a 'fence' in Brighton, the police found in his cornucopia of stolen jewellery the missing heirloom. He had not followed his cardinal rule of passing on stolen goods or breaking them up as quickly as possible. The fence led them on to the real crook who worked in our jewellery shop. Apparently he had argued bitterly with Dave about the apportioning of work, had a violent quarrel, and stolen the heirloom more as an act of revenge than out of weakness or cupidity. Dave was never reinstated.

Feeling somehow menaced, I left the firm shortly after Dave's departure and got a better job at 27s 6d a week in the Creda Electric company in Tottenham Court Road, a good wage for those times.

The journey from Bethnal Green was shorter than the previous one, and the job very interesting. I acted as assistant to the secretary, who handed me all the jobs she could not tackle herself. She was so much under the domination of her boss that she hardly had time to move. Once I heard her sobbing in the toilet cubicle adjoining mine. I didn't dare ask her what was wrong, but had no doubt that whatever the problem – work or love or both – it was due to the boss.

As I had no shorthand, which seemed essential if I wanted to climb up the secretarial ladder, the only one I could then see, I went to evening classes in Mansford Street, not far from my home. Here I studied for a very lowly Royal Society of Arts exam in English, Arithmetic, French and Shorthand. The young teacher who taught us arithmetic was rather shy, but I could see he had his eye on me in the nicest possible way. Though poorer than some of his pupils, he was a day-school teacher and obviously going places – a good catch for anybody so inclined. I wasn't so inclined. I wanted arithmetic and shorthand, not love. And that's what I got: totting up sums, down and sideways in rows and rows of columns. Though I never acquired a taste for maths, even now many years later I can manage doing small sums manually more quickly than by using a calculator.

The man who taught shorthand was quite different from the sweet and shy teacher of arithmetic. He was what I then always thought of as a 'feely' man, an arm round the back, a touch on the hand, an 'accidental' brushing against other parts of your body . . . very feely. If this happened more than once in a cinema, where men of that ilk sometimes took themselves, I had my own very potent weapon, learnt from my mother: a piercing Cockney scream. The rare offender was quickly removed.

I got my Royal Society of Arts certificate with distinction – not much of an achievement after a high school education. The exciting part, however, was that prizes were given in the form of money. With that sum you purchased your own prize and handed it to the form teacher. It was then inscribed and presented to you at the prize-giving ceremony.

In a City bookshop I bought the complete works of Shakespeare in one volume, a wonderful prize (First Year Shorthand), with an introduction by Sir Henry Irving. It has proved invaluable not only for the more obvious reasons, but for crosswords and my part-time stints of teaching English Literature. Nobody any longer needs to read Shakespeare's sonnets or poems to pass an exam based on his work. Yet if they glance at those stirring words of Henry V before Agincourt ('Once more unto the breach . . . dear friends') they would probably never again use the term 'material breach' as they so often do today.

From Mansford Street I went on to WEA (Workers' Educational Association) classes. What a brilliant and benevolent institution that was. The number of people who benefited from the teachers, company and instruction received at the various venues is incalculable. Short-term or recreational classes or three years' in-depth tuition in subjects like economics or philosophy were all available. The trunk load of books that came with them for borrowing by the class was relevant not only in subject but to the needs of the audience. Wonderful, wonderful experience! Wonderful, wonderful people! Their learning and expertise were needed especially during the 1930s when there was so much trouble at home and whispers developing into shouts, of trouble abroad. Political opinions in England were becoming polarised between the left, mostly of idealistic young Communists, and the often equally idealistic right wing supporters.

During my work at the electric company I noticed an advert for appointments to the Civil Service by competitive examination. That seemed a little more up the ladder, though leading to heaven knows what, I still wasn't sure. I decided to try my luck, and at the examination centre met half-a-dozen school friends from my class at Notre Dame. Results of the examination were sent out by post. It was easy to find my name with the three initials 'I.E.J.' in front of my surname Crawley. I came first in the subject of General Knowledge, with nothing much else to boast about. However, the average overall mark was sufficient for me to be listed in the section 'the following candidates are successful'. Alas! I saw none of my former schoolmates listed. They probably did far better by 'failing'. In some years very few candidates passed and others next on the list might be called up. No matter how high your marks were, compared with previous or future years, only those listed as successful could be sure of a job.

So I became a Civil Servant and learnt, to my chagrin, that it was not all milk and honey. The wages at 25s a week were half a crown lower than at Creda Electric and I was more than a year older. Being 'posted' to the Savings Bank Department in West Kensington meant a big hike in fares, leaving a still less take-home pay. Traffic was getting denser every day. It was not an easy journey from my home in the East End almost to Hammersmith but I decided to use to use my old bike, now getting a bit battered.

The work itself was quite easy and not unpleasant. Our department was furnished with waist-high long filing trays, alphabetically sorted into UK post offices. In these files were kept records of post office Savings Bank accounts. When withdrawals or deposits were made, the appropriate cards were taken from the file, and the signatures and the amounts scrutinised against duplicate slips sent in by the post offices. If everything tallied, the cards were taken by another set of operators into a small glass cubbyhole. This housed a huge and noisy machine (hence the cubbyhole separating it from the main room). Card numbers were punched onto a huge sheet that fitted into this machine, a forerunner of the computer.

Certain girls had such a reputation for accuracy that they were often called upon to show visitors from all over the world how the machine worked. Doubtless owing to a blip in the personnel department, I became one of these girls. Demonstrating to high-ranking officials how the machine worked, I always made at least one error and hastily covered it up by showing my 'learners' that when an error was made, the machine registered it with the red-inked letters 'ER' in the margin. Unfortunately these letters turned up so frequently that eventually my officials were transferred elsewhere, and for a little while so was I.

In our office was a reputedly lesbian pair, though as in school, the word was never used, and again nobody thought much about it, except to notice and remark on what we called 'cows' eyes', which passed between the two. They were such a nice couple . . . and obviously integrated with each other so well, it seemed reasonable and proper for them to live together – cheaper in any event. I never once thought of a sexual connotation, though it may be that in any adult love relationship there is some element at least of sexual attraction.

The rest of us took little notice of our odd but so likeable couple, and met for theatre and other outings. I was also press-ganged into joining the hockey club in spite of my protests that I had only ever played lacrosse, the nuns at school feeling lacrosse was better for our deportment than bending over hockey sticks. In my tiny green handbook – not more than 3 inches long, with the silver lettering 'SAVINGS BK DEPT, WOMEN's H.C. 1937–8' – I note that as a member of the First Eleven we beat the Old Ashfordians in an away game at 7–1. A week later, on 23 October, we beat at home the Crown Agents at 3–1.

Few workers or even schoolchildren in the twenty-first century are as lucky as we were in the twentieth to get time off for playing games. It always had to be Wednesday afternoons, and we always had to make the time up – usually by evening work. But it was well worth staying on for a 12-hour day to get such an opportunity.

The compensation of working in the Savings Bank Department during the 1930s was the very high calibre of the staff and being a member, if not exactly of a band of brothers – for the place was staffed almost exclusively by women – of a group of colleagues all of whom proved to be very good friends.

I began writing short articles for provincial papers in Liverpool and Birmingham, and a regular column for *Red Tape*, the journal of the Civil Service Clerical Association. I also entered and won an essay competition on a subject I've since forgotten. The prize was a cruise to Italy, out by train, back by boat. Imagine . . . Italy! My father saw me off on the night train. It would go overland to places like Rome, where everything seemed so ornate; Naples, where I froze in a bitterly cold February and understood the saying 'see Naples and die'; and Milan, where even the roof and church door of the cathedral were so beautiful. Dad was sure this trip was a dastardly plot by a white slave traffic organisation and I would be spirited away and never come back by boat as planned.

Supervisors, in spite of gimlet eyes on their underlings, were extraordinarily helpful and generous in their private lives. I had to ask one of them, a Miss E.I. Hall, for my holiday entitlement to be brought forward from the summer months. Her face always seemed so stern, a look accentuated by large glasses and an elderly hairstyle. I so admired her upper-class voice and authoritarian manner, but they also frightened me to death. She would surely not let me take leave so early in the year, when bank withdrawals were at their highest.

Why did I need the time off, she wanted to know. Was it for a funeral? No, I told her and explained about the cruise. Her next question left me worried. 'Have you got anything suitable to wear?' she asked. Perhaps coming in by bike to the office meant my appearance wasn't up to the mark?

'Oh yes. Lots of things,' I assured her, hurriedly.

'There will be dancing on board and perhaps a few evening entertainments. You will need an evening gown.'

'Oh yes. I'm getting one before we go.'

Evening gown? I had never even thought of such a thing. Then Miss Hall invited me to her palatial-looking home in Barnes, which she shared with a sister. She took my measurements in the most professional way and made me my first and most beautiful evening gown, of pale green taffeta. It was covered with silver thread motifs and tiny pink rosebuds. With slightly bouffant short sleeves, it had a matching coatee, lest I should feel cold on deck. Not only did she herself make this evening dress, she also bought in a high-class West End shop a fashionable dark brown woollen suit, ideal for chilly days or nights and for different changes of blouse underneath.

I have never forgotten her kindness. Similar acts come from many quarters, in war as in peace – just as cruelty beyond belief and which one can never even conceive is also perpetrated by members of the human race.

On that boat returning from Italy, the love bug bit me at last. I fell head over heels in love with Charles, one of the young cadets. He was so handsome that he melted every female heart on board. His eyes were of a deeper blue than the Mediterranean, his lovely Scottish burr was sweeter than the music of a pavane on a guitar. I thought he was in love with me, but every girl he spoke to thought he was in love with her. I met up with him once or twice later when his ship docked. In vain. I had no chance. Neither did he. When war broke out, his ship the SS *Athenia*, carrying young British evacuees en route to America, was struck by the Germans and sank (off Ireland?) with a terrible loss of life.

That came later. Now I had to return to the Savings Bank. Through friends made there, I learnt about the Youth Hostels Association. The Shears twins, who enjoyed walking holidays, recommended to me an organisation to which they belonged. Through looking this up I discovered the Youth Hostels, as good in their own way as the Workers' Educational Association, and so much better for overnight stays than the pubs recommended by cycling associations, where I always pushed the furniture up against doors which wouldn't lock.

I went for cycling weekends, and later holidays, to places all over the south of England, to Cornwall and Devon, to Sussex, Essex and Kent, and to Wales. One of the great joys of my life, and an odd advantage for a girl, was that my mother never worried about me – at school or elsewhere. When I heard other girls say that they had got to be home by this time or that or their mother would get worried, I was so relieved not to be bound by such a restriction. It gave me the most exhilarating sense of freedom when I no longer had to be my brother's keeper.

My decision not to have anything to do with men lest I got tied in the trap of marriage weakened after the Italian cruise and meeting with Charlie, the handsome cadet. Much of the fun of staying overnight in the hostels was the male company. In some hostels, such as the one at Marlborough, small jobs were handed out to all arrivals. For example, washing up after supper and breakfast was shared among the persons allocated for that job – a good way of discovering whether you could get on with your partner. Discussing the merits of various routes, hostels and bikes was another form of camaraderie. Bedrooms were of bunk beds and strictly segregated between men and women. I never once saw this rule violated in all the nights I spent in the hostels in England or Europe, which I visited later.

If we did not have a sleeping bag we could hire one, but few of us did. We carried our own. The best were made of very light Egyptian cotton.

You slid into them and used them as sheets in between whatever coverage was provided in the hostels. I do not recollect ever once feeling cold, but then I didn't go for cycling holidays in December. It was bad enough travelling to work on a bike in the winter months, without adding to the pain by a cycling holiday in an English winter. If we liked anybody we met at the hostel, we set off together to the next stop on our route. The get-out clause was simply a change of route. This was a kindly excuse for saying goodbye in the nicest possible way.

My next romance after Charlie, the lovely cadet, came about this time – not from cycling, but very unromantically from the public baths. Our house had an outside tap, no bedroom light, not even the old gas mantle, and no bath. Public baths were provided by the local council in Abbey Street (now a listed building). You paid your money at the desk, got a beautifully clean towel, and were ushered into a large enclosed cubicle. The attendant outside turned on the tap and water gushed into the bath. You called out for more, hot or cold as you fancied. Then, after a lovely soak, you went home all warm and clean, however dreary or cold the weather outside.

The borough council later set up public baths in Old Ford Road. These included not only slipper and swimming baths but a hall, where famous boxing bouts took place. I met one of the boxers at a dance there, a welter weight named Arthur Danahar, and for a short time went out with him. He was fairly short but very good looking, with lovely long-lashed eyes and a wonderful line in talk. I let him take me home one night. We walked back from the dance together.

'Do you know who I am?' he asked.

'No, I forgot to ask your name. What is it?'

'Arthur Danahar,' he announced, obviously waiting for some flattering response.

'Arthur Danahar. Irish are you? I'll try to remember it. Arthur Danahar.'

'Haven't you ever heard of me?' he asked, 'Welter weight. Won lots of fights.' Getting more carried away he added, 'I've got a fight soon for the welter weight championship of Great Britain.'

'Mmm. That sounds marvellous. What is a welter weight?'

Fame lives in different worlds, all self contained. My reply was as great a set-back to him as to a famous football player or pop star overlooked by the paparazzi. It intrigued and disappointed him so much to find out that there was somebody in the district who actually didn't recognise or know of him, that he asked to meet me again and I agreed.

Our little romance blossomed slowly, as most romances did in those days, except for the passionate couplings described in the press and occasionally tried out in real life. I thought I was in for one of them when, after making some banal reference to the stars, Arthur said in a husky voice, 'I feel real hungry for you.' It was quite thrilling . . . and terribly daring.

We never progressed much farther. He took me out to several boxing bouts, where I usually enjoyed watching the audience more than the fighters. He also took me to meet his parents. Staying overnight in the country cottage where they lived, it was so bitterly cold I felt frozen and lay awake all night. I longed for my own tiny bedroom with the candle which I could blow out when I got through the next chapter of my enthralling book borrowed from Bethnal Green Library.

For a change it wasn't an uplifting one, an economic tract, a volume of Proust, or some tales by the wonderful French short story writers like Maupassant. No, it was one of those where the brave hero overcomes every obstacle put in his path by some evil man or monster to prevent him rescuing a damsel in distress – and of course ultimately marrying her and living happily ever after. And here I was in some frozen cottage, thinking of the battered old oil stove my father borrowed from Harry Meadows next door and put out for me to warm the room. How I missed its comforting glow and the dancing patterns on the ceiling.

The romance cooled down at this point and never hotted up again. Arthur's father, who also acted as his manager, imagined himself to be a shrewd operator. He gave his son strict instructions never to write to me or any other girl on any pretext whatsoever. He feared a breach of promise case. Perhaps he was right to be careful. Girls could sue for compensation a man who promised marriage and 'let her down'. Taking phone calls in the Savings Bank was rather too public for my liking, and there was no phone in our house, so communication thinned down and died.

My last glimpse of Arthur was when I saw him fight for the national welter weight championship of Great Britain against Eric Boon at the Albert Hall. *Sic gloria transit mundi.*

18

PIVOTAL CASE

After I started working in the Savings Bank, as well as keeping up my sporting activities in England, I began to take more interest in events abroad. In Germany the Nazis had doubled their seats in the Reichstag. Hindenburg relinquished the reins of office to Adolf Hitler, who became Germany's new Chancellor. Unknown to many outside that country, Jews were already being persecuted there and in 1936 Pope Pius XI condemned the sterilisation of over 56,000 'inferior citizens'.

In 1935 the Italians invaded Ethiopia and officially annexed the country the following year. After several revolutionary episodes, following the abdication of King Alfonso XIII civil war finally broke out in Spain. There were 'show trials' of alleged traitors in Communist Russia, and later the execution of generals.

At home, economic peace and prosperity seemed as far away as ever, a dream, a mirage. Coming off the gold standard did not improve matters. Jarrow, a northern English mining and shipbuilding town, had 67 per cent of its people unemployed. Two hundred of them organised a protest march to London. I saw them, shabby yet proud after their heroic trek, arriving in the West End streets. Everybody sympathised with their plight. Some provided cash to repair the soles of the walkers' boots. Parliament offered nothing. The vigorous support of the Communist Party helped to sustain them.

The Welsh miners at Dowlais took heart, however, from the visit of Edward VIII. After 1934, when the worst mining disaster in twenty-one years took toll of 262 lives, nothing much was done to improve the pits, but hearing of the awful conditions in which miners still worked – or did not work at all, which was worse – Edward said, 'Something must be done.' Other than increasing the revenue of newspapers and magazines worldwide by scampering off with Mrs Wallis Simpson, the abdicating king did nothing.

If MPs or king could do nothing, what route was open to a teenager like me, circumscribed by religion, gender and upbringing, to influence these events? The civil war in Spain appealed to thousands of young Communists, but I had no training in nursing and could not volunteer as a soldier, even if I had the commitment. Yet I desperately wanted to help alter the unequal society in which I lived. Writing about the evils that I saw was not enough, and unless I became SOMEBODY it would never be enough.

All I was doing to help others or to change the system, other than writing pieces for newspapers and magazines, was acting as a Girl Guide lieutenant to a troop in Bermondsey. Hardly the beginnings of a march on Rome – or anywhere else for that matter. The guides were not much younger than the Captain or me, but both she and I enjoyed our work with them and felt it worthwhile. We took them for occasional weekends in the country or outings to a place called Allhallows-on-Sea, which looked like mud flats but spelt seaside to the girls of Bermondsey. Evenings in the church hall were not all fun and games – they had to do homework for the badges they wanted and there was a good spirit of competition among the different patrols as to which ones could get the best results.

One evening in February, Marie Kelly, the youngest of our troop, came in very late and very agitated. Before I had a chance to ask what the matter was, she rushed up to the Captain and said, 'Can you come round to our house quick, please, Captain? The midwife ain't got round there yet and Mum's having a baby.'

'You go along with Marie,' the Captain said to me as if delivering babies was something I did every day. 'You've got lots of certificates for one thing and another,' she added.

'What good are shorthand and swimming certificates for delivering a baby?' I asked her, hurriedly.

'You've done lifesaving . . . It'll be as easy as peeling a potato. Mrs Kelly's had . . .' she looked at Marie. 'How many is it?'

'There's seven of us, but come quick, please, Captain. Dad's got a bit of work at the docks and except for the kids, Mum's all on 'er own.'

'What do I know about babies?' I whispered desperately to the Captain. 'Not enough to cover a postage stamp. Can't you go?'

'Would do, but somebody must stay here to see everybody off and lock up. After that I've got to be in Wood Green.'

That was a long journey from London Bridge. Beaten, I turned to Marie and said, 'Captain can't manage, so I'll be coming with you.' Marie looked even more worried, as well she might, when she heard this.

As we hurried out of the door, I hissed in the Captain's ear, 'For goodness sake ring for an ambulance as soon as ever you can, in case the midwife doesn't arrive,' which God forbid, I muttered to myself. All I knew about having babies was where they came from, not how they got there or exactly how they came out. Judging by the films I saw and the rare mention of childbirth in the books I read, how they got where they did seemed a very much happier situation than how they came out.

We waved goodbye to Captain and the guides much more cheerfully than I felt. Marie looked no happier. Outside, it was dark and cold. I tightened my coat. Rain threatened.

'You show me the way, and I'll follow you.'

We half ran, half walked through tortuous rows of rabbit warrens, dodged under an arch and came to a mouldering street of terrace houses with most of their roof tiles missing. We got to one where a string was threaded through a hole in the door. Marie pulled the string and pushed the door open.

'Mum's in here,' she said, showing me the door leading into a front room. Outside huddled a few children, a little younger than Marie. There were no sounds coming from the room other than a strange mournful moaning interspersed with sobs. I pushed open the door. A huge bed took up so much space I barely managed to squeeze inside the room. On one side was a bowl with a little water. Mrs Kelly lay on the bed looking distraught, her hair in sweated strands about her forehead. Hearing the entry of someone into the room, she turned her head sideways, and as if speaking to herself, murmured 'Thank God, somebody's come . . . me water's already broke.'

She looked up. 'Are you the new midwife?' she said and then gave a loud moan.

Her legs were open. I could see the crown of a baby's head between them. I threw off my coat onto the bed.

'Quick! Get me a towel and a bit of cotton!' I said to Marie, but in case there was no such thing as cotton in the house, snatched from around my neck the string which held my whistle.

'You'll only need the next push and the baby will be here,' I said to Mrs Kelly, hoping I was telling her the truth. She turned her head and then a few minutes later gave a huge push and a high pitched yell. The baby's head came down, such a tiny little head. Now for the shoulders. With my left hand supporting the baby's head, I slid my right one under and along the little body. The rest of the baby almost slipped out, cord still attached.

At this moment Marie came in with a bit of cotton thread.

'I took it from a needle where Mum was sewing up a coat.'

'Good girl.' I snatched it from her. 'Got any scissors?' I called out. If none appeared I would cut the cotton with my teeth. 'They're on the mantelshelf,' Marie answered, and got them down herself. With a clean handkerchief from my pocket I hastily wiped over the scissors, hardly antiseptic practice, but my manageable best. I waited a while until I saw what looked like a pulsating movement in the cord, cut the cotton, and made two knots in the cord about 3 inches from the baby's belly. Saying a prayer in case I was cutting off some vital organ, I severed the line between the knots.

'You've got a lovely little girl,' I told the mother and asked Marie to get me a towel to wrap around the new arrival.

''Ere take this sheet. I kept it special for the new baby,' called out Mrs Kelly, waving an ancient bit of folded linen. She tried to pass it to me, then slipped back with a groan of pain. I grabbed the sheet, wrapped the baby girl in it, laid her on the bed and put my jacket over her while I got ready for the placenta to emerge.

The newborn infant did not cry. Didn't babies always cry as soon as they were born? Was that after the placenta emerged or before? I had no time to think. Mrs Kelly was showing signs of pain. I waited a few moments in case another baby came out – which, thank God, it didn't – then guided out the placenta and dropped it and what remained of the cord into the bowl at the side of the bed. It was all a bloody mess and the baby was still not crying.

Now that her labours were over Mrs Kelly looked round and picked up her baby.

'What's wrong with her?' she asked. 'Why ain't she crying? There's not a bloody peep out of her.' She gave the little one a slap and called out, 'They always cry. Why ain't she moving? Not stillborn, is she? Jesus, Mary and Joseph, not stillborn! Can't you shake 'er or do something?'

She looked at the little one and began rocking her back and forth. Then she burst into a fit of sobbing, interspersed with slow, eerie moans. These were not the sounds expected of a woman in labour or after it. But what did I know? Nothing . . . all theory. She raised her head. 'Too late,' she whispered. She seemed hardly able to speak. Her voice was husky as if after great exertion. 'Too late. You're too late. Everybody's too bloody late . . . stillborn.'

I ignored the awful words and saying, 'Quick! Give her to me,' took the baby roughly from Mrs Kelly, unwrapped the sheet covering the tiny unwashed newborn and picked her up. She looked so still, so lifeless, so helpless, with such tiny limbs. Her skin was warm, still covered with a coating of amniotic fluid. I thought it should be like the white of an egg. It seemed thicker than that, more greenish-yellow. Perhaps she had swallowed some of it. She hadn't moved, hadn't yelled, yet wasn't that how newborn babies took their first breath? And what if they didn't? Was I supposed to stimulate her into life? But how? It might be possible: I had seen so many people brought back to life when almost everybody had given them up.

If she were already dead, I would be doing no harm in trying to do whatever I could to revive her. But supposing I did nothing? No time to ask questions now. Already I had used up lifesaving seconds. Perhaps I ought to have tried to get her to yell before I tied up the cord? But I was dumb ignorant.

I pulled over the bowl from the side of the bed, then holding the baby upside down by the legs, smacked her bottom. Was there a faint response? I gave her another slap, slightly harder this time. Greenish-yellow mucus escaped from either her mouth or her nose. A slightly softer slap caused another discharge of mucus from her nose. Still no other response. I made a hasty prayer to my favourite St Jude, he of the despairing cases, put my mouth over the baby's nose, made a suction noise as if drawing breath and took in a horrible mouthful of mucus. Then I did a similar operation over the mouth. More mucus. I spat it into the bowl.

Pushing in the baby's cheeks to open her jaw, and terrified of damaging her tiny lungs, I breathed very softly into her mouth – in out, very softly, in out, in out, slowly, softly. I had seen one extraordinary case of revival after drowning and another case where a young man, pulled onto the seashore only seconds after he disappeared under the waves, tragically did not respond at all. Perhaps we would be luckier.

Was that a movement in the little naked body? There was a big shudder like a trembling fit, and then a tiny mew like a cat, followed by a full-blown cry, then more and more yells. I could not believe it. Mrs Kelly raised her head, put out her arms and yelled. 'Christ, she's come back from the dead, that's what! Does 'appen sometimes though I never thought it would to one of my lot.'

I wrapped the bit of sheeting round the baby again, then passed her to her mother. Shaking her head she looked at the little bundle and said sadly, 'Poor kid. She doesn't know what she's in for but 'ere she is and 'ere she stays, with 'er Mum. She's been born for a purpose. Must've been meant to come back like that. Born for a purpose she is. I sure thought she was a goner, but you never know what the Almighty's got in for you, do you?'

'That's true. We'd better get a drop of warm water to give the little one a wash. Then we'll see to you.'

'There's sure to be some hot water in the kettle on the stove.'

She called to her daughter. 'Marie, show the lady where the kitchen is.'

I followed Marie to the kitchen. Our own had improved a bit since I started work, though it was nothing to boast about, but this one was in a terrible state of repair, bits of paper hanging from the ceiling, stained walls, an uneven cement floor covered with shreds of rotten matting. No time to think about that . . . there was a job to be done. The kettle steamed away on the stove. Finding no bowl, I helped myself to the largest saucepan that I could find.

'Is the cold water in the yard?'

'Yes. There's a tap out there. I'll show you the way.'

Carrying the saucepan, I followed Marie into the yard near the communal lavatory at the back of the house. The kitchen's electric light, shining through the uncurtained window, helped me find my way to the outdoor tap. Marie turned it on. I washed my hands, scooped a bit of water onto my uniform to clean it up a bit, then fed some cold water into the saucepan.

Following Marie back into the kitchen, I gradually filled the saucepan with hot water from the kettle, using my elbow as a thermometer until the temperature seemed right enough for washing a baby.

'Can you find me a towel anywhere, Marie?'

She lifted one from the washing line that ran across the kitchen ceiling from one corner of the room to another.

I took the towel from her and tore a piece from the bottom.

'Oh you shouldn't 'ave done that,' said the young guide. 'Dad won't be able to dry 'isself when 'e gets back. When Dad's at work, 'e always 'as a wash when he gets back.'

'Tell him there's no washing time tonight. It's celebration time for a new daughter for him, a sister for you. Your lieutenant will buy him a new towel, and a new sheet as well when she gets home.'

We went back to the bedroom. The new arrival was crying lustily. Marie followed me.

'Let's give the little one her first wash.'

Mrs Kelly reluctantly handed over the new infant. I slid her gently into the saucepan. In spite of her being so tiny, she barely had enough room to sit down. I used the torn bit of towelling to squeeze water over her from the head down. 'That's shut 'er up for a bit,' laughed Mrs Kelly as the yells subsided, 'but it won't be for long'.

After a few seconds I took the baby out, dried her in the rest of the towel, then laid her next to her mother on the drier side of the bed, and covered her up. A knock came at the door.

'One of you kids can open it,' I told the oldest boy. He had peeped inside the bedroom door from time to time, his face a mixture of interest and fear. He and two other siblings who had been told to get into bed had crept out to see what was going on. Still and silent outside the bedroom entrance since I arrived, the oldest one now rushed to the door, glad to be able to move, to help, to do something. The midwife came in.

'Am I glad to see you,' I greeted her.

'Called out to an urgent case on my way,' she said, taking the whole situation in with one perceptive glance.

'The baby's arrived. I've cut the cord but it will need seeing to. You'd better have a look at it. And the baby took quite a long time before she started breathing, though she seems all right now. I've done nothing for the mum. She needs to be made a bit more comfortable.'

'I'll look after her now.' The midwife opened her case. 'Thanks very much. You're from the Guides that Marie belongs to down by the bridge?'

'Yes, I look a bit of a mess now.'

'Can't be helped at times like this. Well I won't keep you any longer. Thanks for coming along.'

'Marie's been a great help. Are you sure you won't need me any more?' Feeling almost as exhausted as the poor mother who had just given birth, I hoped it was all right to leave now.

'Plenty of help here,' she laughed.

'Better you than me.' I laughed. 'Goodbye Marie, see you at Guides next week, and let me know how your new baby is coming along,' I said, and left.

19

FUTURE IMPERFECT

After Mrs Kelly's delivery, I was lucky enough to get a bus from London Bridge to Bethnal Green Road, where I got off at the 'Red Church'. Without a coat, wet, bloodied but unbowed, I walked home through Pollards Row, and thought about the future. Something was obviously wrong that Mrs Kelly and others like her should live in abject poverty, without a chance of climbing out of the pit into which life had placed them, while others had far more wealth than they could ever spend. Mr Kelly's wages would never be enough to support his family comfortably. They would be in an even worse situation when, as a casual labourer, his job suddenly ended leaving him without work. The unspoken reaction of politicians to problems like this was that people should not have children they could not afford to bring up.

After being at the birth of Mrs Kelly's eighth child, I saw that some women had little choice. Yet surely it was wrong to expect them to go on giving birth for nearly every year of their fertile lives, unless they chose to. Men, too, should somehow be able to control their hormones or whatever led them to behave as they did. What was the answer?

I felt like becoming a disciple of Marie Stopes or her followers, yet my Church taught that contraception except by 'natural means' was wrong. I knew nothing about 'natural means' and had heard of the so-called safe period, when sex was possible without conception following. This belief I strongly distrusted, though without any personal knowledge. Even among the faithful, the safe period was called the

169

'Vatican lottery' because it was so unreliable. In my usual ignorant way I assumed, for the time being at least, that the doctrine of the Church was right.

Joining a political party seemed the only answer to ridding the world of the obvious inequality that existed. But which party? A question easily answered by most people in the East End – the Young Communist League, or for the less revolutionary idealists, the Labour Party. There seemed no alternative. George Orwell's book *The Road to Wigan Pier* revealed the terrible standard of living he 'enjoyed' over the tripe shop, but he described socialists as 'vegetarian cranks in sandals' – hardly a recommendation for joining them.

Unable to find the right political niche, I followed my mother's inclination towards the Liberal Party. Strangely ignoring his womanising lifestyle, she was a great fan of Lloyd George. He was responsible, so she believed, for introducing state pensions (albeit with numerous exceptions). That was the reason why she always voted for our local MP, the Liberal Sir Percy Harris – never Labour, because 'It's the poor what gets the blame; it's the rich what gets the pleasure; ain't it all a bleedin' shame?' The poor were too easily corrupted by the smell of money. Unfortunately, Harris became a Labour politician to save his seat. My father, being Irish, had no time at all for the Welshman Lloyd George and his policy on Ireland. It was bound to bring bloodshed to that country for many years to come.

I somehow missed the chance to cast my first electoral vote, but went to the Workers' Educational Association classes and all the meetings I could find, including those at Speakers' Corner in Hyde Park, to hear invective and diatribes as well as less prejudiced points of view. No place was too far if the subject was worthwhile. I joined a course of evening lectures in Arkwright Road, Finchley, no small distance to travel from Bethnal Green at night. It was given by Sir John Marriott, an authority on the Middle East. That area seemed doomed for trouble in the future and I wanted to know more about its background and history. There were also the exciting debates and discussions at Whitechapel's Toynbee Hall which attracted socialists in every hue of pink and red: Jews, a sprinkling of Catholics and a large majority of atheists.

The first time I went to one of these debates, the lecturer began giving us his ideas on events happening in Europe. When he had finished speaking, he looked around the assembled throng and asked, 'Any questions or comments?'

The hall was unusually silent for a few minutes. 'What do you think about the chances of war? Do any of you have any opinions on the subject?' the lecturer continued.

A young man at the back of the class put up his hand.

There was a groan from some of the people surrounding him as if he were well known and so were his comments.

'Yes, I do and these are my views,' he began. Then, taking the *Daily Worker* from his pocket, he began quoting a few paragraphs from it.

'What are you reading?' asked the lecturer.

'The *Daily Worker*.'

'I don't want to hear the views of the *Daily Worker*. I want to hear what you think. Give me your own views.'

'My views are the same as the *Daily Worker*'s and they will always be the same,' the young man replied didactically, and having outlined 'his' views, sat down.

That was the general tenor of the class. Enthusiasm for the cause of socialism inspired everybody there. It was the answer to poverty, squalor, unemployment and all the evils of the time at home and abroad. Young people stood on street corners selling their paper with every bit as much devotion and enthusiasm as the Salvation Army sold their *War Cry* in the pubs. It was impossible not to be infected by the political fervour expressed by anyone under 30.

In Bethnal Green, there was a small but growing clique of Oswald Mosley followers, mainly because there seemed no alternative to Communism. Suspicious of Soviet Russia and all its works and pomp, they formed a nucleus of objectors to that cause. Many were later easily seduced into the Blackshirt organisation.

I could not team up with the Communists and their watchword of 'religion is the opium of the people'. As a Catholic, the Blackshirts were also anathema to me. I wanted to 'do' something other than writing little articles, helping to run a Guide company or selling newspapers propagating the 'cause', so asked at work if there were any jobs in South Africa for which I might be eligible. I had not been vaccinated, as was the practice before being accepted in the Savings Bank, and gave the reason that I was a conscientious objector (!). This seems to have been the reason why my application for a transfer got no further.

And then came the 'Battle of Cable Street', 4 October 1936. With the same kind of insensitivity as religious factions showed in Northern Ireland by parading through one another's 'territory', Oswald Mosley decided to stage a march of his followers through Whitechapel. I had not yet taken part in a demonstration, but had to go along to this one. It was history in the making. Crossing Bethnal Green Road to Vallance Road and passing one of the Kray Gang's homes on the way, I took up my stance in Whitechapel, not knowing that I would be one of a crowd of 100,000, most of whom were geared for a fight with their enemies, some 7,000 Blackshirts. Everywhere flags blazoned out 'They shall not march'. The heightened feeling between the rival factions was almost palpable; as if all were breathing their individual hatred and excitement into the air around me. Any minute surely a mine would be touched off and the force of its explosion blow everybody up, never to demonstrate again.

A Jewish tailor and his son were suddenly thrown through a plate-glass window. Then along came a bus with a driver too loyal to his employers for his own good. It proceeded so slowly along the crowded street, it hardly moved at all and was eventually stopped by the force of the crowd. A couple of men tried to prevent the bus from continuing its journey. An argument ensued. The driver was dragged out from his seat. Screaming, he was thrown into the milling crowds like a fox to the hounds. God alone knows what happened to him. It was the most terrifying sight I had ever witnessed and showed me the awful strength of the masses; as if the minor emotions of each individual were added together and multiplied exponentially until they became a force beyond human control.

Until the Second World War, only the near confrontation with a murderer matched for me the horror of that scene. I wished I could do something but what could a 19 year old do? I did not stay a minute longer but squeezed my way through the crowds to the comparative safety of Vallance Road, praying that I would always be able to retain some semblance of humanity even in a crowd baying for blood. Eighty people were injured that day, including fifteen police. Lorries were overturned all along the streets to prevent them bringing down the barricades at Cable Street.

It wasn't all doom and gloom in that decade of the 1930s, however. There were happier events: Amy Johnson, the 27-year-old daughter of a Hull fish merchant became the first woman to fly from Britain to Australia, in a second-hand Gipsy Moth airplane. What an astonishing achievement, and after only a comparatively few hours' instruction. In 1936 Jesse Owens beat all his rivals at the Olympic Games, carrying off four gold medals, to the chagrin of Hitler, anxious to prove Aryan supremacy.

In the next year came the answer to my quest for an organisation less revolutionary than the Communists, a party working towards a more just society. I found it in the Catholic Social Guild, just right, it seemed to me, for the needs of that time, propagating ethical ideas and working for a better world without destroying the old one.

I read its brochures, then dived through manuals and magazines to find weekend and summer holiday courses. Provided by trade unions, the WEA or branches of Co-operative Societies, many were free for young people. These courses were wonderful occasions not merely for the intellectual widening of horizons, but the emotional and physical ones too.

I met the peeress Barbara Wootton at one of these. She had lent out her estate for the summer course. Lean and tanned, with beautiful legs, a patrician face and lovely head of blonde hair, she may not have been in her vernal youth, but to see her moving around the tennis courts as gracefully as a gazelle was an advertisement for whatever lifestyle she followed. One of my Communist friends coined a name for peers and other 'nobility' who became members of the Socialist party. 'Worker aristocrats', he called them. But Professor Barbara was truly converted. Indeed she married a taxi driver, George, a real Adonis some 20 years younger, so I heard, than Barbara.

She once did a lecturing tour in the USA, and at that time in the 1930s women were not regarded as wage earners and not as much else other than either carers or trophies for men. When she and George were returning to the UK, only George was asked if he had any earnings to declare. He had none. Barbara did not reveal her own. 'I didn't exist for them,' she said, 'And as I never existed, I could earn nothing.' It was a new slant on *dubito ergo sum*.

Romances of a sort came and went, including those at a WEA weekend where some London School of Economics tutors were teaching us politics and (being marvellously good looking to our immature eyes) gave us lessons in even more interesting subjects. I used to meet one of these tutors at assignations very late in the evening. He was glorious: tall, bronzed, a wonderful tennis player. With his head of thick reddish brown hair, those lovely blue eyes for which I've always been a sucker, and a glorious smile . . . what woman could not fall in love with such a good looker, even though he was married to a brilliant American? I nearly but not quite lost my virginity – for men were unusually gallant in those days, and though they might have enjoyed a fling, it was never quite over the top. I was absolutely enchanted with Bill K. of the LSE. . . . The feeling seemed to be reciprocal, but fear of what might be kept us just on the right side of caution, while showing me some of the delights of love.

Another tutor, Dr Conze, a Jewish refugee from Germany, was more of a realist, deeply concerned with the way Hitler was pushing his way forward in Europe. Soon the Nazis would be eating up Austria . . . where next? And what was anybody doing about it? Few of us were so bothered. Other people, and even our own grandparents, might have been persecuted for their beliefs, their religion, their colour. We had not been. We only knew that immigrants were a suspicious lot, always looking over their shoulders at some non-existent threat to their lives.

We also knew that at some time Hitler would be restrained. Of course he had fortified the Rhineland. And why not? Of course he had invaded Alsace. And why not? Weren't the Alsatians half German anyway? Of course he was about to swallow up Austria, but the Austrians would surely welcome him in. They all belonged to the same Germanic tribe, did they not . . . and anyway who cared about Central Europe? Or about treaties? The reparations were a ridiculous impost. If Hitler had to be stopped, then someone would do it before he threatened France and the Netherlands and then Britain. Nothing to worry about.

It was at one of these weekends that I heard of Plater College, Oxford. It was very similar to Ruskin College in Oxford except for its being based on Catholic social teaching rather than the more radical and left wing approach of Ruskin. I had read of these and similar colleges where adults who had missed out on their education could continue learning. The colleges and courses looked very attractive, but I was earning a reasonable wage, enough to keep myself in frugal comfort as well as adding a bit to the family exchequer. A year's leave was not like an afternoon off for playing hockey where a Wednesday taken out for sport could be made up by overtime. If I left to enter a college I would get no wages and not be able to get my job back, for the Savings Bank was not prepared to release me. No earnings, no job . . . a big decision.

Much as I wanted to learn more about politics and economics or why the curse of unwaged unemployment – from which our family and others suffered so often – seemed without any solution, there was no way I would give up my job. Full-time study in anything other than science and engineering where a beneficial end product might be discovered or developed was a luxury, and so there had to be ample money to pay for it.

Then somebody told me or I read about scholarships. Apparently the London County Council offered senior scholarships, with a grant attached, to successful entrants to these adult colleges. It seemed a wonderful opportunity . . . too good to be true, and maybe it was, for an exam had to be passed to qualify for the grant. I looked at the pros and cons. There were more cons than pros. The grant covered fees and pocket money; it did not cover the loss of wages and I could not be released from work without losing my job.

Remembering how lack of money could blight lives, I decided that this exciting future would have to be temporarily foregone while I carried on with evening classes. However there was no harm in meanwhile having a shot at whatever grants were available and saving what little cash I could from my wages. I knew that many aspirants to Plater and other similar adult colleges made tremendous sacrifices to get in. I was not of their mould. For me, my job was too precious to give up, a philosophy, like much else, soon exploded by the Second World War.

But that time was a long way off. I investigated further, pressed the powers that be as hard as I could, and won what might be termed half a victory. If I got a grant from the LCC or anywhere else, AND passed the entrance exam to the college of my choice (which had to be acceptable to the Savings Bank) I would be allowed an academic year off, that is 9 months from October to June. Better still, I would be able to return to work at my normal pay during university holidays, and have my job back in the following September.

This was absolutely marvellous news. What could be better – except that it was half a victory, for the normal Diploma course in economics and political science at Plater College was for two years, not nine months. Not to worry . . . one step at a time. As the Chinese philosopher Confucius said, 'a journey of a thousand miles begins with a single step'.

20

ASPIRATIONS

In 1937 I was 20, still living at home, and had done nothing much with my life so far. Efforts at trying for grants from the LCC and other 'charitable' bodies had received no reply, which is always a bad sign.

My father was relying on casual work when he could get it and my mother still had her minuscule wages as an office cleaner. My own had gone up since I started in the Civil Service some three years before, so life for me at least was looking rosier. My brother was having some difficulty in finding a job that suited him.

'Don't be so fussy,' I said when he turned down a local one that seemed a good opportunity. 'Take anything to start.'

'Who wants to work there? And for that money?' he retorted, as if there was an infinite number of jobs for a 17-year-old lad to choose from, instead of unemployment still being well over the million mark. But though he did not appear too concerned about not working, I felt sure he would find something soon. He would soon get bored playing his accordion or interminable records at home. Perhaps too, my father would get a job that would keep him from finding solace, for his lack of a better one, in the conviviality of the public house. I still went out to the pubs on the occasional Friday night when he had a few bob in his pockets, to steer him drunkenly home. Yet without the 'drink' he was so lovable, interesting and kind, so strong and brave in my eyes, and would prove even braver in the future.

Sports activities, study evenings, seminars and weekends took up most of my 'leisure' hours. In any spare time left, there were youth hostel cycling holidays to the south coast and elsewhere. Sturmey-Archer three-speed gears could 'upgrade' a bicycle, making it quicker and easier to ride, so that previously impossible hills could be tackled. Never quite understanding the mechanics of the gears and how they worked, I invariably chose a speed that made me pedal round at a furious pace when I should have gone slowly, and almost leisurely when my legs should have been turning the bicycle chain fast enough to send out sparks. As for the impossible hills, I still had to push my way up them as before.

Scotland was therefore a little too far away for the speed and length of stay that I could manage. But there were many other beautiful places in Britain within range of Bethnal Green for a cyclist who could not change gears. Devon had exciting roads, with winding bends and steep downhills (1 in 7) into Porlock and the Lynton and Lynmouth valleys. The uphill stretches needed a long slog and strong lungs and much more time than a cursory glance at a map might suggest.

Though too far away for weekends, Wales was near enough for a longer stay. Cycling along the Barmouth–Dolgellau road, surely one of the most beautiful routes in Britain, and ignoring safety-first – the primary rule of road users – I looked across the horizon towards the magnificent expanse of Cardigan Bay. A slight mist pervaded the air and half shrouded the huge sun, but its rays embraced the whole area in their warmth and splendour. As the mist cleared away, the view grew sharper and sharper. Like a magnified photographic image it became absolutely breathtaking. I felt an extraordinary sense of elation, as of a privileged person allowed, like the lunar astronauts and first conquerors of Everest, to see a wonder of creation. Allied to this feeling was the almost depressing sensation of extreme isolation, the sudden realisation of the insignificance of self in a world too large for the human frame.

But in every exploration, however exhilarating, however mundane, there is always the necessity of getting back on track, so I continued on to Snowdon, which I climbed for the first time and which temporarily cured my fear of heights. I then 'tackled' Cader Idris. Nobody attempted, fortunately, to steal the bike left down below.

In spite of all this activity something seemed to be missing. Would a holiday in Europe show me a new path to follow? The fare for a passenger with a bike from Dover to Calais was a mere 25s, just about one week's wages. Overnight stays at youth hostels in Britain and abroad cost very little, as did the breakfasts and packed lunches. Some of the bigger hostels provided a hot evening meal at real bargain prices.

Having worked out the costs of a holiday in Europe, I teamed up in the summer of 1938 with two friends to arrange it. Pat Sullivan also worked in the Savings Bank. Full of good humour, she was a very sweet-tempered girl with whom I played tennis occasionally at her club in Hanwell, west London. Tennis is a good method of discovering the temperament of friends and enemies, but I didn't need any such gauge for Kathleen Davidson, another friend, whom I met at a church function. She lived in 'buildings', our usual term for council flats, in Brady Street, quite near my old school, St Anne's.

Kathleen was a very clever and most stimulating companion who could reduce you to mincemeat with one of her shafts of acerbic wit. Tall, with a most fascinating face, rather like the film star Merle Oberon, she had almond-shaped eyes and a beautiful complexion, not quite white, not quite brown, as if she were a European who had spent all her life outdoors. Kathleen later married a Canadian who fell in love with, *inter alia*, her Cockney accent, of which she was very proud. She eventually went off with him to Toronto as a GI bride.

As neither Pat nor Kathleen had bikes (Kathleen said she would not be seen dead with one – but then, I hoped, neither would I) we planned a walking holiday. We would train to Dover, take the ferry to Calais, and then mostly walk as far as we could get through France and south towards Germany. It is said that travel broadens the mind. Sometimes it can do the opposite: reinforce opinions already held. This trip certainly did that.

As a result of some very bad planning on my part, I made two major mistakes in plotting out our route. First, I calculated miles into kilometres incorrectly, inverting the '8' and the '5', so that the mileage to be covered always appeared less than it actually was. I got away with that mistake only because I had erred on the side of safety, arranging to cover only a very small mileage per day.

The other mistake was a major one not so easily overcome. I completely ignored the terrain. It is nothing to walk 5 miles in a day, but to climb 5 miles up Everest is a different proposition altogether. True, we weren't climbing Everest, but on some occasions it felt like it. Again I had a fallback – namely that all the hostels had been booked in advance.

After ploughing all day through mud and rain up some everlasting hill that never went down at all, we arrived one evening at our hostel about midnight. All credit to the man in charge of the *Jugendherberge* somewhere near Baden-Oos in the Black Forest. After an initial outburst, he took us in and provided us with warm bedding and hot soup. Our ideas of Germany and its people went up several notches. We watched the Pforzheim Fussers play the Stuttgart Kickers at football and acquired a taste for *Apfelstrudel* and *Kirschtorte mit Sahne* that has certainly never left me. What it did for Kathleen and Pat I have yet to find out.

Going through the Black Forest, traversed by so many tourists, we saw little of the Germany behind the scenes. Yet there was one quirky situation which should have caused us to think. Looking in a shop window in Heidelberg we noticed the word *Juden* in large letters, stuck on the plate glass. It was such an odd word in such an odd place, we stopped to look and read the smaller print underneath. It seemed to say (though except for the words 'please' and 'thank you' as befitted three convent girls, our knowledge of German was practically non-existent) that Jews were forbidden to use that shop.

This seemed so peculiar that we stopped a passer-by and tried to ask him what the notice meant. He waved his hands to indicate he knew nothing, saw nothing, did not intend to find out anything anyway, and quickly scuttled away.

We went on, slightly bemused but not enough to worry about what was going on. Like so many people we were completely unaware, and remained so long after our visit, that the German economics minister, Walter Funk, had forbidden Jews to deal in jewellery, property or precious metals and that Jewish businesses were to be closed down by specially appointed executors. So we arrived home with only good impressions of our first tour abroad, especially of Germany where everybody seemed so friendly. Our impressions of the French were that they were cold, unfriendly and inhospitable people, not a bit like the romantic lot we saw on films. They also had terrible lavatories, far worse than the modern ones in Kathleen's or Pat's homes and worse even than mine in Bethnal Green. That at least could boast a chain.

Neither did they understand our French accents and our wish for water instead of wine. Funny people, not a bit like the clean and jolly Germans. I did however feel a grudging sympathy for the French mothers when I saw the graves of so many soldiers killed in the First World War.

Two days after I got home, a letter came from County Hall. My fees would be paid if and when I went up to the Catholic Workers' (later Plater) College, Oxford. I could hardly believe my luck . . . then stopped. It was all very well getting the fees paid, but what about the job? Perhaps I could now influence the Savings Bank Powers That Be still further. Their attitude had been that if I took time off to go to a recognised adult college of further education, I had both to get a grant for my fees and pass any entrance exam or interview set by the College. Unless these two conditions were fulfilled I could not have my job back.

With the grant already in the bag, Father O'Hea, Principal of the Catholic Workers' College, arranged for me to have an early interview. He appeared happy enough to accept me, but emphasised what I already knew from the brochures, that the Oxford University Diploma in economics and political science taken at the College was a two-year course combined with ethics and moral philosophy. Only one previous entrant had tackled it in a year.

'To get the best out of the course and your stay in Oxford, you don't want to shorten it. You will find that two years is hardly enough,' Father O' Hea began, and continued saying that the Diploma examination was taken at the end of the two-year study period.

'It seems a pity to miss the opportunity for that qualification. Besides, there are the philosophy and ethics courses with lectures kindly given by excellent University dons as well as our own Father D'Arcy at Campion Hall. They are an integral part of our study here and every bit as important as the economics and politics.'

I nodded.

Further, he continued, in a shorter stay I should miss savouring the whole experience of Oxford life and study. He did not quite put it in those terms, but I could see he was very much against my desire for a 'quick fix'.

Fortunately, his sympathies in this instance ran counter to his logic. If I showed promise (a horrible phrase) Father O'Hea said he would try to arrange the possibility of my taking the Diploma examination in one year instead of the usual two.

Elated by this news I went back to the Savings Bank. I should now be able to influence the Savings Bank authorities and get them to let me start the Oxford course as soon as possible. I pestered this official and that and finally got what I wanted: an academic year off, starting in the following October, returning to work at normal pay during the Christmas and Easter holidays and having my job back in the following September. This was simply marvellous news. I could not believe my luck – not only to have the chance of studying at Oxford but getting my job back at the end of it, and even being able to work at the Savings Bank during University holiday periods. It was not only a magical city I should see, but all the people I could now look forward to meeting in this new environment, the students, the lecturers, the staff at the college in Walton Well Road, and its housekeeper Mrs Padmanahba who looked after their material needs as Father O'Hea looked after their spiritual ones, and of course Miss Margaret Fletcher. She supervised the lady students and was, so rumour reached me, a real grand dame. Early in October 1938 I left Bethnal Green to meet them all.

21

REALISATION

Anything I say about the time I spent at Oxford will certainly sound excessive, especially to the hundreds of young men who came back from the war to finish a degree course and found the place a skeleton of its former self.

Nevertheless, in spite of being the very antithesis of Evelyn Waugh's *Brideshead*, Plater College figures in my imagination exactly like that huge estate surrounded by lawns, with a grand entrance and steps leading to an even grander hall. In terms of harsh reality Plater College could not have been more different. Situated in the very ordinary street of Walton Well Road, it was a very ordinary building about the size of two combined large houses, without a single feature to commend it. And *Brideshead*'s chapel with its coloured glass windows and galleried entrance bore no resemblance whatever to the one in which we worshipped in Oxford.

That looked far more like the makeshift places in huts and pubs where Mass was sometimes 'celebrated' – if one can use so grand a word – over seventy years ago in remote outposts in Britain. I used to kneel on the wooden floor in those pubs and try to concentrate on the ceremony and celebrant priest instead of looking at the poster advertising 'Guinness is Good for you' irreverently above the altar, and showing a foaming glass of the liquid.

What Plater lacked in architectural distinction it more than made up by the quality of the students, staff and the University lecturers, many of whom provided their services at no inconsiderable cost to their own schedules. The driving force at the College when I went up was the Principal, Revd Leo O'Hea, an incredible man, always generous with his time and a fountain of sympathy for anybody going through a bad patch. As well as being a generous-hearted man Father O'Hea was well known and respected by politicians, local councillors and trade unionists for his ideals of social justice, and his determination to see things through. Behind his chiselled, almost gaunt features lurked a keen sense of humour.

The male students of that time, including the formidable Billy Woodruff, studied and lived at the main College building. Women students did not lodge there but with Miss Margaret Fletcher, who provided accommodation for them in her house in Woodstock Road. She had a clear strong voice: you heard every word she spoke. According to Joe Kirwan – one of the students, later to become Principal – Miss Fletcher had no feelings about regional accents but wanted to ensure that everybody was understood when speaking in public. To this end she made the men read Shakespeare aloud. The girls were excused this chore, though in retrospect it could have added something to our studies.

The men knew little, except by hearsay, about our regime under Miss Margaret Fletcher. This was not their fault, merely due to the paucity of women students. I was the only woman to go up in 1938/9, of the dozen or so applicants who were accepted. I may have been the only woman who applied.

Margaret Fletcher was the daughter of an Oxford vicar. Having become a Catholic in 1896, like most converts she took up the new 'credo' with an enthusiasm surpassing that of the most evangelistic saint. She founded the Catholic Women's League in 1906 so that Catholic women's voices could be heard not just at parish but at national level. Father Plater's efforts to start up a college where young people who had missed out on higher education could learn about politics and economics from a Catholic viewpoint aroused her interest. So keen did she become on this project and so concerned that the eventual College should be open to men and women alike, that she offered her own home in fashionable North Oxford as a hostel for women students. This was a most radical idea indeed for those times when few women were able to take degrees and Cambridge graduates had to use the awful title of BA (tit) to indicate they had passed the same degree as men.

Margaret's house was in Woodstock Road, near Somerville College. A large Victorian villa, its spacious rooms were filled with many of the features – frescoed ceilings, friezes over the architraves, brass door handles, leaded lights and candelabras – that bastions of today's consumer society would give their eye-teeth for.

Strangely enough, after our initial intake of breath at all this splendour, we never consciously noticed any of it again. Perhaps few of Miss Fletcher's 'girls' ever quite realised how lucky they were to get such splendid accommodation with such an extraordinary person.

She was not exactly young when I first met her in 1938, but nobody ever thought of her as old. Her opinions were too forthright, her presence too formidable, her energy too obvious. Though she lacked the regal appearance of the similarly solidly built Queen Victoria, she possessed many of her features: the plumpish face, the dark clothes, the habit of always sitting upright at the dining-room table, and a very straight posture when she walked.

A woman of many parts, she was also a keen gardener – though cutting the hedge was delegated to others – and an amateur painter, with her own studio at the top of the house. This impressed us greatly. A real painter with a real studio!

Full of her own interesting ideas, she tried to educate us in the way she thought we should go. As an example, there was the question of the pigeon pie. In my native Bethnal Green we early learnt to eat anything and everything put before us. Sometimes the mere sight of food made us salivate. Miss out a meal, and it might be a whole day before anything more appeared. But to eat a pigeon! Even when the family next door ate their pet rabbit for dinner one Sunday, I understood why, though the idea of their consuming their very own pet upset me for days. Now, as we sat at Miss Fletcher's dining-room table, she rang the little bell in front of her. Winnie, her pretty young housemaid, came in bearing our evening meal, a pigeon pie. The thought of eating pigeons, those birds that waddled around the feet of passers-by in Trafalgar Square, nauseated me. I made a show of eating the pie but left most of it on my plate.

'Eat up your supper,' said Miss Fletcher, as a mother to an obstinate child.

'I'm not very keen on pigeon pie, if you don't mind.'

Why could I not dream up a better excuse? . . . some allergy perhaps? But I had never met anybody with an allergy to food, only to bee stings.

Miss Fletcher peered over at me with a stern glance.

'You girls may have to travel all over the world,' she said. 'Possibly to act as ambassadors for your country and be asked to dine with people whose cuisine and culture will greatly differ from your own. It could give great offence if you refused or dallied with the food they offered you. The giving and accepting of it is a token of hospitality. Get used to trying different meals and be careful of refusing whatever you are offered, lest you offend.' What could I say in answer to this? I finished the pigeon pie.

Today Margaret Fletcher would be called a Tory diehard. Everything the (Conservative) government did was always right. She regarded herself in some ways as an extension of the College and the University, and had what would now be seen as rigid moral attitudes. Doors were closed at 10.00 p.m. If any male visitor were brave enough to call at the house, Margaret would be present. If he wanted to take out one of 'her girls' for the evening, a chaperone was necessary. This situation caused some resentment among the impecunious students, forced to pay for three people on an outing meant for two.

Her somewhat rigid moral attitude did not extend to her social conscience. She was as forward-looking an employer as she was a social pioneer. The weekends were therefore sacrosanct for her two maids: Winnie, who served at table and did light jobs about the house and

Mary, who was Irish and did all the cooking and certain other jobs. Mary could hold her own with Miss Fletcher at any time.

On Sundays we always had a cold lunch so that one or both of the maids could have the weekend off, a very unusual 'concession' in those days when a maid-of-all-work was just that.

As well as expanding our culinary expertise, Miss Fletcher also tried to extend our cultural vision. Occasionally we would be invited to a musical evening given by one of her friends. The friend, usually a lady called Miss Spooner, could have played Rachmaninov with all the brilliant interpretation of a concert pianist – and probably did – but it was temporarily wasted on the girls as well as the men. We attended for no musical reasons whatsoever. But coming as we all did from impoverished backgrounds, the girls at least were greatly impressed by the splendour of what was quite an ordinary semi-detached villa, its contents, and the occasional food so graciously handed out. We might have imbibed a sense of style. Who knows?

Though Margaret's politics were even more rigid than her moral principles, all of us basked in the hospitality and standard of living she provided so generously and which was an education in itself. Without her we might never have savoured the joys of Oxford at all. In our different ways we all gained from being there. Margaret Fletcher wanted such gains to be passed on to others, as she herself had passed on her advantages to us. College students came from and went all over the world to do just that, and doubtless to eat far worse – and often far less – than pigeon pie.

22

PER ARDUA

In 1938 war clouds hung heavily on the horizon. Britain put up sunshades. We ignored how Germany had already swallowed up Austria and was now looking at Czechoslovakia to satisfy its voracious appetite. Instead we took pride in our record-breaking achievements of that year: the liner Queen Mary ran across the Atlantic in just over 3 days, Sidney Wooderson did his half-mile in a record-beating time of 1 minute 49.2 seconds and Yorkshireman Len Hutton scored 364 runs at the Oval, overturning Australian Don Bradman's previous record by 30 runs. That levelled the series, and helped England's test match victory. It should perhaps be mentioned that the 'Don' fell and broke a shin bone in the game.

Politicians made an effort at stabilising the worsening political situation by recalling the British ambassador from Berlin. The Prime Minister said that Britain could give no guarantee of automatic assistance to Czechoslovakia if it were attacked. He tried, however, to allay the fears of historians who remembered that a far-away little town of Sarajevo had triggered the conflagration of the First World War. Surely another small country like Czechoslovakia would not set alight a second one? For such harbingers of doom, Chamberlain offered what was meant to be a palliative, '. . . if war broke out it would be unlikely to be confined to those who have assumed such obligations'. These 'obligations' included those of Great Britain and France.

In September, after a conference between Chamberlain and Daladier and the dictators Hitler and Mussolini, a peaceful solution to the Czech crisis was signed. The Czechs were not present. It was agreed that 'occupation by stages of the predominantly German territory by German troops will begin on 1 October'. The 'predominantly German territory', the Sudetenland, was to be gobbled up in pursuit of the militaristic *Drang nach Osten* philosophy.

War seemed to have been put on hold, at least for a while, after the Sudeten agreement, so I began my new career as a 'mature student'.

Our studies at Plater College were very well organised. Newcomers like me were given a piece of thin cardboard, 8in × 6in, on which to plan our work for the forthcoming term. Into the Monday to Saturday slots, morning, afternoon or evening, we filled in the list of lecturers and lectures for that particular term – Michaelmas, Trinity or Hilary – and where the lectures were to be held. They might for example be held in All Souls, in Schools, Campion Hall or other places. It was best to opt for a series of lectures which covered the particular subject on which we were working that term.

We also got the names of lecturers or professors to whom we had to report with any homework they gave us. Depending on the type of homework, we chose our lectures for the week or term. They were quite voluntary so that if you didn't turn up, nobody was apparently any the wiser. You just lost out on a vital part of the course. 'Gus' of Notre Dame would have approved of this system, for another of her little mantras, said in Latin of course, was 'Learn or Get Out'. Lurking in the background for Oxford students was that threat of being 'sent down' (never used at Plater College) or for undergraduates the possibility of failing or getting a fourth class honours degree. (I was told later by a university colleague who had one that this was an exceptional achievement which needed fine judgement to achieve – too little study meant failure, too much meant missing out on all the other possibilities that existed. She was extremely proud of her fourth class degree and flaunted it as if were some *cum laude* distinction.)

Books recommended in a lecture were easily available on loan from the many well-stocked libraries. Organisation, timetables, homework and marks were the outer signs of student life at Oxford. There was a spiritual and cultural side too, so intensely pleasurable it was almost sybaritic. We were in no way threatened by our background, or the creeds of others. We did not have to suffer for our beliefs.

Our survival, even our comfort, was assured. This period, so happy and exciting, did however, have a downside: it occasionally induced a feeling of guilt. Why had I been given such an opportunity when so many people were missing out on food, shelter, even the basics of life? I understood the feelings of those Jesuit priests who decided it was not their vocation to teach at private schools and so gave up a fairly easy-going existence in at least one public school to become missionaries overseas.

At Plater College all that we had to do was study . . . and such study . . . books and more books . . . no hardship for those who had learnt to read, not in prisons or by candlelight. However much we owed to the inspiration of dedicated idealists and even our own limited endeavours, we knew that our getting to Oxford was also due to communal efforts made for us by co-operative societies, educational associations and trade unions, religious and charitable organisations and the people within them who all helped us on our way. We understood Margaret Fletcher's desire that when our time at Oxford was over, we should try to pass on to others some of the advantages we had gained from our stay. But first we had to take our exams. Idealism without work is like an oyster without a pearl.

23

AD ASTRA

As one of Miss Fletcher's 'girls' I knew how lucky we all were in having a private study bedroom and what might be called a common room. We could get together there and discuss anything we wanted – which was certainly not confined to moral philosophy or National Income statistics 1814–1914.

Hilda Humphries and Belle Waddington from Manchester had both already completed one year of study, so I saw less of these flatmates than they did of each other. Hilda was a short, frail-looking girl obviously still suffering the effects of her father's death the year before. Her face was petite and pale, her brown hair short and rather thin. She gave the impression of a lost pixie. I could not place her attractive accent. Belle was quite different, rosy faced with a big hearty laugh, thick dark hair worn fairly long, beautiful big eyes and a very forthright Manchester voice and manner. She rarely hid her feelings. A sense of humour she possessed in plenty. Subtlety was not one of her ace cards, but nobody could ever take offence whatever she said, for though her words might sound harsh to softer southerners, they always contained a grain of sense.

On one occasion the little necklace given me by Mrs Silverman long ago, and which I sometimes wore, slipped out from under my blouse where I had temporarily tucked it.

'That's a nice necklace,' commented Belle. 'Birthday present?'

'No, it was given me by a Jewish lady for my First Communion.'

'By a Jewish lady for a First Communion?'

I was tempted to take a leaf from Mrs Silverman's book and say, 'By you a rosary is a suitable Chanukah gift?' but did not want to enter a long discussion, so replied, 'Odd I suppose, but no odder than me giving a Jewish boy a present for his Bar Mitzvah. And you couldn't expect a Jewish lady to buy a cross, could you?'

Belle puckered up her face a little as if thinking about this. I took the necklace off, showing her the tiny charms hanging from the chain.

'The lady who gave me the necklace thought it would be a nice present to remember her by, wherever I went. She asked a friend to add on the little charms. I've bought a few more since. The ones with letters on are hers.' I pointed them out.

'I see them . . . an aitch and a y . . . yes and a few more. What do they say?'

'Mrs Silverman said they spelt *Lekhayim*. It means "To Life". Funnily enough I didn't wear the necklace very often afterwards. Wasn't allowed to when we wore school uniforms but later on it seemed rather a nice thought and a way of remembering her kindness after she died. I often recognised it when Jewish people greeted each other, you know a bit like the old Irish crowd when they come into a room, and call out "God bless all in this house."'

'Better than "Heil Hitler", any road,' Belle said amidst our general laughter.

When I met a group of students from Queen's College, originally from Yorkshire, I found they were almost as forthright as Belle. My mother had bought me a fox fur, all the rage at that time in Bethnal Green where I strutted around in it for a time. I should never have taken it to Oxford, but wore it for an evening with George Grasby, one of the students from Queen's. He looked at me while I waited for the complimentary remark, and said just what he thought, 'Jennie! That awful fur! You look like a suburban housewife.'

He was quite right, the fur was completely inappropriate for Oxford – and it was just the sort of remark Belle would have made had she seen me setting forth in it. On this occasion she was out enjoying herself so I missed her comments. So much the worse for me. I was more sorry for my mother than myself, but smoothed over her disappointment that I wasn't ever going to wear the fur again by pointing out that it would make an ideal birthday present for one of her friends.

A good-hearted, very friendly lass, Belle got on well with everybody including all the men students. She eventually married one of them, Phil Murray. He had to face some stiff opposition.

I went out with George Grasby several times thereafter (without the fox fur). He and his friends were all on Hastings awards to study history. Harry Pitchforth, a scholar, entitled to wear the longer gown on that account, was very clever with dates – historical ones of course. George, in the same college, came from a small Yorkshire village and had a wonderful fund of literary quotes. These greatly appealed to me because I had never heard them before, including the Shakespeare ones, and because of their relevance to the particular occasion.

We were drifting down the river in a punt on one occasion when we were nearly capsized by a chap so entranced by his passenger that he was staring down at her quite unaware of the passing traffic on the river.

'I hope he can swim. He nearly fell in,' I said as we passed him.

'A consummation devoutly to be wished,' quoted George.

When we were very innocently sunbathing (in those days it was possible) in one of Oxford's lush green meadows, George came out with the first lines of a small poem by Leigh Hunt so utterly charming it more than compensated for his remarks on my fox fur. I've remembered the verse ever since.

> Jenny kiss'd me when we met,
> Jumping from the chair she sat in;
> Time, you thief, who love to get
> Sweets into your list, put that in!
> Say I'm weary, say I'm sad,
> Say that health and wealth have miss'd me,
> Say I'm growing old, but add,
> Jenny kiss'd me.

Truth compels me to add that I never jumped up from any chair to kiss George, not even when I met him later in Yorkshire. I must have been a really frosty student and had there been a few more girls around, probably would never have been punting or sunbathing around the Isis with such eligible young men.

We all enjoyed our leisure. In such a place, so near the Cotswolds and its lovely villages, how could we not? There was the cinema too. One of the joys of seeing films in the Oxford cinema was the occasional pithy, witty or droll outbursts of the audience, always loud enough for everybody to hear. They added to rather than detracted from the interest of the film, though not perhaps in ways that the director or scriptwriter intended. One interruption in a film I particularly remember.

On this evening, the cinema was showing a very old film of Edgar Wallace's 1911 book *Sanders of the River*. To appreciate the reaction of the audience it is necessary to understand that different colleges might have more students from one area than did another. Yorkshire scholars, for example, with Hastings awards for history, attended Queen's. The few miners or trade unionists might attend others, including our own or Ruskin College. Balliol attracted a fair proportion of UK students and also had a number of black and white African Rhodes scholars.

The film we were all watching that night, starring Paul Robeson, tells of the problems of a British colonial servant trying to keep peace among the natives. Already out of date in 1938, it was an obvious target for caricature. The film reached that clip where two boats, filled with local tribesmen, race frantically down an African river. A couple of Oxford 'blues', acknowledging their college's higher proportion of black students, clapped, cheered and finally yelled out 'Row up Balliol!'

The blues, whether Oxford or Cambridge, would have been thrown out for far less in our native Smarts cinema in Bethnal Green Road, or the Excelsior cinema off Pollards Row. Our East End cinemas had a reputation to keep up.

Working for the Diploma was not beyond us, though looking at some old exercise books, the amount we got through appears quite formidable. I was very lucky to have a photographic memory, able to remember figures and facts and anything written down in front of me – and not merely overnight. What I heard rather than saw, however, never stayed with me for long, which is probably why I can rarely remember a line of music or adequately mimic a foreign accent in spite of a large vocabulary acquired from seeing the words of that language.

In the beginning of the second term, Trinity 1939, Franco swept into Barcelona and a month later, his 'rule' was recognised by the British Government. In spite of Labour MP Clement Attlee's ferocious censure of Chamberlain, the resignation of Señor Azaña, President of Republican Spain, made all protests futile. In the same month Pope Pius XI died. Though he had spoken out against Nazism, priests were still being persecuted in Italy and Germany and he failed to heal the rift between Church and state. More rifts appeared in the European political landscape, with the Germans marching into Prague and Hitler having his eye on Danzig.

During this time I had some long conversations with Bill, another student, the son of the Foreign Secretary, Lord Halifax. Bill was going through a personal crisis. Like most at Oxford during that period immediately before the outbreak of the Second World War, we were all solidly pacifist: no war for any reason whatsoever except self defence. We argued half the night away on the rules of a just war as enunciated by Aquinas. Only if somebody invaded our country could we legitimately take up arms against them. There were other clauses to remember, and for Bill the added difficulty of being the Foreign Secretary's son.

He thought it would be unfair to take advantage of an education that allowed him to debate the rights and wrongs (if any) of modern warfare, when men who had not been given such advantages had no choice but to join whatever branch of the military needed them. We discussed this dilemma for so long that Bill and his pals arrived too late at their college to get in. One of them had already climbed over the walls. Bill, about to follow him, was stopped by the University's own police patrol. 'You needn't bother to climb over, Mr Woods,' the proctor said coldly, 'I shall open the college doors for you.' Bill was 'gated' for a week. When war broke out some months after this conversation, he was one of the first to join up, having probably come to the conclusion that 'the hottest places in hell are reserved for those who, in time of moral crisis, retain their neutrality'. He was, I believe, badly wounded.

In the summer our University Diploma examination took place. We were supposed to wear dark suits, rather like an orchestral group, for this important occasion. My mother, determined that I should not be outdone by what she always thought of as the Oxford toffs, went over the top, buying for me a short black cape lined with white silk, and a blouse to match. My fancy hat was more suited to a ladies' day at Ascot or a wedding ceremony than a very formal written examination. I must have taken it off before actually sitting down in front of the papers, but certainly wore it in the group photo taken afterwards.

The results of our Diploma examination would not be out for several months. I was very anxious to pass. This seemed like my last chance to move upwards, though to or for what, I wasn't quite sure. I doubted that I would ever be able to alter the world's ills, but getting an Oxford qualification was at least a beginning. The political outlook seemed daily more threatening and the climate of 1939 full of war clouds. The future looked so bleak, there was already talk of closing the College for the next academic year and perhaps even longer. I was not due back in the Savings Bank until September, but could volunteer to start earlier than that. Another European trip might be the last chance to travel abroad if Hitler decided to march through Poland. He had already made a pact with Russia, securing his eastern flank and making it easier for him to attack. His well-trained panzer troops would face little resistance from the besieged Poles, squeezed between twin juggernauts coming from east and west.

First year students had nothing to lose by a European trip. They had no exam results to wait for and their first year of further education looked like being their last. All that they would lose by going abroad would be a little time and a little cash. Nobody foresaw the possibility of internment in a foreign country for the duration if war actually broke out. Jim Smith, a miner from Durham, joined me. So did John Hennessy, who attended St Anne's church in Vauxhall.

A few more threw in their lot with us and we decided to go on much the same route as with Kathleen and Pat the previous year. This time, however, it would be a cycling tour with about 20 to 45 miles a day. My pace was about 15 miles an hour, but remembering the difference caused by the type of terrain, I kept the mileage low. We would be able to travel much further by bike than we could the previous year when our itinerary was mostly hiking or by train.

Little did any of us realise, as we set off in July 1939, that hostilities would begin a few weeks later and that poor Jim Smith, who had worked for years in the pits, would lose his life in the war. Our main objective was the Rhineland and southwards on to the Schwarzwald (Black Forest). German youth hostels were efficiently run, clean, cheap, some situated near towns, some in open country. Safe paths through any forests were clearly marked.

My old youth hostel card, half of which has survived, shows that we left Dover at the end of July 1939 and took the boat for Ostend in Belgium. The fare for each of us with a bike had not gone up since the previous year and was 30s. Many of the stamped entries on my hostel card are no longer clear, but we appear to have stayed for our first night in Bruges.

My first big shock was at a bridge crossing the Rhine; perhaps it was Duisburg. I cannot remember the name but the scene is etched on my memory. Facing me on the opposite side of the river was a big placard bearing the words in gigantic letters, EIN REICH, EIN VOLK, EIN FEUHRER as if advertising to the folk on our side, like a market trader in

Bethnal Green Road, that he had 'no connection with the firm next door'. In front of the placard were some children playing, happily unaware that they were of One empire, One people, One leader.

How worried and sad that sign made me. I knew that in many countries people displayed giant pictures of their political leaders, doubtless to show their loyalty to those in power and to prevent themselves from turning up as the accused in a trial of traitors or spies or suddenly disappearing altogether. But Germany? It seemed incredible to me that cultured, intelligent people as I had found the Germans to be should make such a show of their leader. It was like having a placard across the white cliffs of Dover publicising in glorious technicolor our gracious Queen, King, Prime Minister or whatever.

How ignorant I was of what was going on in *Deutschland über Alles*. Even when much later I heard more, it seemed too terrible, too repellent to be true. This refusal to believe evidence, to brush it aside as a lie, rumour or distortion of some kind because it reveals such incredible, terrible facts, is one reason why evildoers get away with so much for so long.

After a bit of fuss with a couple of guards at the bridge, we crossed over to the Reich. I looked back. There to my even greater surprise was another placard which I had not seen from my original vantage point. In equally large letters, it spelled out LIBERTÉ, ÉGALITÉ, FRATERNITÉ. Fortunately there was no leader mentioned, and though the French are probably one of the most patriotic nations in Europe, the sentiments displayed on that placard could never be regarded as xenophobic. An equally sad picture, however, was that of the children playing nearby. Would the French and German groups be killing each other in another few years? Before pedalling on, I fumed that war seemed to be the only way of resolving disputes between countries.

Our entries on that trip through France, Belgium and Germany included Dullegreete (Belgium?) and then in clearer print, Cologne, Coblenz, Rüdesheim, Karlsruhe, the picturesque town of Heidelberg, and fringes of the Black Forest to Baden. At this spa, the station master called out in a loud voice to every arrival, 'Baden-Baden, umsteigen Baden-Oos'. We had no idea what he was saying but we kept repeating it almost like a catchphrase or slogan for several nights afterwards. After Baden, we cycled off to Kolmar and almost down to Switzerland.

Throughout our travels we saw – but then would we have expected to? – no signs of war preparations, other than young men and boys all apparently hiking to somewhere or other, complete with identical knapsacks and invariably singing marching songs. This did not disturb us, as it might have done had we been aware that these young men were perhaps preparing for a war that could break out while we were still in what would become enemy territory.

The only discussions we had with young people were very limited because none of our party spoke German. In the youth hostels all that the Germans wanted to talk about, or perhaps all that we could understand, was the Duke of Windsor and his abdication. That was forced on him, so the walkers and cyclists firmly believed, because he did not want war with Germany. We could not convince them otherwise.

On the rest of our route home we learnt a little more. We got off our bicycles looking for a place where we could have a coffee. As we wheeled our bikes along the cobbled street, we stopped at a small shop and looked at some newspapers stacked in shelving in the front. I cannot remember their names but you certainly didn't need much knowledge of German to see that peace in Europe was fast fading from the agenda. I picked one up and held it out to the others of our party.

'Doesn't seem too good,' I said.

At that moment, the shopkeeper came out, looking irate. I could not think what had annoyed him. Perhaps picking up the paper, and worse still, commenting on it in public, was not proper behaviour? He shouted at us, and unlike most shopkeepers in Germany at that time, did not appear to be of a pacific nature. Discretion being the better part of valour, we made a hasty departure and sought our coffee in another village.

24

BORDERLINE

There was a kind of furtive air about this *Kaffeestube*, as if by serving us the waiters were engaged in some illicit operation. It gave me, at least, a feeling of disquiet. What was happening in the wider world outside? Perhaps war was imminent? It could not have been declared or we would surely have already been picked up as spies or enemy aliens.

We were coming to the end of our holiday and nearing the border at Venlo. Our next stops on our homeward route were at Honville, Sedan, Virelles, Champigneuilles. In the distance, we heard the sound of a train. Escape, I thought, with the same kind of desperate optimism that spurs on refugees. Once we're over the border, whatever may be happening in Germany, at least in France or Belgium we'll be safe.

'There's a train coming in. Let's dash for it.'

Everybody stood still, amazement on their faces.

'I'm whacked out,' I said, using a female ploy.

'We'll have to move fast,' Jim answered, succinct as ever.

Used to making quick decisions on a bicycle tour like ours, a spokesman said hurriedly, 'You go for the train.' As it neared the station, he encircled a dissenting group and shouted, 'We'll cycle back and meet up in London. Cheerio then, everybody.' With a quick wave of the hands, our united party abruptly broke off. A train pulled up into the nearby station.

'Rush for it!' Making a tremendous sprint, quite unworthy of a whacked-out female, I matched the deed to the words. Astonished, John and Jim followed. Pushing our bikes in with a combined effort, we just managed to clamber on board the northward bound train. It started off with a groan and a grunt towards our salvation over the border. The carriage in which we landed was packed with passengers. They appeared a frightened, furtive lot, as well they might, nearing a border that could change their lives. Like tube passengers on a packed commuter train, they didn't take our entrance too kindly as we shoved our way inside.

We stood, a silent phalanx of odd English travellers, by the doorway, our backs to the corridor. Our tickets were valid only from Venlo. Could we pay the surplus on the train; at the end of the journey; or would we be turfed out before the border? Staring out of the window, seeing little except the thickening shades of twilight, I hoped, rather stupidly, that our stance might hide us from the eyes of any inspectors coming along the train before we reached the border.

We were almost in sight of the crossing point when two men came along the corridor, yelling for tickets: '*Fahrkarten, bitte. Fahrkarten.*' Were they *Zollbeamter* or German *Polizei*? Neither was welcome. We stared more fixedly at the window. The reflection showed that they had stopped and were eyeing our bikes up and down. No hope now of getting over the border unnoticed. They pushed their way towards us. One of the men looked particularly sinister.

He asked for our passports and tickets. It appeared, as we suspected, that we had not paid enough for ourselves and our bicycles. He wrote down a figure, held it in front of us, then put his hand out, obviously waiting for the cash. His manner was hurried, but reasonable, almost courteous. So far so good. I had misjudged him. I bent over to take some cash from my carrier bag. The little necklace which Mrs Silverman had given me so long ago slipped out, dangling on my shirt. I had meant to pack it in with the rest of my belongings for our last few days and had forgotten to do so when we left the *Jugendherberge* that morning. I now asked myself whatever possessed me to take such an object into Germany at all? Perhaps wearing the necklace was a gesture of defiance?

The officer's attitude changed abruptly. Courtesy disappeared. Now in the guise of Herr Sinister, he pointed to Mrs Silverman's gift and gestured that he wanted it off. I became concerned. This was not a man to trifle with. I handed him the necklace. He looked at it, got out a small magnifying glass such as watch repairers use, focused on the chain, and shouted, 'Aus! Aus! Steigen Sie aus.'

We understood he wanted us out, but as the train was still rolling on, this was not possible. He pulled a chain over our window. I sensed rather than saw a tiny huddle, almost a group shiver, run through the other passengers in the carriage. Had these stupid English foiled their chances of getting out of Germany . . . or were they wishing us good luck?

The train ground to a halt. Herr Sinister disembarked. 'Folgen Sie mir,' he yelled in the manner of those who think understanding of a foreign language is helped by shouting the words more loudly. His aide, who had stood silent so far, shoved us and our bikes in the direction of his boss. Pushing us onto a platform of fractured concrete, he yelled, 'Schnell! Schnell!!'

The railway 'halt' where we unceremoniously landed looked like an abandoned allotment gradually losing the battle against nature. A few wooden shacks showed that the area once knew human habitation.

We glanced at the departing train. What did the future hold? Not for the first time, I wondered whether we should have gone on this cycling trip at such a fraught time in human history. Now in this silent emptiness, the night encompassing us, buildings and trees fading into darkness, I was uncertain if we should ever get home again.

Illustrating by rough gestures that we were to move faster, Herr Sinister led us across this railway halt, towards a small wooden building in a state of almost terminal disrepair. All the window panes were out, a few boards stuck in their places. He told us to leave the bikes outside. Doubtless they would be scrutinised minutely afterwards. Afterwards? After what?

'Inside!' he commanded, kicking open what had once been a glass-panelled door. At this point we should have made some daring action as they do in all the best films . . . pushed him into the building, shut the door after him, knocked out the second-in-command standing behind, and sped like the wind into the arms of rescuers, for further hazards yet to come. We did no such thing. Thought is inimical to action. We stayed put.

'Schnell! Schnell!' Herr Sinister now yelled, aiding our entry into the room with an angry shove. Following us closely, he switched on the light. It dangled from the ceiling on a frayed bit of flex which swung softly to and fro. That slight movement, that tiny tremor, seemed as sinister as our captor himself. The light flickered on. It revealed a small, dank room which felt as strangely cold as if it were a December night instead of a midsummer evening. Old brown patches on the ceiling showed where summer storms had left their mark. Fading yellow posters of timetables long since discarded were just managing to cling onto the wall. Again I thought of a film set. In this one, gangsters tortured their victims and neither gangsters nor victims were ever found again. I reminded myself that this was real, and nobody had been tortured . . . yet.

'Sit down,' Herr Sinister ordered. I sat. The boys remained standing.

A stale smell hung about the place as if it had not been used for a long time, except perhaps as a convenient pissoir for passers-by. Would the next hour be our last, more particularly, my last? Somebody had translated the letters on my necklace. I was a Jew. Who else would carry round charms reading 'To Life' in Yiddish, particularly when they were disguised by other charms fitted in between? There was no room for doubt. I was obviously some sort of spy. Questions, questions, questions . . . I could answer none. Murmuring 'Geschenk', which I thought meant 'gift' or 'present' proved no use at all.

Herr Sinister turned his attention for a moment to the others. I was terribly frightened for them. Were they to have their trousers pulled off to reveal whether they were circumcised? An aberrant thought suddenly occurred to me about a meeting with the author Harold Rosen in London's Festival Hall, when he told me a joke which became the title of his book, *Are You Still Circumcised?* After having made his way in the world, an immigrant goes back to his mother in Russia. 'So what happened to your side-locks and beard?' she asks him. He tells her that he can't go round like that any more. Everybody would think he'd just got off the boat. He reveals also that he hasn't a Jewish kitchen with milk and meat dishes kept separate, doesn't go to *schul* on the Sabbath and no longer keeps his head covered with a *cuppel*.

His mother, as she hears about her son's downward path to perdition, becomes distraught. She rocks from side to side, until she finally gets up enough courage to ask him one last question, 'But you're still circumcised, yes?'

This was not the time for such thoughts. Defiantly believing, like many other dupes of the time, that there was no real anti-Semitism in Germany I had taken Mrs Silverman's necklace with me and worn it. Too late to have a rethink now. Jim Smith was being questioned.

'Sie? Jude?' asked Herr Sinister. Good old Jim, I thought as, immediately getting the crux of the question, he shook his head. Pointing to himself as if to say 'Me, Tarzan, You, Jane' (some Jane!) he began vigorously miming the action of shovelling hunks of coal. Miner was the occupation still on his passport, not the most usual job for a person of the Jewish faith. Miner, Jim showed himself to be. Who would have thought salvation from Herr Sinister to come in the unlikely form of Jim Smith, that solid northern rock, trousers too long and tucked up with bicycle clips making creases round his ankles; Jim Smith, grizzled crop of thick curly hair clipped close to his head, a short, solidly built fellow whose only claim to good looks was in his lovely grin and steely black-lashed blue eyes; Jim Smith, tough, lovable, mature Oxford student from the coal mines of Durham.

Jim did the trick. Herr Sinister rapidly changed to Herr Willkommen. 'Ja, ja' now became the lingua franca. Coffee appeared from some mysterious source while we waited for the next train, and were politely shown onto it. We got back to Dover without further incident, so my old youth hostel card recalls, in August 1939 . . . and stayed overnight in the hostel there. Another month and we would have been too late for a boat back.

It was a lovely warm day with a cooling breeze coming off the Dover shore as we cycled back to London in August 1939. The road, beautifully asphalted, unlike many of the routes on which our bikes had wobbled abroad, was the only place where one of us (me unfortunately) got a puncture. I let my sex down badly by being so glad, yet again, to have male companions on the way.

Yet in spite of blue sky, the asphalted road so different from the cobbled roads of Europe, and the sense of freedom that Britain always conveys, I, at least, felt weighed down by a pall of gloom. Our journey had shown us a far more menacing scene than we ever knew in Oxford. War clouds were darkening the future for us all, the boys more than me, for I had a job to return to – or hoped I had. They might be called up for military service or feel impelled to volunteer. We wondered how long it would be before we should have another holiday trip to the Continent – or anywhere else for that matter. It was the last ever for Jim Smith. That lovely lad, sturdy miner from Durham who had spent all his life from the age of 14 in the pits and whose presence saved me from possible internment in Germany as a spy, was killed serving in the Second World War.

When we reached London we stopped at a Lyons tea-shop – a brilliantly inspired innovation by 'Joe Lyons' to provide reasonably priced meals for an aspiring working class. Customers were served by very attractive waitresses nicknamed 'Nippy' girls. The Lyon's Corner House restaurant 'up west' was under the same management and also staffed with Nippies. They wore black uniforms with short, frilly white aprons tied round their waists and little black and white bandeaus round their heads. Nippies added more than a touch of normality to an increasingly abnormal world. They lifted up the spirit with their attractiveness and the efficient and happy way in which they served their customers.

The Corner House equated with the Savoy or the Ritz for those not quite rich enough to dine in either of those establishments, but who hoped to reach that social rung one day. The Corner House also gave diners the chance of hearing live music played by a band of violinists dressed in romantic gypsy garments that matched the romance of their tunes – an ideal place for courting couples as I later discovered.

We left our bikes outside and sat down at the nearest table. In August 1939 nobody would pinch them. Faintly in the distance we heard the muted voice of Vera Lynn singing 'We'll meet again'. Though competing with some famous names like Judy Garland and Deanna Durbin, her clear sweet tone and its ringing sincerity soon made her the 'Forces Sweetheart'.

Now, however, we were just hungry, thirsty and slightly tired travellers, taking little notice of any background music. Sitting down at the nearest table, we ordered three cups of tea at 2*d* a cup and three buns at 1½*d* each. The buns were delicious and the cups of tea tasted like a heavenly brew after our trip abroad where tea was never available and thirst always had to be satisfied with the inevitable coffee.

Our satisfaction at such an enjoyable meal turned to consternation and embarrassment when the bill came. We had not yet changed our little remaining foreign currency into English coinage. Hastily foraging in our pockets for the requisite amount, we managed to collect enough between us to leave 'Joe Lyons' without owing him a thing except our thanks.

Now for the last leg of the journey homewards . . . Jim had a long trek to the north of England, but hoped for a lift from a friendly lorry driver on the way. John started off for south London.

As we left for our various destinations, we called out, 'See you soon' – such a casual parting, so often and so easily said. We made no fixed arrangements to meet up with each other. As a miner, Jim could have become a 'Bevin Boy' exempt from military service. He volunteered to join the army. I never saw him again. Even if he had not become a war casualty, later movements, bombings, job changes and war service soon made a reunion impossible. We had to get back to our ordinary lives. But those ordinary lives had gone for ever. They would be swallowed up like much else in the maw of war and our lives would never be ordinary again.

Meanwhile, I went back to Bethnal Green.

25

PANIC STATIONS

My 'translation' to Plater College, Oxford, from my home in Bethnal Green in London's East End was over. Gone were the wonderful buildings, cobbled streets, the spires, the cyclists whizzing round between the colleges, the lawns which needed only a little periodic cutting and a few hundred years of watering to keep their luscious carpet so green.

I saw and loved all these wonders. I breathed in the lovely early morning atmosphere when the Isis is bathed in mist, when everything is quiet and serene and only birdsong disturbs the dawn's tranquillity. I was as smitten by Oxford's beauty as a besotted lover; enchanted by its golden summer architecture and autumnal gravity, by the black-gowned figures flitting through the twilight. Now I was back to Square One, to the Bethnal Green home where I was born.

The biggest change for me had been due not to Oxford's beauty, but to a whole new lifestyle: of being whisked away from a shared house without any of the basic amenities which modern families take for granted, such as a bathroom, indoor toilet or electric light, and magically transported to one where there were two maids, where all your food was provided for you without your ever having to help in any way, not even to take a share of the washing up, where you no longer had to work for a living and your only commitment was to do your best in an exam to be taken at the end of the course. I kept to my books. It was one of the most wonderful years I had ever known.

The other students who started with me – miners, trade unionists, factory hands, unemployed workers – had looked forward to the normal two-year course and a qualification which could change their lives. Being able to cram most of that course into the period from September 1938 to July 1939, I was luckier.

Now with a war looming on the horizon, Plater College (which had not yet altered its name from the Catholic Workers' College) was contemplating a 'shut down'. If it did, the first-year students who had begun with me would never finish their course. Their hopes of a University qualification, and much else, would disappear like dandelion seeds puffed away by the wind.

When Chamberlain came back from Germany, waving the document he thought would give 'peace in our time', it seemed as if peace at last had won through. Prime Minister Chamberlain was as naive as I. On 3 September, a few weeks after Jim, John and I returned from Germany, came his chilling announcement: Germany had invaded Poland 'and . . . consequently this country is at war with Germany'.

War! My heart sank. Who could possibly ever have foreseen after the terrible bloodbath of the Great War that an even bigger maelstrom threatened to engulf the world? Had no lessons been learnt? The refrain never stopped going through my head: 'We are now at war.' What next? Within seconds, the answer came. An air-raid warning wailed through the streets. Later on, that sound would become horribly familiar. What could such a warning signify immediately after the announcement? If anything was destined to put fear into the hearts of normal London citizens, it was surely the sound of an air-raid warning so soon after a declaration of war. Were we, like the unfortunate Poles, to feel the wrath of a 'blitzkrieg'? Would fire bombs be used . . . or a land mine? None of the possibilities was pleasant. Perhaps gas would be preferred.

I was on my usual way to church that Sunday morning, and had reached Brady Street buildings in the Whitechapel half of Vallance Road when I heard the sound which later was to become the forerunner of death, devastation and destruction. My friend Kathleen Davidson lived in a flat on the fourth floor of the buildings. We were long-time friends. I climbed up the steps to call on her. Climbed? Well, I tried to climb but was almost knocked down by a stampeding rush of people fleeing from their homes in panic. You cannot credit the nature of panic unless you see it before your eyes as I did in Whitechapel on 3 September 1939, that first day of the Second World War. It is like an infectious disease that spreads with incredible speed from person to person.

I saw families hurrying, almost tumbling down the stairs in their haste to leave. Any news the next day about the calm reaction of the people in London on hearing this air-raid warning certainly wasn't true of Brady Street buildings in London's East End. People were running up and down the stairs putting on gas masks, taking them off, carrying them along with anything else they thought useful in an air-raid. Mothers tucked their babies under their arms along with whatever else they could manage. Gas masks dangled on the arms of children running alongside, mystified by the scent of fear.

Fathers too, home from work or unemployed, felt in duty bound to accompany their families out of the building . . . to what? There was no air-raid shelter downstairs or anywhere near so far as I knew, so where were they all running to?

What they were actually doing was not running to anywhere, but away from, from a threatening unknown. The unknown – always there in front of us – becomes in war time either especially fearful or, like a helpful guide, directs us to an apparently safer, happier situation that often turns out to be far more threatening and dangerous than the one from which we have escaped.

Eventually I worked my way through the throng, got up the stairs, rang the bell and waited outside the door on the fourth floor landing. Kathleen, one of the most unflustered people I have ever met, came out. Nothing ever caused her to turn a hair.

'Coming to church?' I asked Kathleen.

'Might as well,' she replied laconically. 'If we're going to be blown to smithereens, might as well be in church when the end comes. Besides, it looks better.'

I did not feel anything like so equable. In spite of my confrontation with 'Herr Sinister' in Germany and now the declaration of war, I still retained my pacifist convictions. Perhaps some last-minute peaceful solution might be found? Alas! I soon learnt that when war actually breaks out, it is a long time before it stops and meanwhile impossible to remain a pacifist.

To pick up a gas mask means somebody arranging it for you; to buy any overseas produce means a sailor somewhere has to bring it into the country for you. How can you remain a pacifist and eat food supplied by people risking their lives to save you and others from starvation? If you took a leaf from Berthold Brecht's 'food comes first, then morals', you might be able to manage it. That's probably how the 'Cambridge spies', Burgess, MacLean and Philby, managed to equate their consciences with their Marxist beliefs and keep their traitorous connections with the Soviets for nearly twenty years.

Because of my objections to war for almost any reason, I had never collected a gas mask. To do so meant relying on others to do work I would not do myself. Now as I saw everybody round me carrying these horrible signs of real war, I realised that once such a conflict began, you were in it for good or evil. You could not remain neutral. You had to be for it or against it. If for it, you did your bit, gave it your all and became a hero or villain depending on who were the eventual victors in the war, or you just lay low and took what was coming to you. If against it you had to become a spy or a Quisling or hope you would be allowed, as few countries other than Britain ever allowed, to protest or become a conscientious objector. You could not stand aside.

Kathleen put on a light coat and joined me on the stairs from which, like Horatio on the bridge, all but us had fled. After so much panic, the air-raid warning proved to be a mistake, due to some mechanical failure.

What a moment to have a failure. The Germans themselves could not have timed it better. We got to St Anne's church and found it strangely deserted. Even the ceremony of the Mass seemed to have diminished in strength and power. We went home both of us deep in thought, wondering what the next weeks would bring.

What they brought to me were two things: first, the loss of my pacific stance. Was I going to collect a gas mask or not? I collected one, took it home, found it almost impossible emotionally and physically to wear it, and never tried it on again throughout the whole of the war. But the action of collection meant that I could no longer believe myself to be against the war. Like it or not, I was involved.

The second loss was that of my job at the Savings Bank in Hammersmith and being transferred elsewhere. It was the job which I had imagined coming back to and the first dent in my armour of security since I started there.

Shortly afterwards, on 17 September Russia invaded Poland. Two days later Moscow agreed with Germany on the partition of that devastated country. Wedged between Soviet and Russian forces, Polish officers decided, as the lesser of two evils, to surrender to the Russians: 60,000 were killed, 200,000 wounded and an estimated 700,000 were taken prisoners. Many other so-called 'socially dangerous elements' were sentenced to hard labour. Divided between two dictatorships, Poland suffered the horrors of both.

Yet in the UK, Communist idealists of all kinds held firmly to their political convictions for many years after this political volte-face by Soviet Russia. They ignored revelations about labour camps, purges and trials. Some of these UK 'idealists' did not leave the party until Russia invaded Hungary in 1957 or even later when the Berlin wall came down.

I heard that all the Plater entrants passed the university Diploma. Of my two flatmates, Belle married one of the male students Phil Murray, went back to Manchester and took up a teaching career. Hilda got into Somerville. After achieving a good degree she went into the Civil Service.

One of her classmates, William (Billy) Woodruff, later served in the forces with distinction. He returned to Oxford via one scholarship or another and climbed his way to professorships in many different countries. Writing about his early beginnings and very movingly about his war experiences, he achieved best-sellerdom.

Against the threat of an all-embracing war, the fact that I also had passed the Oxford University Diploma in economics and political science with distinction in several subjects, and top marks of all candidates in economic history, seemed a complete irrelevance. Father O'Hea said that if he had known I would get such high marks in such a short time, he would have made greater efforts to find me a tutor in economics so that I would have done better in that subject. It was a good thing perhaps that he didn't. Following my brother's example of learning from my 'failure', I did the same, eventually ending up as a senior lecturer in economics and writing a book on monetary theory.

Many waters were to run under many bridges before that happy Elysium arrived. In Bethnal Green, I contemplated a different scenario.

A few days after bidding farewell to the Plater boys I went to a political meeting at Toynbee Hall. Some Jewish fellows were there that evening. Though they had their own meeting places, they often turned up at Toynbee Hall. That institution, understandably in view of the events in Germany, was a centre of left-wing opinion and growing more so.

Many East End Jews, particularly the young, saw in Communism the only way of altering the British political and economic system to achieve a fairer society. Hearing of more and more oppression of their fellow religionists in Germany, their beliefs became even stronger, as did those of their opponents who regarded the Communist system as even more malign.

It was at that meeting I met Morrie. He asked me to go to a dance with him in a location I can't now remember, except that it seemed rather a 'high class' one. Perhaps it was the Hammersmith 'Palais'. That was almost 'up west'. Among all Morrie's other talents, he was a very good dancer and a patient one, too.

I took an instant and almost dangerous liking to him. Exceptionally attractive with his blue eyes and lovely head of ginger hair, he was 6 feet tall, well over the average for most young men of those days and in that area. But I liked everything about him, his intelligence, his looks, his ethics, his politics. He was a 'liberal' Jew, though he also never made any secret of his religion.

His father was a rich and well-respected local East End tailor with his own business and a very practical and kindly wife. Kindly though she was, I doubt if she would have favoured a marriage between her son and a *goy* like me, though such a possibility never entered my mind.

Our relationship moved forward much more quickly than either of us was really prepared for. Impending war, like an impending execution, concentrates the mind wonderfully and does a lot to speed up responses. Neither Morrie nor I found our respective faiths a barrier to friendship. What I, at least, failed to realise was that a platonic friendship between a young man and woman is, in the long run, very unlikely to continue in that fashion. One of the pair always loves more, desires more.

Religion, practised in our own way, became more of an interesting talking point than a cause of dissension. This is possible for two friends of different faiths and sexes only when both are able to compromise . . . not an easy path to follow and one that, when both are young, usually ends in giving up either the friend or the faith. For the time being, however, our liaison seemed to be progressing beautifully.

After a lovely evening we were walking home when Morrie held my hand and started singing, 'Bei mir bist du schoen'. It was such a lovely sensation to hear him so happy. I even felt I might eventually tie in my lot with him. Then he stopped singing and blurted out:

'I've decided to join the Palestine police force.'

I could not believe him. 'The Palestine police force? But why? What possible reason can you have for going out to Palestine?'

'I just feel things will change out there if a war comes, as it surely will, and there will be a need for a good police force. Promotions are likely to come soon. But I don't want to go out alone.'

He asked me if I would join him and emigrate to Palestine. I can't think now why the Palestine police force should have attracted him. His mother was horrified.

'Oy vay! For why you want to go out there?' she asked him. 'Such a country. So you don't like living with me any more?'

'No, momma, it's hard to explain,' he replied.

This was before a new state of Israel was born out of the horrors of the Holocaust. Possibly Morrie hoped that by being in the area he would be able to help in some way. Much as I felt we could make a good life together, I could not envisage it in Palestine. Further, friendship between people of very different religions was one thing, but marriage was another. Morrie had asked me to go out with him. He had not suggested marriage and I certainly was not ready for such a big step.

I was too entrenched in my East End cocoon, too lacking in an adventurous spirit, too steeped in the miserable memories of unemployment, and not yet goaded by starvation or persecution to try my luck elsewhere. Sadly, we parted. Like taxi drivers hearing the tales of their passengers, we never know the ending of the many people we meet on our journey through life, so I never discovered how Morrie fared in his new environment, though I heard from his mother that he had left England.

Soon afterwards, my services being apparently needed elsewhere, I moved from the Savings Bank to offices vacated by the Automobile Association near Leicester Square. Certain advantages came from this new 'posting'. It was nearer Bethnal Green than was Hammersmith. That meant less travel, slightly more money in my pocket. The outlook from the new headquarters in Fanum House was also far more lively than looking out onto Blythe Road, West Kensington – if you could manage to look out at all. Now I could see lively Leicester Square and the current and forthcoming attractions at the cinemas nearby. I greatly enjoyed the spectacle of queues daily filling up the Square.

The work at the new offices was breathtakingly boring, mainly mechanical and requiring the minimum of intelligence, which is perhaps why I was posted there. Anybody who gives up a job with reasonably fair wages to study and earn nothing at a time when more than a million people are unemployed must be a bit stupid, it appeared.

Our work dealt with preparations for the issue of ration books, a job which opened up all manner of opportunities for anybody of a garrulous or fraudulent disposition. I could have been labelled the former, though in this case the work was too monotonous even to pass an iota of gossip about it to anybody. As for fraud . . . so far I wasn't tempted to help myself to a few extra ration books, though had I been afraid of starvation, I might well have thought differently.

By some perverse logic, Kathleen was offered, like many others at this time, a post in the Civil Service without having to take any exam whatsoever, at a higher level and therefore a higher wage than those of us who went in by the normal examination route. This kind of management from above caused a great deal of unrest among employees hoping for promotion after a three- or four-year stint on lower levels.

The Civil Service 'union' was helpless. Nothing could be done. Already the mantra 'Don't you know there's a war on?' was being played. A strike was out of the question. The attitude of the powers that be was that more staff were needed for particular posts and had to be enlisted before they were snapped up elsewhere. It certainly seemed an unfair policy, not merely because of the higher wages, but in Kathleen's case an appointment to a branch of the Customs and Excise (a much more prestigious service than the rather lowly Savings Bank) and in offices not far from Tower Bridge, almost within walking distance of her home.

I should have taken courage in both hands, packed up my job and looked for something else. What one should do and what one actually does, as everybody knows, are two quite different things. The welfare state had not yet come into being. I was a weakling, too afraid to risk being out of work and a burden on my family. Opting for safety, I stayed where I was.

As well as the loss of my former job at the Savings Bank, I lost all contact with friends there and found it difficult to make new ones. No more Wednesdays off for sports, though that was a small price to pay in war time, even for a 'phoney' war with no attacks, no invasion, no bombing, only a false air-raid warning given out by the British.

However, apart from athletics and swimming, in which I still took part, there were other chances of meeting new friends. In the East End, as well as political meetings, dancing was another common way of meeting people of the opposite sex. Girls were expected to sit out on chairs provided round the wall, hence the name wallflowers. They might be asked to dance by any of the men present and take their chance of whom they got. No picking and choosing for them, though they could fake tiredness or some other lame excuse if the partner were particularly gruesome. Some poor girls might sit the whole night through waiting to be picked up by a not especially attractive man.

I met up with Maggie, an old school friend from St Anne's, quite by chance at a dance in the local church hall. She was now 'walking out' to use the fashionable expression of those days, with a very personable young man, Charlie McGuire. He had a safe job, reasonably well paid, on the railway. They intended to get married in the following year, the summer of 1940.

More important still, I met Frank Hawthorne, or perhaps it is fairer to say he met me. He relates that I spoke some words of German to him. If so, they were probably the only German words I knew – something like *guten Abend* or other trivia picked up in my recent holiday, a cheeky way of showing off that I had been abroad. Big deal . . . a somewhat similar ploy to one used at that time and later by some men, of carrying around a book with an erudite title, to impress a girl.

No such subterfuges need be brought into play today. Liaisons and sexual encounters seem to offer no problem to anybody, young or old. It does seem odd therefore that in spite of (or perhaps because of) this, there are hundreds of advertisements by men and women looking for somebody offering tender, loving care, with preferably a bit of dosh to go with it, like some form of dessert to the main offering.

At St Anne's I again met John Brannigan, a former student of Plater College, back home in Poplar and an important personage, a local councillor, no less. Retaining his trace of an Irish accent, as modest and religious as ever, he was an attractive and amusing companion, and a very good card player, to boot.

Political meetings or educational gatherings such as those at Toynbee Hall attracted a different crowd. When Frank and I first met at St Anne's it was a coincidence unlikely ever to happen again. An aircraftman in the Royal Air Force, which he had joined anticipating a war surely going to come, he was home on weekend leave and staying with his widowed father in the tiny cottage, almost like an almshouse, nearby. I had gone to St Anne's because it was expected of Plater College students that when they left Oxford they should try to help their own communities, at work or in their trade unions. It was the only occasion Frank and I were both at St Anne's together.

The two words of a foreign language that I spoke on meeting Frank (though I cannot think why) apparently impressed him to such an extent that, young as he was, or perhaps because he was too young to know any better, he made up his mind then and there, unknown to me, that he was going to marry me. Maggie foretold this would happen. 'Never,' I retorted, laughing. In spite of my brief encounter with Morrie, I had successfully avoided the marriage trap so far. To be caught in it . . . never. For a woman, marriage was the end of all ambition, and I still hoped to change the world even at this late hour.

Even if my ambition wavered, the memory of my efforts at acting as an emergency 'midwife' in Bermondsey to a woman having her eighth child was enough to keep me single – or so I thought. Alas! At the age of 22 and even with a newly acquired Diploma I had much to learn. Frank proved a very adept teacher.

26

ALL CHANGE

Life proceeds in a straight line only chronologically. Though one year precedes or follows the next, each brings different challenges, different experiences. Going from Bethnal Green to Oxford in the year 1938–9 was one of the biggest changes in my life. Others, equally important, but not so pleasant, were now about to spring on me. Though I lived through two years of the First World War, from 1916 to 1918, I was too young to know anything about it. By contrast, I felt the full force of the Second World War from its outbreak in 1939 to its conclusion in 1945. It changed my life every bit as much as if I had changed my race, sex or religion.

First of all there was the relationship with my parents. Absence is supposed to make the heart grow fonder. That was true as regards my mother. During my time away in Oxford, I learnt to appreciate her more, her extraordinary honesty in the face of so much poverty and so many temptations; the way she held on to her Protestant ethic of right and wrong (including a favourite phrase 'Pay up and be respected'); her way of always keeping her word to employers as well as to neighbours and friends; her fearless forthrightness – unless faced by an officialdom she could not understand; her boundless energy and quick Cockney repartee; the hardships she endured as a child without ever moaning about them in later life; and the impact on her of losing all her family except her father, when she and they were so young: mother, two brothers and a sister.

Now in her mid-forties, her thin dark hair, which she wore in a bun at the back of her head, showed no signs of grey and never did throughout the whole of her life. Her complexion was fair to sallow, except after an outing, when she became pinker and browner. Her main claim to beauty came from her lustrous brown eyes, different from my father's hazel ones, more soulful. Though always neat when she went out, I never saw her in anything remotely 'stylish'. All I ever noticed about her figure was that she was full-breasted but far too energetic ever to get fat. Unfortunately, having had rickets as a youngster, her legs already showed signs of the bow-legged stance that became worse as she got older, though they never stopped her 'mooching', as she called it, round the markets.

It was true she never thought about righting the world except that around her, which meant family. So what? For them at least she would fight to the bitter end, determined never to sink in the mire of London's East End.

I began to understand the reason for her shortness of temper when times were hard and she lashed out at me for some misdemeanour or other. I understood too, though could not sympathise with, her attitude to reading as a waste of time, her feeling that there were always more important jobs for women to be getting on with. If you had time for reading, then you should be 'doing' something useful: sewing, machining, typewriting, peeling potatoes, cooking, scrubbing or washing up. TV and the couch potato were a long way off.

Though Mum had never looked in the Catechism of Christian knowledge, she knew as much about the danger of the mortal sin of sloth as did Sister Mary Austin (Gus) of Notre Dame, though Gus, being a Latin teacher, referred to it as *accidie*. Both women certainly knew about sloth's contrary, the virtue diligence. As far as my mother was concerned, just sitting around with an open book was itself akin to sloth, an admission card for the fires of hell, so I could never read or study at home without a terrible feeling of guilt. I lost that sensation completely at Oxford, where everybody was reading or learning something, except those waiting on those who were reading or learning something.

Happily, in adult life as in childhood, I succumbed to the lovely, irresistible lure of the printed word. But sometimes when I sit still today instead of chasing around 'doing' something, the guilty feeling comes back to haunt me like an unloved ghost. It used to leave me only when reading or researching certain books or subjects became part of my job. I managed eventually to read for pleasure by persuading myself that I was learning something . . . which was probably true.

By contrast, Mum fully understood that to be good at music you had to practise it, and practise it often. She had been very impressed with one of my father's sisters who used to lock her son in a room and did not allow him out until he had done an hour's practice. The technique seemed to work for he could certainly play the piano. I never could in spite of the lessons for which my mother paid from a lean purse, and which gave no return (except possibly as a by-product, the stimulation of my brother's latent musical gifts).

Whether the locked-in practice session was of any use to my cousin, I have no idea, for he joined the army as soon as he could, got married, was sent off to the Far East shortly afterwards and was killed during the Second World War, without ever seeing the daughter born after he left.

My mother's attitude towards music remained steadfast. Music was different altogether from sitting about doing nothing except reading books. They would never bring you in any bread and butter, whereas playing any kind of instrument, as long as you could turn out a tune, always earned you a penny or two even if it only came from busking on the streets – so my brother Jim was able to play whatever and whenever he liked.

As well as Jim's music, our home in Bethnal Green was also full of Mum's delicious brand of Cockney humour, mixed with the occasional Jewish phrase. It could so easily deride the social climber who was 'Eton and brought up' or the too richly bejewelled celeb who became in Mum's vocabulary 'Diamond Lil', while the woman only aspiring to be Diamond Lil was merely 'dressed up like a tuppeny 'alfpenny 'ambone'.

The down-to-earth patois of Bethnal Green was not merely streets but a universe away from the donnish North Oxford competitiveness and intellectualism with which I'd grown familiar and where I'd lost the last vestige of my East End accent. I held on to it for home use until much later when I sent a script to the BBC, and was so incensed that after all my efforts to learn to speak 'proper' I was asked to read it in a Cockney accent. I climbed onto my high horse and decided not to broadcast at all.

I also saw more clearly why my mother had such an empathy with my brother and his girlfriend Bella. They were all like each other, spoke the same language, enjoyed the same music and tunes (an area from which my tone deafness completely excluded me) and had the same aspirations, which I did not share. Though well attuned to the news, they took little interest in politics, economics or sport, which were for me of such concern.

As a child, I was 'different' if only in my constant hospital sojourns. In my teenage years, my determination to remain single and childless (the two in those days went together) was not at all the 'normal' attitude of a young female East Ender. Coming to terms with people who are physically, mentally or spiritually different from oneself is not an easy task and it works both ways.

Mum added on some Catholic principles (church on Sundays) to the ethics of her Protestant upbringing. She also celebrated Jewish feastdays, sending at those times good wishes to all her Jewish neighbours and friends. She had no knowledge of Jewish history and never showed the slightest interest in Judaism, though she picked up a few phrases, including some swear words and a curse which she occasionally used to a Gentile. She was certainly interested in Jewish feast days, mainly because of the food with which they were celebrated. We munched matzos without ever bothering that the leaven excluded from matzos represented sin which we had to eliminate from our lives. As for the gamut of kosher cooking . . . it was so unbelievably rigid that I wondered how any poor Jew could ever comply. Perhaps fasting was the only way.

We knew nothing about the battle of the Maccabees in 165 BC when the Jews returned to a devastated Jerusalem and found one lamp burning in the Temple that lasted for 8 days. This miracle, celebrated as the Festival of Light, meant for us the chance of some fascinating oil-fried food: latkes, doughnuts, chicken and apple fritters. We gobbled these down almost as quickly as they came from the pan. The apple fritters with their combination of oil, sour apples and sugar tasted especially good. We never bothered one iota about the oil's religious significance.

As superstitious as ever, my mother might easily have become a Catholic if the Lord had punitively shown her the unwisdom of her Protestant ways. After my childhood bout of diphtheria, which led her to send me to a Catholic school, however, the Lord never showed any further displeasure, so in spite of the persuasiveness of several of the nuns at St Anne's, Mum never moved further along the Catholic route, except in one somewhat macabre regard.

Still comparatively young, she became concerned that as a Protestant she might not be allowed to be buried with my Catholic father in the same cemetery. She therefore bought a plot of land at St Patrick's Catholic cemetery in Leytonstone. It was the only bit of real estate she ever bought in her life. Though I could never understand her reasoning, she was determined to be buried with my father when they eventually both died.

I noticed too, much more of her generosity than when I was younger, and when she doubtless had to watch every penny. Her brother, killed in action during the First World War, had left her a few pounds in the Savings Bank. She gave some to her father, which helped him out in hard times and probably saved him from the ignominy of the workhouse. The rest she regarded as blood money only to be used for a very good cause such as her burial plot or an extreme emergency.

The possession of that money in the Savings Bank (where it would be eaten away by inflation), and the fact that my father had a temporary job, caused my scholarship grant to be reduced from £12 in the first year to

£9. Mum never thought of moving the cash elsewhere as a sophisticated investor might do, but by my second year at high school it was too depleted to make any difference to the grant. An odd incident in 1939 when war was on the horizon had a big impact on my mother's later life and also gave me a clue as to where the money had gone.

She came home one day with a huge bag of vegetables and dumped them on the kitchen table.

'Guess 'oo I met on the way back from work?' she asked my father.

''Ow the 'ell should I know?' Dad replied, rather impatiently, hardly looking up from the paper which he hoped would show him the winner in the next day's races.

'You'd never believe it. Tim Collins.' She waited expectantly. No reaction came from Dad other than the mumbled 'Whoever's 'e?'

'Don't you remember?' She gave a quick look at me. I was sitting at the other end of the table, a pen in my hand and a book at my side, pretending to be absolutely engrossed in the permissible act of writing. My ears were wide open.

'Don't you remember?' she asked my father again. 'That chap, you know,' I saw her give another sidelong glance at me. Rashly assuming I was not interested in the conversation, she continued, ''E was in some sort of trouble. Didn't tell me what. Wouldn't do, but I guessed it was bad, an open and shut case. 'E had to pay some solicitor or lawyer to get 'im out of it, otherwise it meant the nick.' She shook her head. 'They were such a nice couple. I couldn't let him ruin his life and his wife's could I when that bit of money saved him from jail?'

'I've caught on now. Wasn't that your brother's money? I thought you were mad at the time, giving any of it to a chap like that. Practically a stranger, 'e was. I told you it would never come back. You should have let 'im stew in his own juice,' said my father. 'Nothing to you, 'e was, nothing.'

'Well it was blood money. Couldn't use it except for some good purpose.'

'Plenty of those around,' said my father. 'What about me. Ain't I a good purpose?' He looked up at her with one of his charming grins which could melt the Matterhorn.

'Anyway has he brought any of it back? He's had it long enough.'

'Well, sort of.' She opened the bag. 'He's got a stall in Spitalfields now. He recognised me on my way back from work, and filled up the bag with everything he could find.'

'Handy, but a bit of veg don't amount to much, does it?'

'He told me that I should never go short of vegetables for the rest of my life and he'll pay me 'is owings next time he sees me.'

'Another *spiel*. Tell me another one do,' sang my father, getting wiser as he got older.

'I bet 'e means every word 'e says.'

And he obviously did for as far as I know, my mother got her money back and never went short of fresh vegetables even during the worst blockades of the war.

Though I got the gist of my parents' conversation I never quite discovered why the mysterious visitor needed to borrow the money, but guessed it might be for somebody to defend him in a court case. My mind ran over all sorts of intriguing possibilities – blackmail, abortion, forgery. I guessed it was abortion, a heinous crime in those days, almost equivalent to murder, which some people would still assert it is, but I never did find out.

Though my relationship with my mother seemed to have improved after my time at Oxford, it somehow grew a little colder with my father. Dad had always been so handsome with his thick head of hair, now almost totally grey, his lovely long-lashed hazel eyes with their tiny gleams of green, and his fresh complexion. And he was such an interesting companion during our walks to Mass. Now he looked gaunt, his skin the colour of parchment. I did not know of his worsening health. Nobody ever spoke of such things unless they were almost at the point of death.

He now had a full-time job with a measure of security and mates he saw every day. So he no longer relied on me as he had so often done in the past. His job entailed cutting up iron bars to customers' specification. This was done on benches in the open air outside the factory building on good days and thought to be easier and better for the men than cutting the metal sheets inside the workplace. Nobody was then knowledgeable enough to know that the inevitable releasing of metal dust particles into the air was almost as prejudicial to a worker's health as the smoking of cigarettes.

The few men with whom Dad worked all succumbed to the same terminal disease. Nobody cared overmuch about health and safety, especially the men themselves when there were so many others without jobs at all. War would soon change that situation, but not yet. The firm ultimately went out of business. Compensation culture and the welfare state were a long way off. No worker, unless he belonged to a strong trade union (a move never contemplated by my father), would risk suing his employers for compensation as a result of an accident or illness caused by working for them.

Dad still smoked his cigarettes, but with wages coming in regularly every week he was rich enough to buy his own packets of Woodbines. He also cut down his drinking to a round at the pub with a few of his pals, mostly on a Friday night.

Mum also had her job as a cleaner in the Children's Hospital, Hackney Road. Save for the stairs, which were harder on her knees than the floors, and the rather stiff attitude of some of the management staff, it was much easier than being a charlady in the City. She did not have to get up so early and the hospital was only 5 minutes' walk from home. Working in the wards was particularly enjoyable for her. She had a real gift for communicating with small children. The occasional opportunity to cheer up a sick child or to have a little chat with convalescent patients was a welcome bonus.

Love can often grow up between very young and much older people, whether related or not. The age difference can also be the source of such a profound lack of understanding that it grows into a cruelty and hatred which leads to murder. Some mothers love their tiny babies with a passionate devotion, but show little affection for them as they develop, and there are parents who are quite hopeless with their small babies, but wonderful with the same children when they grow older. My mother's hospital job was almost a throwback to the happy days when she was the maid-of-all-work for the Waterman family.

She came home from the hospital at midday to make my father's dinner, and often went back again for a night shift. Dad had two rather strange inhibitions. Having been in his younger days a carman with two horses to control, he got used to travelling by horse and cart and disliked other forms of travel. An hour's journey, or perhaps a little more, was about as much as he could stomach. The second inhibition was never going into any kind of café. This might have been due to a kind of shyness, though it never seemed to stop him from entering a pub. His refusal to go into a café or any other similar eating place made my mother almost as bitter as about his getting drunk, and often led to quarrels. She felt she could get a much better job if she were able to work a full day instead of coming home at midday to make sure Dad had a cooked meal.

Fearless and independent as she was in many ways, Mum was still rooted in the conventions of working-class married life where (provided there was something to cook) women always cooked for and stayed by their men, no matter what. Dad, however, occasionally took over the baking of the Sunday dinner. He did this very well indeed, so on these occasions my mother's heritage of rigid Protestant and Jewish observance of the holy Sabbath stood her in good stead.

Preparations for my friend Maggie's wedding were going ahead for the summer of 1940. Meanwhile, after our first meeting at St Anne's, Frank saw me home and with the perspicacity he showed on many later occasions made a note of my address. He sent me a letter as soon as he arrived back at his quarters and, without waiting for an answer, followed it up with another the next day.

The letters were so unsophisticated and the spelling was so awful I corrected them and sent them back. Even if he couldn't spell, he was one of the most intelligent young fellows I had met since leaving Plater College: pleasant, a good companion and, a very big point in his favour, a Catholic as well. But I wanted no entanglements and he seemed very young, though he would never tell me his age. He asked me to correct his spelling and took no umbrage at my returning his corrected letters and kept on writing, his spelling improving with every missive he sent. He told me later that he often made deliberate mistakes in his letters, so I should write back.

Although good looking and tall, with thick dark hair and lovely 'hazely brown' eyes, it was Frank's 'positive' attitude that attracted me the most. He was never depressed or boring, always interesting and cheerful, whereas I alternated between moods of depression and ecstasy. He fortunately kept all his lively characteristics throughout his life and even today at 86 is never boring, always full of new ideas and with all the energy of a man at least 10 years his junior.

As an aircraftman in the Royal Air Force, stationed in Norfolk, he managed to get back to London for the occasional weekend when he would take me out, with Maggie too. Charlie McGuire, her fiancé, working on the railway, often had to do unwelcome shifts so weekends were not always possible for him. The three of us went on Saturday nights to Lyon's Corner House and listened to the gypsy band.

Frank was a very good dancer, dividing his attention fairly equally between Maggie and me. Though not endowed with any sense of musical rhythm, I eventually learnt under Frank's expert tuition (for I had forgotten Morrie's) to distinguish between a waltz and a fox-trot and even managed the tango. Frank performed this dance with great flair, devising all manner of fancy steps which I greatly enjoyed.

In the background to our developing friendship was the 'phoney' war. In 1939 the UK seemed strangely immune from attack. After the invasion of Poland from the east by the Soviets and by the Nazis from the west, others to fall were Denmark and Norway. In April the Nazi invaders were in command of all of Norway's main ports. The British navy entered the fray and sank ten German destroyers. British and French troops landed at Narvik, but neither army was properly equipped for Arctic operations.

Prime Minister Chamberlain told Parliament that Hitler had 'missed the bus', but if this were true he managed to board a faster one. Chamberlain also declared that the Allied strategy of war trade agreements was destroying German economic life, and British naval action was stopping Swedish ore supplies reaching Germany through Norway. These 'agreements' were wishful thinking. England was still grossly unprepared for war.

Save for the couple of false air-raid warnings and the obvious signs of war preparations, with shelters going up and sandbags going down, the year 1939 in Britain ended in comparative calm.

That was not the case in 1940, at least for countries overseas. In March, after a heroic defence of their country for 14 weeks, Finland conceded defeat in a war in which the Russians lost a million men. A few weeks later the German foreign minister saw the envoys of Belgium and Holland. He told both those countries that to protect their neutrality against an impending attack by the British, the German armies were crossing their borders. He did not tell them that the blitzkrieg on the Netherlands had begun.

The Belgian army began to disintegrate in the face of the German attack. The Dutch fended off that on The Hague, but Rotterdam, subjected to an aerial bombardment, soon fell. Neither Belgium nor Holland had learnt the lesson of Poland.

Neither had England, it seemed, but at least we had the Channel as our defence against an invading army. In London, going off to work every morning, I found the labelled queues of children departing for safer villages and towns an immensely poignant sight. After the Nazis swept into Holland and Belgium it would surely be the turn of the French and

British troops defending the Channel coast. Against a background of mounting military catastrophe, Chamberlain asked for a vote of confidence. The Labour opposition refused to cooperate; and he offered to quit in favour of Lord Halifax. The opposition refused to serve under anybody but Winston Churchill: only he commanded the support of a majority in Parliament. On 13 May 1940 his first message as the new Prime Minister was to say 'I have nothing to offer but blood, toil, tears and sweat.'

In the next few weeks Belgium and Holland surrendered. Queen Wilhelmina offered the Dutch merchant ships to the British, and had the gold and diamond reserves of Amsterdam loaded onto warships before she and her family sailed to Britain to continue the fight. These brave gestures were of little help to the French and British. Defying the widely held idea that the Maginot line was impenetrable, the Germans first skirted it, then thrust through Luxembourg and the Ardennes. On 14 May General Rommel led a tank attack against French forces near the Belgian border, broke through the Maginot line, turned north and drove deep into the territory defended by the British and French.

Hampered by refugees fleeing from the German invaders, the British and French fought bitterly all the way but soon found themselves encircled on the Normandy coast. With their backs to the sea, they faced 750,000 German troops. How were they to escape, if at all? At this point, on orders from above, the German heavy armour was halted. Hitler feared the tanks would be bogged down in the marshy land along the coast.

This extraordinary pause in the fighting gave the British troops the chance to escape. Operation Dynamo came into force. A huge contingent of big and small ships, destroyers, ferries, fishing vessels and even holiday cruisers all sailed off to help rescue from annihilation the remnants of the British Expeditionary Force, and the Belgians and French and other troops fighting alongside them.

The little ships picked up the men who were wading out to sea in an attempt to escape from the bombers above and the guns on shore. Leaving the Dunkirk coast littered with bodies and battered metal, the survivors were strictly disciplined: they were more orderly, so one survivor said, than a bus queue. Over 300,000 of them got out.

Belgium surrendered. France could not hope to survive the exodus of the Allied forces and on 25 June also surrendered, a few weeks after Italy declared war on Britain and France. The humiliation for France was total. Half of the country was to be put under occupation.

In England we heard of these events with mounting dismay. Seeing them on newsreels was worse. The evacuation of Dunkirk, which gave us so much joy and hope, was – we had to remind ourselves – a victory actually born out of defeat. London opened its biggest air-raid shelter to cater for 11,000 people. Sir John Anderson introduced prefabricated shelters of corrugated iron, made in sections to be bolted together. They were distributed for use in back gardens or anywhere else where there was space to spare.

By the summer of 1940 Britain was Hitler's only remaining enemy. A rumour circulated that German troops were being issued with English phrase-books in preparation for a landing in Britain. My imagination ran riot, wondering which phrases they would use.

Much of our armour was rusting on the French beaches. The Home Guard were training with broomsticks because guns could not be spared. Australian and New Zealand volunteers were arriving but they needed time to train. Although conscription was now in force and 2 million men between the ages of 19 and 27 years were called up, invasion posed a threat with which the British army was not familiar. At any time we might have to face an air onslaught with only a handful of trained pilots to ward off the enemy. If those young men failed, what would be our fate? We held our breath and waited for the Germans to land on our shores.

At this point Churchill encouraged us with one of his famous wartime pieces of oratory, speaking a few trenchant words that put fire into our bellies. 'Let us therefore brace ourselves', he said, 'to our duties, and so bear ourselves that, if the British Empire and its Commonwealth last for a thousand years, men will still say, "This was their finest hour."'

Even before hearing those words, the most cowardly among us knew that we would never concede an inch of our land without the most fearsome fight.

27

THE 'BLITZ', 1940

The total strength of the German war machine was now focused on the defeat of Britain. Churchill was already setting up small resistance pockets in case the enemy should ever land on our shores. Echoing the feeling in everyone's heart, he declared on 4 June 1940: 'We shall defend our Island, whatever the cost may be, we shall fight on the beaches, we shall fight on the landing grounds, we shall fight in the fields and in the streets, we shall fight in the hills; we shall never surrender . . .'.

The first daylight raid on Britain by German bombers was a foretaste of what the future held. And what the future held was first the targeting of RAF airfields and radar stations. This preliminary strategy was designed not only to destroy installations, runways and aircraft but, just as important, to reduce the number of available pilots before the planned invasion of Britain. In those historic air battles the RAF was not easily to be destroyed. Though that small force of pilots was outnumbered in the air by four to one, they managed to destroy in one day alone ninety-nine enemy planes for the loss of twenty-two of their own. Seeing comparatively little return for their efforts, the German high command put invasion plans temporarily on hold and decided instead to demoralise England by air battles over London. This would force our obstinate island into submission and eventually into signing an armistice. Why should – and more to the point – how could Britain hold out against the whole weight of the German Luftwaffe? In effect, as soon as Germany decided against destroying Britain in the air, the Battle of Britain was won. Churchill acknowledged this in his tribute to the bravery of those young RAF pilots on 20 August: 'Never in the field of human conflict was so much owed by so many to so few.'

Germany sent its first wave of bombers on the late afternoon of 7 September. Some 350 of them, escorted by almost double that number of fighters, let loose their devastating load over London. Before long, it seemed as if the whole city was in flames.

Two hours later a second group of raiders, guided by the fires lit by the first, began another attack. And so it went on, night after night, the hideous wail of air-raid sirens, followed by the noise of planes, bombs, anti-aircraft guns. In that first night more than 400 people were killed and 1,600 badly injured. Thousands more were made homeless.

If you were unlucky enough to be in the wrong place, you saw large parts of London on fire. Not far from my home in Bethnal Green, St Paul's cathedral stood out against the flaming red sky with Wren's mighty dome seemingly immune from the flames around it.

Everywhere you saw devastated buildings. You might hear the screams of the injured; more unlucky still, you heard nothing or were screaming yourself.

That was merely the beginning of what became known as the 'blitz', a period of intense bombing that lasted almost unceasingly for the next 8 months.

War, perversely, had a liberating effect on many women in the UK. Their labour was needed to produce munitions in the factories, to take over men's places in farms (Women's Land Army), to assist them on gun sites (Women's Army Auxiliary Corps), in the Royal Air Force (Women's Auxiliary Air Force), where they did magnificent work on photographic interpretation, particularly in pin-pointing the V-bomber site at Peenemünde, and as intelligence officers to help at Bletchley in unravelling the mystery of the Enigma code and other intelligence. Voluntary services, largely made up of women, also helped the war effort in all manner of ways. Conscription would come in later for unmarried women, but for the moment, it was just a case of carrying on with our normal jobs.

Nobody was immune from the enemy. Maggie and her fiancé decided to bring forward their wedding date. I was invited to be a bridesmaid. My friend Frank, now promoted to Leading Aircraftman Hawthorne, and suffering the full weight of the Luftwaffe's assaults on RAF airfields, could not come. He still continued to write, especially now that all leave was cancelled.

Maggie's wedding took place east of Bethnal Green at St Margaret's Catholic church in Canning Town, where Charlie had found a small home for them to rent. It was a lovely if slightly worrying occasion. The bridesmaids, including me, had pinky-mauve long satin dresses and little bouquets. The men wore their best suits, smartened up for the occasion. As Maggie came down from the altar, her happy dimpled face was alight with love. At the wedding breakfast there was no sign of the austerity and rationing soon to come. This was the pattern for any happy occasion, to make it really joyful, with food looking as good and plentiful as in peace time. She and Charlie were to survive the war and have a fairly long and happy life together, with seven children, four boys and three girls.

What came during Maggie's wedding celebrations that afternoon was the wail of an air-raid siren. In our finery we rushed for shelter and then . . . was that a salvo of bombs? Under what seemed a horribly thin roof every tiny noise reverberated and echoed with all the power of a Big Ben carillon. I bowed my head more in fear than in prayer. How I hoped for Maggie's sake that we could get through this day at least. I thought how terrible a fate it would be to be bombed on your wedding day, whereas many people might think that the most wonderful way to go. The all clear signal fortunately came only a few minutes after our descent into our underground shelter.

We did not emerge entirely unscathed. Our clothes, covered with dust and debris, sustained the most obvious physical damage. The mental ones went deeper. Being cloistered for even a short time in the air-raid shelter on Maggie's wedding day brought on a burst of severe introspection. At the age of 22 what had I seen? Gone round Britain on a bike and spent a few weeks, purblind, in Germany. What had I done? A few articles in newspapers and magazines all over the place that were probably never read and certainly would never change the world . . . though one on 'a cure for the cosh' introduced the idea of community service as a punishment for crime many years before the concept became actuality.

What did any of that matter? In total the only contribution I had made to the community so far was towards the Guide movement, steering young people into new skills and offering them cheap and interesting holidays. The latter were in any case usually helped by the owners of the estates we occupied: Lord Treowen in Abergavenny (where I swam 100 times round his fountain) and Battle Abbey, where Lady Brassey made us so welcome. Unlike our Guide Captain Edith Clay, who was already a nun, I had made no sacrifices or commitments.

Now in the summer of 1940 I felt an overwhelming wave of despair, as if enveloped in a black mist out of which nothing could be seen, nothing felt nor heard. Your hands fought and struggled to get out of the miasma. In vain. There was no escape. I could never change the world or even part of it. Tomorrow the landscape as I knew it might disappear altogether. How could anybody look forward to a future? What future was there? I must live for the day. It might be the last I should ever know.

Throughout 1940 the East End of London received the lion's share of the bombing, though Buckingham Palace, the British Museum and the Prime Minister's official home at 10 Downing Street were all damaged. Even during a radio transmission from Broadcasting House, a bomb exploded. St Paul's escaped the fire raging round it, which seemed to be a miracle.

Buses continued to take people to work, though they might have to avoid the bomb craters which appeared overnight. Rescue services coped magnificently and 'business as usual' was the watchword. My mother never used the Anderson shelter which Dad had rigged up (don't ask me how) in the back garden. She could not bear the noise of the bombs. If she were working in the hospital she totally ignored everything going on outside, no matter how loud. She just carried on with her work, as if the hospital conferred a kind of immunity on its workpeople. But to sleep in that 'Anderson' in our tiny back garden . . . no, nothing would induce her.

Every night she went off to the underground tube shelter at Liverpool Street or Bethnal Green. My father rarely joined her there. There were all sorts of reasons, but primarily, in spite of his drinking, he was a rather private person, whereas my mother could be very jolly and mixed in with anybody who was not too 'common' and whose language did not offend.

My brother had now joined the Royal Air Force and was either in or on his way to South Africa for further training. That left my father and me at home. Our local newsagent, who had a shop at the corner of Gossett Street a few yards from our house, asked if he could use our shelter as he had no back yard, and consequently no nearby shelter in which to sleep.

I shall never forget his bravery, his complete disregard of the chaos around him, the way he came over, complete with alarm clock lest he should oversleep and be unable to distribute his newspapers punctually to his customers . . . and this at a time when, as darkness fell, the sirens almost immediately set up their wail to tell us of yet another wave of bombers over the city. It was hours before I ever fell asleep, and sometimes not at all.

Everywhere there was noise, bombs exploding, bells ringing to announce the arrival or departure of ambulances and fire engines, against a background of booming anti-aircraft guns. You might get up from a night spent in a tube shelter, pick your way across the rubble to go to your home, and find it no longer there. And here was our newsagent Mr Irons making himself comfortable as soon as darkness fell, ignoring everything around him. I was devastated when I learnt that his son had been killed in the mass prisoner escape from a German prisoner-of-war camp, but it was doubtless a case of like father, like son.

There was another man like Mr Irons that I remember, who worked in our department at Fanum House. He was a temp brought in at the outbreak of war, so I knew nothing of his background. He soon made it clear that he was not bothered by the 'blitz'. He was a Christian Scientist and his belief in an afterlife was so strong that it enabled him to face any kind of impending disaster with equanimity. He ignored air-raid warnings completely, and had an almost fatalistic approach to life, saying, 'If it's my turn, there's nothing I can do about it. So why should I rush about when I can get on with my work?' I too had become something of a fatalist, but my change of heart gave me no extra courage.

Seeing families, including the young children whose mothers refused to evacuate them to safer parts of the country, lining up in the early morning for the underground shelters, reduced me nearly to tears. Instead of getting hardened to this spectacle I grew daily more and more upset by it. By the time I arrived at work I was almost a nervous wreck, not at anything which had happened to me, but seeing what was happening to others. Our Christian Scientist cheered me up no end though I never sat out with him when the air-raid signals went. I so much admired his stoicism in the face of danger, and wished I could emulate it. But I couldn't . . . not then at any rate.

Meanwhile the United States was still not able to give us succour. Doubtless money flowed through the various banking conduits to land in England. Volunteer Americans could also be seen in the London streets, like the many others from all over the world who rallied individually to England's help. In the dying months of 1940 America sold a limited number of military aircraft to Britain, but until Japan bombed Pearl Harbor and brought America officially into the war, England stood besieged and alone.

In the last week of September, shortly after Maggie's wedding, Frank got a day's leave and met me in Hyde Park. He used to speak of it as his university, for in more peaceful days he often went to hear the stormy tirades of the open-air speakers.

It was a lovely autumn day with only a faint breeze whispering that summer had almost departed. A weak gleam of sunlight filtered through the clouds. Not all the leaves had yet been whisked away by autumn gales from the mottled bark of the trees. Those that had, lay mouldering on the ground in little heaps that tempted me to run through them and kick them all asunder before they were swept away by whoever was now tending the park.

Frank tells me that it was in that park he asked me to marry him. Sad to relate for the romantically minded, I do not remember the occasion at all. I remember only going home and saying to my father, without any preliminaries, 'I'm going to get married.'

My father responded in like manner. 'Is it to that chap who comes round here about an hour before you're supposed to go out?'

'Yes, that's right. Frank.'

'Didn't think it could be anybody else. Poor chap. Wants his brains tested.'

It wasn't Frank but me who wanted her brains tested. What had I done? Promised to get married to somebody I had seen less than half a dozen times, about whom I knew very little except where he lived and that he was a Catholic – which at that time in my life scored a lot of points. Indeed, like a *fromm* Jew, I could not have contemplated marrying anybody from another religion. Neither would I have looked at a married or divorced man, or someone who had 'played around'. One who had had a previous girlfriend, rather than several, might be even worse. But then marriage had never until that time even entered my horizon. It was something to be avoided at all costs.

Yet here I was thinking of tying myself for life, for that is what a Catholic marriage meant in 1940, to a young man about whom I knew practically nothing, not even his age. I did not even know what the physical aspect of marriage entailed, except a romantic notion I'd picked up somewhere that it was a kind of physical fusion. How that fusion took place, I hadn't the slightest idea, though after my helping Mrs Kelly's delivery in Bermondsey, I knew the consequences. I had no desire at all for babies; if such a prospect ever occurred to me, I put it out of my mind at once. I didn't fancy it at all.

To women of a later generation it may seem incredible that at the ripe old age of 23, I could be almost as naive as I was in my teens, but there were many women, even East Enders living in an area where Marie Stopes preached the doctrine of birth control to the unconverted, who at the beginning of the Second World War were just as naive as I. And convent-educated girls might have been able to rattle off a bit of Latin, but the word 'sex' rarely entered their vocabulary, certainly not within hearing of the nuns.

That virginal state did not survive the war. The influx of hordes of lonely soldiers using Britain as a base prior to going overseas soon dissipated any 'blissful' ignorance. The American GIs in particular, with their fascinating accents, their disproportionate pay and their lavish generosity in a period of acute austerity, proved irresistible, so it sometimes seemed, to the whole nubile population of the British Isles.

And where were all my noble aspirations to change the world . . . ? Gone with the first load of bombs. Marriage meant my independence disappearing down the aisle. The only world that was about to change, indeed be revolutionised, was my own.

28

WEDDINGS AND PARTINGS

ycling to work from Bethnal Green to Leicester Square in October 1940, I began to adopt a fatalistic attitude to the London 'blitz' and the daily scenes of devastation, at least during the daylight hours. There was little I could do about the carnage around me and I was on the verge of getting married.

Frank was in Hereford on a Group 1 electrical instructors' course. If he passed, he would be upgraded to Corporal Instructor. Somehow our marriage was arranged within the minimum period of six weeks from the banns being called. Why we should have acted so quickly, I can't think. Perhaps he was due for a posting overseas or perhaps, having agreed on marriage, we felt there was nothing to be gained by hanging about. The decision probably seemed to my parents and anybody else who knew of our intentions as if I had committed the awful crime of getting pregnant before marriage, and this quick ceremony was a good way of covering up a terrible mistake.

I cannot remember deciding anything about the wedding, but the arrangements must have been made by Frank or me. I certainly can't see either my parents or Frank's father doing any arranging. We were not going to be married in the bride's home district (Bethnal Green), as was customary, but by special licence in Hereford.

It is perhaps worth recording that a marriage which began on such a low key outlived the church where it took place. More than sixty years after we were married, we visited Broad Street, Hereford, and with a feeling of great sadness saw a board above the church advertising that it was for sale. Being in a very important shopping area, it was probably worth a good deal to a development company. We spoke to a man decorating the altar, who told us that the building was to be demolished. In fact, it was later rescued from this fate.

But in 1940 we were dealing only with the present. We knew nothing about the future. As far as I was concerned, I didn't even know if we would have one. That situation never entered Frank's mind. Always positive, his main consideration was how to get leave. He went round to all his Air Force friends trying to persuade them to forego their off duty entitlement: friendship indeed.

I had already given in my notice at work. As in teaching, no woman in those days was allowed to stay in the Civil Service after marriage. This ban on married women did not apply to any underpaid factory and similar jobs, and was rescinded in 1941 so that women could enter the labour force. Looking back, I am sure that there must have been many women who remained technical spinsters until they drew their pensions, by which time so many barriers had been broken down that women were allowed to work whether they were Mrs or Miss.

I was not allowed to claim the so-called marriage dowry which women received on leaving the Civil Service to wed. The reason given was that my service as a Savings Bank employee was less than the requisite six years. Weakling as I was in so many respects, injustice always infuriated me. I challenged the judgement and, getting no response, went to my MP, Sir Percy Harris. With his help, the Bank ruling was changed so that anybody who gave up her job to marry a serviceman due to go overseas (a requirement soon watered down) got her 'dowry'. Mine came a year later. This so-called marriage dowry was in effect a return of our pension contributions made over our working years. By taking it, as all brides-to-be did, we were unwittingly losing our pension entitlement. But who thinks about pensions when they are young?

Our wedding date was fixed by special licence for Saturday 12 October 1940. A Sunday was not available. That date had a certain advantage in that my birthday being a fortnight later made the disparity in our ages (three years) look more 'acceptable'. We were to have a nuptial Mass on Monday 14 October, an odd arrangement, but then everything about our marriage was odd. I found myself a new job as a kind of problem-solver to the remaining evacuees in the area (many had already returned home) – a job as odd as our wedding arrangements. I could hardly sort out my own problems, let alone those of others.

An oldish lady who had formerly catered for the ministers serving the needs of Hereford cathedral had just lost her visiting canon, and on my rounds almost dragged me into her house. Apparently afraid of getting one of those dreadful East End children billeted on her, she asked if I wanted a room to rent. I found her request like an answer to prayer without even having prayed. My eventual moving in became a chore we could both have well done without.

Frank and I booked bed and breakfast in a nearby hotel for my mother and Frank's widowed father. Sadly, my father could not get the time off work to come to the wedding. Even if he had, the travelling from Bethnal Green via Paddington or Euston to Hereford at that time, when he was in poor health, would probably have proved too daunting.

Wartime weddings displayed amazing ingenuity on the part of all involved. The bride-to-be, families and friends did everything possible to ensure that the big day should not suffer from the austerity that became gradually worse as the war progressed. In spite of severe shortages of material and food, a wonderful show was always put on, giving an extra piquancy to the day. Everybody piled in to help. The bride invariably came down the aisle looking beautifully attired in white, usually with an exquisite bouquet and attended by almost as beautifully attired bridesmaids.

The nuptial feast became a truly memorable one. Food rations saved for weeks were put to use with imagination – dried eggs, dried potatoes and soya flour. The wedding breakfast table lacked nothing. There was even a cake, sometimes of several tiers, which could well have graced the Savoy or Ritz in peace time.

British weddings during the Second World War were a good example of how some people transform a situation in which they find themselves. I found another example of this ability in a transit camp where I once had to stay between the many moves I experienced throughout the war and a couple of years afterwards. The windows of all the wooden huts in which I then lived for short times had old navy blue curtains. Nobody liked them but as we all hoped our 'residence' in the huts would be short-lived (unlike our own existence) we did nothing about the navy curtains, just put up with them – all of us, that is, except one woman. It may have been against the rules to interfere with the 'furnishings' in case they infringed the 'blackout' by letting the interior lights shine out. If so, she ignored the rules, made sure of her own blackout precautions and took the ancient navy curtains down. Having washed them, she managed somehow to bleach them and then enliven them with bright decorative motifs. Her hut stood out among all the others. If any stranger wanted to find her, he or she was told to go to the hut with embroidered white curtains. Naturally enough she became the spokeswoman for all of the women in the camp.

I had no intention of getting 'dressed up' for my wedding, having a faint intimation, almost a hope, that my marriage to Frank would never take place. This may seem very strange to the romantically minded, but marriage was such a tremendous leap in the dark that I felt anaesthetised, in a trance. Some mysterious force was pushing me into a place where I did not want to go, yet I was absolutely powerless to turn back. This feeling may be similar to that of those men or women who sense they have a 'calling' to the religious vocation, but fight and rebel against the idea before eventually 'caving in'. And I have heard of brides who turn back at the altar – a horribly cruel thing it seems to me to do – yet marry the same man afterwards, sometimes several years later.

I was certainly not going to wear a white dress, veil and all the trimmings. I would wear my normal brown coat of a rather nice bouclé wool material. It was trimmed with a bit of imitation fur round the collar and fitted rather well. Round my head, I would tie a brown scarf in a turban fashion as my very fine, not to say thin, hair was always such a nuisance. I went so far as to buy a new pink dress of no particular merit, except that the colour seemed to suit me.

The choice certainly didn't suit my mother.

'Pink!' she exclaimed when she saw it. 'Whatever made you get a pink dress? You know what they say about pink . . . old maid's last chance.'

Last chance or not, that was what I intended to wear. Then at the station she gave me her second and final bit of sexual advice. She looked round furtively. Lowering her voice in case anybody around the station could overhear this erotic conversation, she whispered, 'Have you got a nice nightie?'

'Yes, yes,' I replied hastily and got on the train.

That, along with the botany I learnt at school, was the sum total of my sexual education. Over a lifetime such lack of knowledge has done us no harm.

Frank managed by a combination of bribes and threats to get weekend leave, four coloured chits giving him four days' leave – a real luxury in war time. Our Saturday wedding ceremony was very low key, similar I imagine to the plainest of register office marriages. Walking down the aisle to the front of the church, nobody with me, I experienced moods of such acute elation and depression it was like being desperately intoxicated. What was happening? What was I doing? I could not believe that I was getting married. I must get out now, and think over this step once more. Soon it would be too late. But it was already too late. Frank came out of the front pew in which he was waiting, and stood by my side. He looked so happy, so proud, I felt almost guilty. Had I led him astray, used feminine wiles to get him to the altar? No, I knew that, whatever had prompted us both to the altar, that at least was not the reason. We must have said the right words, signed the right papers, because we got the wedding certificate, which we still have.

After the ceremony we walked down to Hereford cathedral to have our photos taken. St Xavier's church, where we tied the knot, had a rather poor entrance and in spite of being a 'pukka' Catholic church, did not provide such a handsome backdrop as did the twelfth-century cathedral's lavish walkways. Frank's father, my mother, Frank and I all looked exceedingly happy and made an attractive foursome. Then we went back to the hotel where we had booked rooms for our respective parents, and enjoyed a wedding breakfast of sorts.

I draw a discreet veil over our wedding night: we were both virgins with a lot to learn. Frank was kind, passionate and emotional. Suffice to say I was not quite the best of respondents, but as I have mentioned earlier, he was a good teacher. If there is chemistry in love, I sadly lacked it, but fortunately Fate had provided me instead with a Bunsen burner. Sometimes over the years as the result of a tempestuous gale the light flickered to such a tiny flame it seemed on the verge of dying out altogether. In a different kind of weather, it burns with the dazzling brightness of a lighthouse beam. Historian Lady Longford, married for over fifty years, and whom I met much later, was once asked if she ever contemplated divorce. 'Never,' she replied, 'but murder often.' That sums up our early married years.

Monday morning when we had our nuptial Mass was quite a different occasion from the Saturday ceremony. Our parents had gone home and we were on our own in the church, save for a few regular and obviously very devout attendees. I did not feel so anaesthetised in this ceremony as I did on Saturday. The realisation had dawned somewhat painfully that I had made a commitment. Come what may, for better or worse as promised in the ceremony, I must stick by it. My life now would radically change. Too late for any regrets, for all the changes I would now never make in the world. I had to get on with the rest of my life, a different existence that would be tied up with Frank's. Of one thing I was sure, it would never be boring. He was scientifically gifted, full of ideas and would bring new interests into our life together. If he moved upwards, so would I, if down . . . well I wasn't sure about that. As I walked out of the church, a well-wisher came out of her pew. She gave me a little statue wrapped up in tissue paper and said, 'It's just a thought, my dear; just wanted to wish you a long and happy married life together.'

The news of the wedding had probably been announced in the notices of the week. Otherwise how had a complete stranger not only known of our wedding, but even packed up a little gift for the unknown bride? Or perhaps she was a regular churchgoer and had seen our marriage on the previous Saturday. Whatever the reason, her gift and good wishes provided an elation and excitement out of all proportion to the value of the gift. It somehow uplifted me with happiness that lasted not only for that day but for many weeks afterwards. Her good wishes have certainly come true over the intervening years.

Frank went back to camp that evening so we had a passionate farewell (we were learning fast) in our rented rooms. Then he left and I was alone. He came home for some weekends afterwards but during the intervening days and empty weeks I found that being even a part-time housewife was an occupation for which I had little interest and even less talent. Frank soon came to share that belief. Trying to cook a carrot cake I translated cloves in the recipe into cloves of garlic. He tried his best to eat the finished product but gave up after a mouthful or two. A few burnt offerings cooked on the landlady's stove revealed my ineptness even more. But the *coup de grâce* almost came when I ironed his uniform trousers and put the crease in the side instead of in the front. We had to put the trousers under the mattress to remedy the mistake.

That I had to share the kitchen with the owner of the house and take our meals from there, through her living room and into our own rented room, was not the best way to begin married life. Quite apart from the danger of accidents carrying hot soup or stews down a long corridor from one room to another, there was an unstated bar on Frank entering the kitchen. This was not so much an interdict put down by the aged owner

– she would probably have welcomed a chat with a young man. But until Jamie Oliver and other TV chefs altered the picture, it was very unusual for any man, other than a professional chef, to enter a kitchen – almost equivalent to emasculation. As for cooking anything, even an egg, that was almost as bad as pushing a pram: so unmanly it was enough to make a man the laughing-stock of all his mates.

Had I started married life with a kitchen we could call our own, who knows what might have developed. But that was the situation I inherited. It lasted for years until, spurred on by one of the children, Frank decided to make his own bread. He did it perfectly, keeping the family entertained throughout the whole process from beginning to end. Furthermore it was excellent bread. Truth impels me to say he never repeated the experiment.

My many imperfections as a houseworker meant this was not the life for me and I fear it was not the life for Frank either, though he never groaned about it at all. The part-time job I held as a kind of conciliation officer for evacuees came to an end as the children settled down more happily or slowly filtered back to the areas from where they came.

I pottered around Hereford for a bit, then managed to obtain a job in a greengrocer's. Apart from the minuscule wage, the only advantage of this lowly paid job was to ensure that, with rationing becoming more stringent, I could get an onion or two – and our landlady certainly loved her onions. I was also first in the queue for any luxuries like bananas, but standing out in the cold all day, my fingers froze so much I could hardly weigh anything accurately. I did not last with the greengrocer for very long, looked round for something better, and briefly contemplated joining the forces. Doing this when Frank was still in England did not seem a sensible option. Even if I could not provide gourmet dinners, there might be alternatives I could offer to a serving airman. Six weeks later all options closed. I discovered I was pregnant.

29

HOME FIRES BURNING

My first reaction on realising I was pregnant was utter disbelief. It was almost impossible to take this idea on board. Then I remembered my mother's one bit of sexual instruction. During a certain time in the month, I should not wash my feet. Only twice in a woman's life did this law not apply: when she was expecting a baby or had turned 50 years of age. Well I wasn't 50 yet, and had long since discarded the idea of not washing my feet at a certain time in the month (where did she get that idea from, I wonder?). Only one possibility remained. No matter how unbelievable or indeed how unwelcome the truth, I was pregnant.

Frank's reaction to the news was similar to my own, but he took it more calmly. Against his job of servicing aircraft damaged by enemy flak quickly enough for pilots to go on another mission, my revelation was comparatively trifling. Until we had built up our army or supplemented it by overseas aid, the RAF was England's only defence against the enemy attempting to land on our shores.

Abortion never even remotely occurred to us. We were wedded not only to each other but to the Catholic faith. Frank needed to do nothing and there was little he could do outside his job. What should I do? Except for getting confirmation of what I knew to be true, nothing also seemed to be the answer. So for the moment, life continued as normally as it could in war time. I thought of returning to Bethnal Green. Apart from Frank's presence and the cathedral with its famous Mappa Mundi, what was there to hold me in Hereford? Apples, cider and sheep?

Premature partings always happen in war time, yet leaving Hereford and a new husband seemed an odd thing to do so soon after getting married. A few months later a solution appeared. Frank was promoted to Sergeant with a posting to RAF Henlow. That meant I could go back to London and get a job for a few months before my protruding belly revealed I was not alone. Meeting Frank was fairly easy in Bethnal Green. Henlow was not all that far away, certainly more accessible than Hereford.

We spent Christmas Day with my parents. It was as joyful as the festival, peppered with bombings, could be in war time. Lucky to get any leave at all, Frank had to go back to base shortly after our ersatz Christmas pudding. Mum went to Liverpool Street tube, Dad, Mr Irons the newsagent and I into the Anderson shelter, preparing for the nightly bombing attacks. Both my parents had jobs. Mum was still a cleaner at the Hackney Road Children's Hospital, which had mercifully survived the bombing. Dad was also working, cutting up steel bars in Whitechapel, and my brother was training in South Africa.

For the first few weeks of the year 1941, I found myself on my own for most of the day. That suited me fine. While looking for a job I could write a few articles for the provincial and Catholic press. As well as the *Catholic Herald*, I also had a few pieces in the *Catholic Times* and *The Universe*, but the *Herald* seemed to be more interested in questions of social justice. That's where I sent the odd article whenever I got a spare moment. Humour, such as it was, went to either the *Liverpool Post* or the *Birmingham Post*, where I got the comment (from which editor I can't remember): 'Like to see more of your work, without prejudice.' What that implied I didn't quite know, but I welcomed the chance to earn a bit of pocket money.

Frank had been allotted a marriage allowance. It was usually given only to older men in uniform. Now the ruling changed to take cognisance of earlier marriages occasioned by war. Similar to the small sum paid to servicemen who supported their parents, it stopped me from feeling too dependent on my husband for my keep. Though early impoverishment made me fearful of taking risks, our East End immigrants – and particularly my Jewish friends – passed on a more useful lesson: the importance, for women, of aiming for some financial independence. This trait I also copied from my mother. She was a wonderful manager and would have to be almost facing starvation before she would allow herself to ask for anything from anybody, even from my Dad, the most generous as well as the most feckless of men. He would give away the clothes on his back to anybody he thought more needy.

The East End was still feeling the full weight of the London 'blitz', as I found at home. My mother took her nightly outing to the underground shelter, usually at Liverpool Street, occasionally at the Bethnal Green tube. Meanwhile, in between the 'scribbling' I also practised some cooking, without too much risk to home and hearth. I need not have worried about home and hearth. They disappeared shortly after my arrival.

One evening my father said he would pop out to the pub with his brother, John. Bethnal Green probably had more pubs in the main road than any other place in Britain. Uncle John had moved with his wife and two children from a tenement building in Whitechapel to a house in our street, a few doors away from our own. I decided to visit an old friend from St Anne's.

Dad told me later about his evening. He and his brother had a few drinks and then started homewards. For a change, the night began quietly. A few stars dotted the sky. Suddenly a noise erupted. A huge firework soared upwards. Flares and flames lit up the streets. The men recognised the signs at once: incendiaries! A fusillade exploded nearby, bringing with it an unreal daylight. Looking round they saw what appeared to be the only shelter, a brick-built lavatory. Rushing in, within seconds they were pressing their hands to their ears to drown the noise of bombs coming down, one after the other, hardly a second apart. The floor trembled with the impact.

'God! Look at that!' said Dad pointing upwards. The sky was filled with blinding flashes followed by flames, flashes and more flames. They stared at the spectacle, more in awe than in fear. Then came a moment of menacing quiet. Like men in the trenches, they waited, immobile, for the next threatening salvo. Nothing. Everything was still, the sudden silence almost more threatening than the bombing, as if somewhere, an unseen enemy was preparing for a final push. Could they dare venture out? Looking up, the brothers suddenly realised, probably having had more than their fair share of drink, that the only reason they were able to see the sky in flames was because the so-called 'shelter' had no roof. They rushed out, laughing all the way home, in spite of more bombs spitting down unmercifully.

I got back earlier than Dad. My mother usually stayed all night in the underground shelter, going straight off to work at around 6.30 in the morning to be at the hospital at 7.00 a.m. It was only a 10 or 15 minutes' bus ride if she went to Liverpool Street, but you always had to be prepared for the worst. I realised that truism even more as I turned the corner of our street. Firemen were playing a spume of water on a row of houses, our own among them. Like the adjoining ones, it appeared to be a sizzling mass of rubble. Hissing noises came from the blackened structure. Fire bombs had caught the outermost house, the blaze spilling over into the others. I moved closer. The upstairs part of our house was damaged beyond repair. The downstairs half had not quite gone up in smoke. It was still too hot to venture inside, though the front door was still standing. At first it appeared that nothing could ever be retrieved from the wreckage.

My few possessions were gone: a doll won in a raffle years ago, the 'Chummy Book' presented to me on behalf of the Duchess of York (now Queen) on the occasion of her visit to the Children's Hospital, the library of books willed to me by the old lady for whom I read her son's letters from America. My mother later recovered some items, including two pieces of furniture given to her by the Waterman family for whom she had worked long ago . . . our great big round kitchen table and a glass and mahogany cabinet of which she was inordinately proud, boasting that it had come from 'Lord Earl Delaware', whoever he might be. My father had nothing of his own except his clothes, including a mac given to him (via my mother) by the same mysterious 'Lord Earl Delaware'.

As our house was now without a roof and almost uninhabitable, we were offered temporary accommodation in a school. One word aptly describes it: awful. But it was not for long. I tried staying in the underground shelter in Liverpool Street with my mother. Much as I loved the camaraderie, the feeling of fellowship that we were all in this together, everybody wanted bombs to rain down on Germany with even greater force than those dropping on us. How could they wish to inflict the same terrible suffering on others? What a prig I was and, with a husband in the RAF, how illogical too. What other reaction could one expect? But I never went into a communal shelter again.

Though the upper half of our house was a shell, we could still access the air-raid shelter in the back garden as well as the water supply. 'Roughing it' in the back garden where the Anderson shelter was still standing with our bunks inside, Dad and I got by. People were now leaving London in droves, searching for rooms and houses elsewhere, so it was not hard then to find other accommodation. The downstairs half of a house in our street became vacant. We moved in: one bedroom for my mother and father; one for me with the huge 'Lord Earl Delaware' cabinet installed by the side of the put-u-up bed; and a kitchen with 'outhouse'. So far, so good.

It was now February 1941. The Germans were no longer content with bombing only our capital. Liverpool had already suffered the attentions of the Luftwaffe, with one of its air-raid shelters having received a direct hit in November 1940. It killed 160 people. Other cities, too, felt the German onslaught. In Bethnal Green we concentrated on our own safety . . . but not for long. In May 1941, Liverpool suffered another attack, becoming, other than the capital, the most heavily bombed city in

England. Eventually 4,000 people died, 10,000 homes were destroyed and 70,000 people made homeless. The reason for the port city's heavy bombardment was clear – the docks and convoys of ships with vital supplies. If we couldn't be bombed out of existence, we should be starved. What the German air forces failed to do, their submarines nearly did.

I had temporarily gone back to a job in Leicester Square, not the same one, but still busy with rationing problems. What would happen when the baby arrived, I had no idea. I had visited no doctor, and for the moment stayed put. Frank then came up with a solution to our housing problem. He was to do this many times in the war years, appearing on the scene like some Galahad rescuing a beleaguered damosel, a role he greatly enjoyed as I did, too. He found me accommodation in Hitchin, quite near his RAF station, with the Steanes: corporal, wife, two children and their granny. They were Irish, a wonderful, generous-hearted couple to have taken in a pregnant mum. The granny was particularly lovable, an endearing character that epitomised for me all the characteristics a granny should have: small, grey-haired, an ever smiling face, incredible patience not only with small children, kind, totally unselfish and with a fund of fascinating memories about the Ireland she once knew. Perhaps I expected a granny to be some kind of saint. She filled the part admirably. Grannies of the twenty-first century look very different – young, smart and efficient.

When the war ended (when would that be?) the family might be comparatively well off. They owned a house in Barrow-in-Furness which they let when they moved to Hitchin. For the time being they appeared to be content with their cramped quarters, which became even more cramped when Frank and I moved in.

The war news grew worse. Under the provisions of 'Lend Lease', the US were now giving England 'all help short of war', which meant ammunition and other supplies. Germany was not halted. Her soldiers invaded Greece and Yugoslavia. One month before our baby was due, they crossed into the Soviet Union, and besieged Leningrad. Britain joined up with the Soviets in a pact of 'mutual assistance'.

That summer, July 1941, was one of the hottest on record. Being pregnant was not physically pleasant. I thought sometimes of the soldiers waging war in the desert. In that inhospitable terrain it must be infinitely worse than being a heavily pregnant woman in the heat of summer. And what about the merchant navy, plying through the freezing waters to get to and from Murmansk and other Russian ports? If the U-boats torpedoed your ship nobody would stop to pick you up. You were just left to drown in the icy seas. As usual, the thought of other people's troubles does little to minimise your own.

I visited the local clinic, where they booked me a bed for the confinement date prophesied to be in July. In that month, while I was at the clinic, my waters broke. Did that mean the baby was imminent? I was told to go home and that the baby would arrive any minute. It did not, and it was days before the first pains of childbirth gripped me. I wish so much I had been able to meet my little newcomer and all the rest of my children with the 'Welcome to the World' greeting which I heard a woman give to her newborn baby on television. It sounded so wonderful, a greeting all mothers would like to give their newly born children.

But I just couldn't. It never even occurred to me. In the Book of Genesis are the words 'in sorrow shalt thou bring forth children', and it certainly seemed that having a child was the most painful and long-drawn-out business possible to suffer. I did not realise how quickly the memory of the pain would go. If that memory did not vanish so quickly, nobody would surely have more than one child.

Childbirth pangs were aggravated for me by a rash that appeared all over my body, apparently due to an allergy caused by the drenching of my nether regions with some kind of antiseptic solution.

Frank bought me a huge second-hand pram from a man whose wife had died in childbirth, hardly a happy omen. Unlike the poor woman who had bequeathed it to us, it proved almost indestructible, however. It transported our children and our belongings to various houses throughout the United Kingdom and later to and from Germany, eventually ending up years later as a garden plaything. Meanwhile the pram served us well as a downstairs cot in the Hitchin house where I returned about a week after coming out of hospital.

Francine, as we named our little newcomer, was not the quietest baby then living. Night after night I got up to carry her downstairs away from the other bedrooms, so that she shouldn't wake up the landlady and her family. It was freezing cold downstairs without heating of any kind. I nursed and fed the baby for hours before she fell asleep and I could go up to bed. Sometimes I even fell asleep myself on the sofa. Frank had to come down and retrieve me, like a lost handbag. The situation was not easy and eventually I returned with Francine to Bethnal Green.

There seemed no prospect of the war ending. Our shipping was being sunk at a terrible rate in the Atlantic and the Arctic by German submarines. The desert war was not going our way either. Mussolini had linked up with Hitler, and late in 1940 the Italian forces had invaded Egypt. North Africa was strategically important because it was the only land-based area from where we could take the fight to the Axis powers of Italy and Germany. In February 1941 the British and Commonwealth forces, particularly the Australians, forced the Italian Tenth Army to withdraw, and almost pushed them out of North Africa. 'Never has so much been surrendered by so many to so few,' quipped Anthony Eden. That situation did not last long. Hitler sent Rommel to stop the rot. Tank warfare must have been particularly gruesome, but fighting in those fiercely inhospitable desert sands he earned the devotion of his men, the respect of the enemy and the conquest of much of the North African terrain.

Those of us at home became more and more depressed as the bad news kept coming, muted of course, from almost every front. Though the RAF was fighting the threat to us from the skies, the only 'victory' so far was Dunkirk. Yet in spite of the deluge of bad news never once did I or any other person then living in Britain have the slightest doubt that one day we would win this terrible war. Only one question remained. When?

30

DISASTERS ON ALL FRONTS

'How could such a thing ever have happened?' Americans asked each other in the evening of Sunday 7 December 1941. On that day, shortly after 8.00 a.m., Pearl Harbor was attacked by the Japanese Imperial Navy in what must be regarded as a brilliant military coup conceived months earlier by Admiral Isoroku Yamamoto. The strike force of 353 aircraft, led by Commander Mitsuo Fuchida, included dive-bombers and aerial torpedo planes. They launched their terrible onslaught on the ships in Pearl Harbor and airfields nearby. Though 29 Japanese aircraft were shot down by ground fire and by pilots from military installations, the episode, from the American point of view, was an unmitigated disaster. As with all disasters, if not God, somebody else has to take the blame. How could so large an attacking force fly to Pearl Harbor without being seen or questioned? Why were there so many ships all together in the dock, presenting such an easy target for a potential enemy?

The Japanese did not rest on their laurels. They occupied Malaya and Thailand, seized Shanghai and later invaded Burma and Hong Kong. Australians of the 2/20th Battalion Australian Infantry Force (AIF), New Zealanders, British and Dutch were captured in Singapore.

In Bethnal Green, as in the rest of Britain, we asked the same questions as the Americans about Pearl Harbor, but weren't so concerned with the answers. We knew that talks going on between the US and Japan had broken down. In the insular pattern of ordinary men and women caught up in any war, about its real causes we knew little – only the results. Having already lost friends and relations ourselves, we understood the agony of grief which so many Americans suffered after and during that incredible disaster of Pearl Harbor.

For us in Britain there was one mitigating factor – it must now only be a short time before America was caught up in the battle raging over Europe. The power of that country would soon bring the conflict to an end. This conclusion eventually proved rather more optimistic than everybody, including GI Joes, had hoped. Nevertheless a day after Pearl Harbor, Britain and the US declared war on Japan. Not to be outdone, Germany and Italy followed by declaring war on the United States. For better or worse, the Americans were now caught up in Europe.

In Bethnal Green we heard in January 1942 that the Australians had defeated Japanese attempts to take New Guinea and now felt safe from invasion. Code breakers discovered that Admiral Yamamoto (of the Pearl Harbor plan) was flying to the Solomon Islands. He was shot down and killed by US fighter pilots.

At home we were temporarily more concerned with domestic issues. Soap was added to the rationing list, which already included clothing and fuel. I thought I might be pregnant again, and again was not exactly ecstatic about it. At this stage my mother volunteered to mind our baby daughter Francine, now nearly 1 year old, while I went to the cinema with Annie, a Lithuanian friend of my schooldays in St Anne's. It was very uplifting to get away for a bit, and a real tonic to see the handsome Tyrone Power swaggering around, always triumphant, no matter what the odds.

Annie's family ran a successful clothing business on the top floor of their two-storey house a few streets away. I confided to her that I was probably pregnant. Single and unattached, she replied, 'Second baby? No problem. It'll almost drop out.' I wanted to believe her. Having a second baby must surely be easier than the first.

On the way back we heard the sound of enemy aircraft. Gruesome enough, it was still more cheerful than the pre-bomb-dropping silence of the V1 rockets that would be Germany's next 'secret weapon'.

'Quick, let's rush over to my place!' said Annie.

Her home in Teesdale Street was nearer than mine. We arrived there breathless. She fiddled with the key for priceless seconds, then pushed open the door. We dodged into the back yard and piled into the Anderson shelter. Already densely packed inside, her family were quite cheerful for the first few minutes of the bombing. As it continued, getting nearer and nearer with each salvo, morale worsened among everybody in the shelter. Strangely enough, I felt no fear, not even the slightest twinge; no fear at all.

'Not to worry. Not for us,' I kept saying at each blast . . . neither believing nor disbelieving it. I felt cocooned, detached from this scenario, merely repeating words to comfort the small girls and their mother sobbing in the corner. The next bomb was indeed for us . . . or so it seemed until we heard it plumbing down onto the houses nearby. The sound was deafening. It shattered our ear drums. Crumbling bricks whizzed out of the air like catapults. Great slabs of concrete fell onto the roof and by the door of our shelter, effectively pinning us inside. Cries for help surrounded me and, from our own group, yelling too. For some reason which I can still never explain, even hours later, when the screaming dwindled away to thin, pitiful calls for help like those of an emaciated kitten, I still felt completely unafraid and cheerful enough to keep morale fairly high, in spite of the fact that we might not be rescued for hours.

'Somebody will get us out soon,' I kept saying, quite uncaring whether somebody did or didn't.

We were eventually extricated from the rubble. Others in the street were not so lucky. Dead bodies and parts of them lay strewn around, while ambulance workers and fire fighters did their best to bring the street back to normal. I hasten to add that once in the street I was violently sick. Not too much courage there.

That experience, however, led to a wonderful offer from Annie's mother. She was so impressed by my behaviour in the shelter (having probably not seen me being sick in the street afterwards) that she offered me accommodation. It appeared that the family, with knowledge doubtless learnt from being immigrants, had bought an empty house almost for peanuts when everybody was fleeing from London. It was a big one in Wembley, north London, with three floors. The family weren't intending to live in it, so I could rent the entire first floor. It had a bathroom and two rooms, one overlooking the front of the house, the other at the side. I could wander where I wanted throughout the whole house, the big untended garden and the huge kitchen downstairs. What a wonderful stroke of luck!

Before I moved in, women older and wiser than less experienced Annie repeated what she had already told me, that having a second baby was much easier than the first. I believed them until Eileen Hook, our Mayor's daughter, discovered the hospital where I was having it.

Tactlessly perhaps, she said, 'That place! For heaven's sake, try not to go there. It's like a butcher's.' This was not exactly comforting news.

Frank at this time was on almost constant duty in readiness for the bombing of Berlin and other German cities. I hadn't seen and would not see him for many months, certainly not much before and after the new baby arrived. Meanwhile I moved into the Wembley house and was amazed, when rationing was already in place, to see the kitchen packed with enough food to last out a siege for years . . . great bags of flour and potatoes, huge tins of vegetables, sugar, fruit and soups. I hastened out in case this was a scene I shouldn't have witnessed, and almost as a penance, spent the next days and weeks tidying up everywhere, including the front garden. It looked quite attractive when finished, though I hardly knew the difference between a weed and a plant.

Furnishing the flat was hard but enjoyable. With savings from my bit of 'writing' money, I picked up some 'toots' for a few pence in places where I knew they were sold and was given or lent others. Though hardly likely ever to feature in an issue of *House and Gardens* or *Vogue*, I was very proud of the home I created.

Now I had to find somebody to mind Francine. She would be 18 months old when the new baby was born in February 1943. My mother could not get time off work without facing the sack.

Finding a babyminder was almost as hard as finding rooms. And that was hard enough. Get your extra pint of milk (government concession) for being pregnant, and if an eagle-eyed landlady found it on the doorstep, she would guess your 'secret' and ask you to leave within the week. Until I got a home of our own I never took any extra milk, inaction for which my bones paid dearly later on. The government eventually 'remedied' the housing situation (until it learnt a bit of common sense) by making tenancies fixed for ever. This ensured even fewer would come on the market and landlords would be tempted into all manner of dreadful stratagems to get possession of houses they had rented out.

A babyminder turned up in the wonderful person of an old lady living alone in a big house across the road. She said minding a baby would be company for her. I surely did not thank her enough. All was now ready for Francine's new brother or sister.

By what form of transit I got into hospital I can't remember. Petrol was rationed and I probably went in by ambulance. Arriving at the hospital, I was shoved into some scratchy gown and left on a stretcher in the corridor. After what seemed hours I was suddenly wracked by a terrific pain. A nurse arrived and wheeled me into the labour room.

Carried onto a stretcher, I felt my legs being tied. This was something totally unexpected. I looked up to see what was holding me. My legs were tied to stirrups at the bottom of a trolley. My knees hung over these contraptions, which were about 12 to 18 inches high, making wider the opening where my baby was to emerge. I felt absolutely helpless trussed up like this. 'Can you let my legs down, please?' I asked the nurse. She replied by a slap right across my face. Perhaps she had been worked off her feet, was at the end of her tether, perhaps she thought I was hysterical. That slap could certainly have made me so, for I was in no way able to retaliate and felt at the mercy of everybody in the room.

I cannot say it was an easy labour. After it was over, the new baby went into one ward and I into another. Cockroaches were crawling from the ceiling, a scene I never expected to see in a hospital. I fell into a kind of doze and woke to find myself soaked in blood. A certain amount of commotion ensued. Sounds and words like 'fever' and 'isolation' reached me through a fog. I was wheeled into an empty room. The baby was brought in for me to feed. Otherwise I saw nobody. I had picked up a non-infectious fever of some kind and would have to stay in hospital until my temperature went down. I had no intention of staying there and after a few days discharged myself and asked my father to take me home.

Poor Dad was completely inept at dealing with this kind of situation. No taxi for him . . . or me either. Why did I not take the bull by the horns and order one myself? Perhaps none was available. We went back to Wembley, picked up Francine, then went back to Bethnal Green the whole way by bus, not an easy journey, carrying a toddler and new baby, changing and waiting for buses in the depths of winter.

Between looking at the tiny frail creature I was bringing home and the little one so excited with the passing scene, I remembered the baby I once helped deliver. Mrs Kelly had obviously not played the 'Vatican lottery' and what was the difference? It certainly had not worked for me. Yet I still held on to the dicta of the Church. Religion rarely releases its grip on its believers until they are well past the age of reason, whenever that may be. I felt in the mood expressed by a little son of mine many years later when I met him after his first day at school.

'Was it as bad as you thought?' I asked him.

'No,' he said. Seeing my look of pleasure and relief, he added, 'No. It was worse.' That's how I felt after my second wartime delivery. I made up my mind then and there that if ever I should have another child, it would be in the maximum possible comfort even if I had to break the law or pay the earth.

That cold weather we experienced on our journey back to Bethnal Green was as nothing compared with what was happening at the same time in Russia. Having reached the gates of Moscow, the German troops, like those of Napoleon's in 1812, were also forced back by that invincible defender of Mother Russia: its winter. The Germans surrendered at Stalingrad in February 1943. In one of the bloodiest and bitterest campaigns of the war, no quarter was given. Men on both sides showed themselves capable of cruelty unimaginable. In the light of what they suffered, the misery of ice, snow and hunger, of burning homes and frost-bitten feet, who dared judge them?

The raid against Nuremberg, the last in the series between November 1943 and March 1944, resulted in the greatest loss suffered by any air force during the Second World War: 665 men. In North Africa the Germans and British were still slogging it out, with neither side completely able to outwit and defeat the other, whereas, with a few exceptions, the Japanese appeared to be carrying all before them in the Pacific hemisphere.

For the time being I stayed at home and did not return to the Wembley house. Like most East End mothers, I put the baby in the pram outside the house to get some 'fresh' air beside the pail of sand kept on all doorsteps as an emergency against fire. The big pram was in Wembley and we used instead a large doll's pram my mother found somewhere. We never worried about a baby being stolen in those fertile days. For some people it might sadly be 'a consummation devoutly to be wished', especially now that the GIs had arrived with their lavish generosity of all kinds when Britain was experiencing so much scarcity. More of concern to most mothers was the soot raining down from the 'fresh' air and covering pram blankets and much else.

The 'tummy button' of new baby Jennifer had not healed up when I left hospital. I had to dust it with a yellow powder after her daily wash in our little zinc bath. I put the yellow powder in its tiny carton on the chair nearby. Francine, intrigued with all these bathing preparations, accidentally knocked over the carton. All the contents, not readily available at chemists, were spilt on the floor. I was so utterly worried and distraught, I smacked her. It was the only time in my entire life that I ever smacked anybody. I never did again and this is the reason why.

When I went outside a little later to check up on baby Jennifer, she was covered with sand. Francine, doubtless hating this screaming arrival taking up so much attention and causing her to be smacked, had taken as much sand as she could from the pail outside and thrown it all over the 'rival'. And so I learnt a very interesting lesson in child psychology.

I soon learnt another, this time a sadder one, about adults. In our street and elsewhere the bombing was becoming less frequent. The 'blitz' had ended. People were trying to return to their London homes – rarely with any luck. Bombing raids and sirens were less often heard, but had not disappeared completely. Tit for tat raids were continuing between Britain and Germany. The East End was a barometer of the civilian population. If it could be demoralised, so would much else of Britain.

My mother still went out nightly to one or other of the underground shelters. The Bethnal Green tube was a deep level one and therefore considered particularly safe by most people. It was now rumoured that the RAF was going to take its bombers into the heart of Germany. Sure enough on 1 March it bombed Berlin. Everybody in the East End was alert to the high probability that the Germans would strike back even more fiercely.

Frank had been working almost non-stop to ensure that all the electrical equipment in our aircraft was properly serviced. He came back on Wednesday 3 March, having got a day's leave to see his wife and new daughter.

The evening started quietly with one or two of our guns showing their paces. As soon as my mother heard the noise she announced, 'I'm going off now'.

We begged her not to. 'It's dangerous to go out. You'll get caught in the flak,' Frank told her.

'Well, I won't go to Liverpool Street. I'll just pop along to Bethnal Green, then,' she said. 'That's not far to walk.'

'Stay here, Sue. It will be safer,' urged Frank. He knew that my mother was even more frightened by these noises from the sky than she was of thunderstorms. Neither did she like the Anderson shelter in the garden.

'You can go under the table,' Frank continued, pointing to 'Lord Earl Delaware's' reputed gift. 'And we'll all join you.' Dad added his persuasive voice and we all scrambled under the table. The crying babies were given a taste of gin or some other alcoholic drink and nearly passed out. We did not stay under the table very long, as it was far too cramped and uncomfortable, and went to bed. Tired out after many sleepless nights, we went off to sleep almost at once. Even my mother stayed at home. She went out as usual very early next morning but came hurrying back within the hour. She told us a grisly and almost unbelievable tale about an accident in the Bethnal Green tube shelter.

'Terrible,' she said, shaking her head. 'All them poor babies. And the mothers. Awful. I don't know how they can bear it . . . but I've got to get back. Just thought I'd let you know what 'appened there.'

'Good thing you didn't go out then,' I told her as she left for the hospital again, though I knew that unless she was at work, even such a disaster would not stop her from going to the tube whenever a raid started.

The accident at the Bethnal Green underground had apparently resulted in many deaths and injuries. Some of the casualties were brought into the hospital. The tale Mum told was hardly credible but I did not doubt it. I had seen the panic on the stairs in Brady Street buildings when an air-raid siren went off accidentally at the outbreak of war. Like Mum, Frank and my father also had to get back to work. I stayed at home, finding out as much as I could about this terrible disaster.

Apparently air-raid sirens wailed out their warning at 8.17 p.m. People poured off buses and out of cinemas to reach the tube before they were caught by the bombers. Within 10 minutes, 1,500 people went down safely into the shelter. At 8.27 there was a salvo of new anti-aircraft rockets, a sound unfamiliar to most people. Berlin had been bombed by us a few nights earlier. Fear that this sound might be the precursor of a dreadful retaliation caused a panic surge into the shelter. A woman carrying a baby tripped near the bottom of the nineteen steps. Her fall caused a domino effect. Unable to move or to be seen because of the blackout, the plight of people on the ground was invisible to those above. They continued to press forward.

At the inquiry into the disaster, the magistrate said that the 'stairway was converted from a corridor to a charnel house in from ten to fifteen seconds. Death was, in all cases examined, due to suffocation and the vast majority showed signs of immense compression.' 173 people died: 27 men, 84 women and 62 children. A further 62 people were taken to hospital. Little knowledge of the disaster leaked out, as it was thought by the War Cabinet that any publicity about the incident would give it 'a disproportionate importance, and might encourage the enemy to make further nuisance raids'.

Not a bomb had fallen; not an enemy aircraft entered the sky. Panic killed the victims. Yet the unfinished tube shelter had room for 9,000 people, with bunks for 5,000.

Unlike other wartime disasters, this one did not leave survivors glad they had survived. Many felt guilt. They had held babies who got crushed to death while they survived.

It is not easy to answer questions like 'How did you get out all right, when my baby is dead?' In some cases, being unable to give an answer meant families never speaking to each other again for years afterwards.

I did not like leaving the Wembley house empty, so went back again, soon after the disaster at Bethnal Green, and was surprised to see that Annie's family had now moved in. They first thanked me for making the house and garden look so presentable, then told me they needed the first floor. Would I kindly move upstairs? This was an attic floor of two small rooms, with no water and no lavatory except in the bathroom downstairs.

I said that I had furnished and carpeted the two rooms she had given me, and it would be very difficult to transfer.

As good fortune would have it, at this point Frank arrived to take up residence. He was due to take an RAF course at the Polytechnic in London's Regent Street. If he passed, there was every chance of him becoming an officer. His arrival eased the situation with Annie's family and for the time being (everything in war time was for the time being) we stayed where we were. But I knew it would not be for long.

Frank passed his exam and, almost like a Christmas present, in December 1943 got his promotion to Pilot Officer. We went 'up west' with the two small children to celebrate, had a bite to eat, then picked up his uniform, the cost of which depleted our savings almost to nil. It was packed very nicely into a suitcase for us by the outfitters and we happily boarded the bus back to Wembley. Imagine Frank's dismay when he picked up the only suitcase remaining on the bus and knew by its weight that it was empty. It was Saturday night, he had no uniform and was due to report for his first posting as an officer on Monday morning.

31

MOVING TIMES

It was getting late. Frank suggested I stayed with the children at Wembley. Annie's family were spending Christmas at their home in Bethnal Green, so happily we would be on our own for a bit. Meanwhile he went off to the nearest police station in Savile Row and reported the theft, giving his name, address and other relevant details.

'Not much hope of getting your uniform back,' said the officer in charge. 'It's a common ruse at Christmas time.'

Frank looked surprised. Who would want to steal an officer's uniform . . . other than perhaps a spy? And then he remembered. In the uniform were a bar of chocolate as a present for the children, but more important were his wallet, identity card and a few unimportant papers. In the light of that knowledge, the theft looked even grimmer. Instead of going to a station as a newly promoted pilot officer he saw himself facing charges in a military tribunal.

'The crook gets on a bus,' continued the policeman. 'He carries an empty case, leaves it in the luggage compartment and waits for somebody else to get on the bus with a suitcase . . . not too long at this time of the year. As soon as he sees his chance, the crook nips off with your case and leaves his own. Bob's your uncle.'

The policeman spread out his hands as if in despair at man's cupidity and stupidity. Then he looked up at Frank and asked, almost as an afterthought, 'Got any kids, sir?'

'Two.'

'How old are they?'

'One baby and one getting on for two.'

'That's it, you see. Ideal. People with young children make the best victims.'

Frank raised his eyebrows.

'You see,' explained the officer, 'parents' eyes are generally more focused on their children than their goods. We'll let you know if anything turns up, but I don't hold out much hope. Still . . . '

When Frank got home, the children were in bed. We spent the rest of the evening wondering how he could get out of this terrible predicament. He just could not turn up at his new posting, somewhere in the north of England, in civvy clothes. To arrive in his airman's uniform was hardly a better proposition. With all the shops shut on Sunday, there was no possibility of buying another uniform, even if we could afford it. We stayed up until past one o'clock, waiting for somebody to call. Nobody did.

I tried St Jude again. No harm in trying, though he, like most of them up there in the heavenly kingdom, had probably forgotten us on earth.

We hardly got a wink of sleep that night. Perhaps it was just as well, for at about six o'clock on that Sunday morning came the sound of a huge rat-tat-tat on the front door. Frank answered it. A police officer stood outside.

'Good news, sir,' he announced. 'Your case has been found. If you'd like to come round to Savile Row, you can pick it up straightaway.'

Frank could hardly believe his luck. Spilling out questions one after the other, he asked where it had been found.

'They'll tell you all about it at the station. But it seems a policeman doing his round came across the case by a bridge near Wapping. If all the contents are inside, you can count yourself lucky. Though an officer's uniform wouldn't fetch much in the black market, the crook, whoever he was, could have thrown the case and contents in the river. Then it would have been a long time before anybody saw it again, if ever.'

Frank made a contribution to the police benevolent fund – gratefully received at Christmas time – and rushed off to the station. Not a thing had been taken from the case except the bar of chocolate. We were overjoyed.

The family came back soon afterwards. I was being edged out . . . understandably, I was an interloper, but where could I go? Frank went off to his new posting in the north of England. Not wanting to wear my parents out with my continual arrivals at their door, I answered an advert for a live-in job in a country house.

It was an absolute revelation to see how some people were 'enduring' this war. The man I assumed was my boss met me with his car at the station. I got in. He showed me a box he kept for collecting cash, to help so he said with his fuel costs. In spite of his piercing look, I hoped he didn't expect me, as the new domestic help, to fund his car.

The house in which he lived was an eye-opener. He and his wife had lost many of their pre-war staff and complained bitterly about how difficult it was to manage without them in war time. They didn't know the half of it. They still had a cook, a cleaner, a gardener and a butler who cleaned the silver over a sink separate from mine where I arranged the flowers. There was a huge garden full of fresh kitchen produce which helped these lords of the manor with their entertaining, though they grumbled incessantly that they could not do this as often or as lavishly as they would like. I was more or less a kitchen maid, expected to do some light housework, occasional cooking, serve the meals, take away the plates and wash them up.

All went well for about a week . . . and then disaster. I was bringing in some grouse – or it might have been pheasant – when a little voice called me. I looked down to see Francine. She had come out of her bed, opened the door of the dining room and was tugging at my skirt. She wanted a story. I told her to go back to bed. She started crying, loud and long. That was more or less the end of my vocation as a housemaid, and it was back to Bethnal Green again for all of us. At least the armies seemed to be gradually getting control in Europe, with British and American forces landing in Sicily and with Italy surrendering.

It was decided to evacuate our road. Dad and Mum weren't intending to move, but I thought I would go with the children. It meant more space for my parents and besides, we might be allocated lodgings in a pleasant country zone. No such luck. When I got off the coach on which we were transported away to safer areas I found myself in Leeds.

'Be careful of your belongings,' whispered the man in charge of our evacuation party – hardly a welcoming introduction to the council estate where we both got off. He knocked on the door of what looked like the least attractive house in the area. We waited until a woman came out, hair in curlers, two children by her waist and a baby in her arms.

'These the evacuees?'

He nodded.

'Bit earlier than I thought,' she said, pointing to the curlers in her hair. 'But glad you've come,' she added, looking at me. 'I was wondering how I could get on with an early shift tomorrow and nobody to look after the kids. You won't mind giving a hand will you? The two big ones, they're 6 and 8, will tell you where everything is. Well, you'd better come in.'

I went inside, accompanied by the officer in charge. He stayed only seconds, taking a few notes, and rushed away. Then I followed the landlady round the house, my spirits drooping with every step I took. Coward that I was, my tenure again lasted about a week. The woman doubtless had more 'guts' in trying to work in war time than did the lords of the manor I had recently met . . . and offering to take in evacuees as well. Having to look after a house and five children as well as my own was, however, a bit too much of a challenge at that time in my life, though I know she meant well.

The local school provided us with emergency accommodation – beds on the floor and the whole gamut of life under siege. Running round the big hall, the children loved it. I did not. A house then became available, occupied, so I was told, by just one other family, also evacuees. It sounded marvellous. Taken there by car, I got out to view our new lodgings.

It looked as good as you could expect in war time: a first floor room for all of us to serve as kitchen, bedroom and for every other purpose, a bathroom and lavatory along the corridor on the same floor. Then I met the other family, a mother and her two young daughters. Both children were suffering from TB. She worried constantly about whether they would ever recover and had been glad to be evacuated to a place near to all of Leeds's medical facilities and, except for the room which I had just been given, to have the run of a whole house. I comforted her as far at I could, but in the circumstances my presence in the house was not very helpful. I was taking up accommodation when, from the health point of view, hers was a far greater need. She and her children would surely be better off in a house of their own. I contacted Frank. He turned up again, in his gladiatorial guise, whisked us out (we got caught up in the Leeds tramlines) and drove us in a thick fog to rooms he had found on a Lincolnshire farm, fairly near his station.

The farmer's wife had a most peculiar habit of sniffing when she went by. 'I have a very good nose,' she once said in explanation. I felt her good nose might be more profitably exploited in the wine trade than on the visitors that crossed her path in the farmhouse. However, the days seemed more peaceful up here, so after surviving a few weeks and with my usual anxiety always to have a bit of spare cash for 'rainy days', I decided to try my luck as a teacher at the local Technical College. I explained to the Principal that I was a tenant at the farmhouse, could only work part time and might not even be reliable for those hours. Furthermore I could not guarantee to teach for a whole year.

'Who can guarantee anything these days?' he said. He was very short of teachers for the opening session next week and was glad to get anybody even remotely qualified. He didn't add 'such as you' as he could easily have done. On the appointed evening another fog hung over everything, this one so dense and thick it was difficult to see your own hand in front of you. Servicing bombers, Frank was on night duty almost continually. I left very early for the College, but had to bring Francine with me. Though the farmer's wife was quite happy for Jennifer to remain sleeping in her cot, there was no babyminder for a toddler. When I arrived, the Principal was not there, and not a soul recognisable as a teacher.

The students were milling around, at a loose end. If the teachers did not turn up soon, they might get a bit rowdy or head for home. After half an hour's wait, the student hubbub grew louder. How on earth I had the cheek I don't know, but I lined them all up in queues for their various classes, sent them into what I hoped were the appropriate rooms, gave them each the same exercise to write – something like 'What I expect to learn on this course' – and took what appeared to be the easiest lot along with me into a vacant room.

What I taught them I don't know, but they looked as if they were interested. Perhaps they should have joined the acting class. The Principal turned up some time later. He had been held up in the terrible fog, as were most of the teachers. They lived farther away from the College than I did. I apologised for the presence of Francine, sitting contentedly at the back of the class. 'She's probably the best of the lot,' the Principal whispered. He seemed to have been very impressed at the way I mustered everybody into classes, and I soon had a very well-paid job, by my standards, as a part-time lecturer. He gave me a reference, grossly exaggerating my minimal 'administrative and organisational ability'. Fortunately he had never seen me in the kitchen. Frank was not often at home, and I paid one of the daughters on the farm to look after the children. Everything went very smoothly for quite a long while, until the following April, when Frank came back one day saying he was about to be posted with yet another promotion to Flying Officer. I gathered he was going overseas.

With Allied invasions of Italy, the occupation of Sicily and the surrender of Italy, the war was going our way at last. I finished my stint at the Technical College, went back to my beleaguered parents in Bethnal Green, and began another almost impossible search for rooms. But this time I was lucky, really lucky. My cousin, the boy who had been locked in as a youngster to make sure he did his one hour's music session, had married a girl who lived with her mother and young child in a suburb adjoining Croydon. Anticipating her husband's return from the Far East – with an optimism that proved sadly misplaced – she was looking for a bigger flat than the pre-war one she now occupied.

The flat found for her by her mother-in-law (my aunt and Dad's sister) was too dilapidated, and with only two bedrooms, too small for her to consider moving from the comfortable maisonette she now occupied. Subject to the landlady's approval, she offered it to me. I took it on like a shot. In the kitchen, the worktop covered an ancient bath. There was a lavatory in the corner with two doors. One led into the small garden, the other from and into the kitchen. Although it made a very short cut from kitchen to garden, you had to be very sure that one or other of the internal catches of the doors was on, otherwise there could be embarrassing situations. The rent for me was hiked up to 27s 6d a week, to be paid in advance.

I was in heaven. In spite of the dilapidation, this first home had some wonderful features: the lovely marble fireplace, the conservatory which one day could be repaired, the tiny garden all our own. In the upstairs flat lived an old lady and her single daughter, both wonderfully kind. What more could we want? Peace on earth was the answer, and that looked as if it might soon be on the way. I pushed my huge pram up a hill to the fishmonger's and joined the queue for fish and chips.

'They've landed!' exclaimed the woman in front of me. I thought at first she was referring to the fish, not the allied landings in Normandy.

'The Americans too,' she added. 'Won't be long now. The men will be coming home soon.'

'Sorry for some of them,' said another. 'Did you hear about . . . ?' Then followed one of those bits of wartime gossip which, regretfully, I always enjoyed. Not now. I did not strain to hear it. I could only think of the men making those landings. The end of the war in Europe might be in sight, but God, how I feared for those men . . . how many would return? The Germans were not going to cave in so easily.

I found myself expecting another baby. This time, as I intended after the last, I was determined to have it in comfort and booked up at Fulmer Chase, in Buckinghamshire, a maternity hospital for officers' wives. In March came some more of those awful V1 and V2 bombs – but they were the last. We were not all that far from London. The children and I slept in the one bed, and never woke up all through the night, though the front windows were blown in and the glass strewn all over the eiderdown. Ceiling paper was torn down and there was further minor damage. Other than getting rid of the glass, and attempting unsuccessfully to repaper the ceilings, I did very little about it and made no attempt to move elsewhere.

The war in Europe ended on 8 May 1945. When all looked lost, allies gone or yet to come, the Royal Air Force in the Battle of Britain saved our island shores from invasion. That tremendous struggle when 'so much was owed by so many to so few', plus British grit and determination to hold on, effectively began Hitler's defeat. Helped by individual acts of bravery in many countries and institutions, Russian manpower and, later, American logistics at their brilliant best, came the allied invasion and final surrender of Germany.

Mussolini had already been captured and hanged by Italian partisans. Hitler had made his will. Aware of the Russians only miles away from the bunker where he and his long-time girlfriend Eva Braun were entrenched, they both committed suicide. So did many of his henchmen, including Dr Goebbels. How did Goebbels, and more particularly his wife, cope with the awesome problem of what to do about their six children? Surrender to the Russians after so much bitter internecine warfare would not get the same treatment as surrendering to the Allies, who were in any case much further away from Berlin than were the

Russians. The whole family took cyanide – though the manner of their deaths has been disputed. When the Russians arrived the bodies were too charred for any infallible forensic evidence.

Frank was overseas, as he had been seen since the beginning of the year. On VJ day, 15 August, after the terrible bombing of Hiroshima and Nagasaki, the Japanese surrendered unconditionally. I took the children in the big pram down to the shops. A young girl on a bicycle whizzed past me. She seemed to be going a bit too fast down Blenheim Gardens, a street sloping into the main road. Like most of us, she was probably overjoyed that the end of the war had come. She did not realise, poor girl, that her end too would come within minutes. I saw her almost dive into the main road, no brakes applied, or maybe they just didn't work. It was a terrible sight. She ran into a bus travelling along towards Croydon, was caught by the wheels and somehow thrown out of them like a piece of old rag.

Leaving the pram on the pavement, and telling the children to be good (a vain hope), I rushed across to see if I could help. Impossible. Yet though I had no idea of her age, she looked extraordinarily peaceful after such a quick and what seemed such a horrible death. A policeman came round in the evening to interview me. I had left my bag by her side. When he saw I had two children, he repeated what I had heard earlier about women with young children. Mothers made poor witnesses. Their eyes were focused too intently on their children. He told me that the victim was a young girl who had come down to our little suburb for a weekend with her grandparents.

Robbie Burns's wisdom, 'the best-laid schemes o' mice an' men gang aft agley', was shown to me in another instance shortly afterwards. Almost as a peace-time celebration (though there would be many street parties) my parents came from Bethnal Green to our little flat for the last Sunday in September. I was repairing the place so gradually that other than the removal of the glass, it looked barely any different from the day when it first suffered the bomb damage. Seven months pregnant, I found the ceilings a bit hard to manage, and that morning was covered in plaster, which I shook roughly off. Mum was making a plum pudding, a 'spotted dick', a Cockney delicacy I absolutely adored.

'You shouldn't eat that,' said Dad to me, when Mum served it after our main course. 'Too heavy for somebody in your state.'

Another old wives' tale I thought, and then I was seized by abdominal cramps. Was this baby going to arrive . . . two months too early? Was all my planning in vain? I asked Dad to phone Fulmer Chase. He was too nervous to do so. My mother had rarely used a phone and did not volunteer. I phoned myself. An ambulance arrived and I was whizzed off. Fulmer Chase was in some ways, strangely, a rather sad place. Many of the women had lost husbands. One had been photographed, I think by the *Daily Mirror*, because just before giving birth to the most beautiful twins she saw her pilot husband dive to his death on a Scottish beach. Our new baby, Michael, weighed just over 3 pounds. Helped by some wonderful nursing care, he came more easily into the world.

I had to stay in the nursing home much longer than I anticipated, but had put some of my 'teaching money' very rashly into the shares of WC French. It was my first taste of 'high finance'. I was sure they could not go wrong when they made ceramic goods, including toilet basins, and they were doing quite well.

I sold them all to pay for the confinement, my stay in the nursing home and the care of Francine and Jennifer, and had a bit left over. Frank came home from his overseas posting shortly afterwards, bringing a huge box of eggs and several other delicacies that we had so rarely seen in the past 5 years. He also brought some good news. We were to join him in Germany in a small hamlet called Bückeburg, just outside Cologne. He had been transferred to Intelligence. The UK, along with Russia and America, were trying to pick the brains of the German rocket scientists, and with his knowledge of German and electronics Frank was delegated to help.

Our move overseas was delayed when the new baby developed measles, though for some reason, neither of the girls did.

'You'll never rear that baby,' said my father at his melancholy worst. We eventually left Britain for a ruined Germany. At the port scheduled for our departure, the children were looked after in a crèche on shore. I almost forgot about them when I boarded the boat alone to find our berth. The harbour master had to stop the boat to reunite us. I packed in some Nestlé's condensed milk for our new son, and to my huge surprise, he thrived on it from the very first day.

Since my mother's birth in 1891, and my own in 1916, I had travelled a long way from Bethnal Green via Oxford and now, in 1946, towards a devastated Germany. With Frank, I would travel further still . . . to find ourselves the last couple to leave Berlin before it was closed to the West and the Airlift, organised by the Allies, save their one-time enemies from starvation; to watch the Berlin Wall go up and men who had never read Frost's poem 'Mending Wall' kill themselves to surmount this one. Then, in a happier setting, we saw the Wall come down and eventually the dawn of the twenty-first century. But that's another story.

ALSO FROM SUTTON PUBLISHING

Children of Bethnal Green

Doris M. Bailey
paperback • £12.99 • 0 7509 3815 3

Doris Bailey recalls the humanity of Bethnal Green's back streets during the 1920s, 1930s and throughout the Second World War. She vividly remembers the endless struggle to make ends meet, the little shops and the people who ran them, street sellers, and the very different world of Sunday School and chapel. Her eye for detail and her sense of fun combine to make this a fascinating study of life in the East End.

'one of the best books to come out of the East End'
DAILY TELEGRAPH

The Way Things Were

Denis Cassidy
Foreword by Sir Bobby Robson
hardback • £14.99 • 0 7509 4037 9

Vivid, moving and personal, Denis Cassidy's depiction of his childhood in the grim and grimy backstreets of working-class Newcastle captures an era that has long gone, a moment in history that will never be repeated. His story is an atmospheric reminder of how much life in Britain has changed in the last seventy years. Were these the 'good old days'? According to Denis, they were just 'the way things were'.

www.suttonpublishing.co.uk
Customer Services: 01963 442030
Email: privatesales@haynes.co.uk